BEWARE OF THE
CABLEGUY
FROM COP TO SERIAL KILLER

BY JEFF KAYE

Polimedia
Publishers

Published by Polimedia Publishers
© 2008 Jeff Kaye

ISBN-13: 978-0-9768617-3-7

First paperback printing
Printed in the United States of America

Polimedia Publishers
100 S. Sunrise Way #A670
Palm Springs, CA 92262
info@polimediaent.com
www.polimediaent.com

This book is dedicated to Buffy Rice Donohue

BIOGRAPHY

Jeff Kaye recently retired as a sergeant from the Reno, Nevada Police Department. He spent the majority of his twenty-four years in law enforcement working in various undercover operations, including supervision of a multi-jurisdictional narcotics task force. Mr. Kaye holds a degree in Criminal Justice and throughout his career has been called upon to offer expert testimony in undercover operations, clandestine lab enforcement, and undercover operative stress syndromes.

Mr. Kaye currently resides in La Quinta California with his wife and two children. He is the Chief of Public Safety for the Desert Sands Unified School District. He is the author of two other books, *Two Faces Have I* and *Mainline*.

INTRODUCTION

I first became involved in the David Middleton case on a cold February night in 1995 while working as a sergeant in the Patrol Division of the Reno Police Department. From the moment I arrived at the site where Middleton's first victim was discovered I knew this was not an ordinary homicide case. The following three years of investigation and prosecution proved my initial hunch to be correct. It also showed me this was a story that, someday, needed to be told.

This is not the story of David Middleton. It is a true story about heinous crimes committed by a man who people trusted and allowed into the inner circles of their lives. My initial research uncovered allegations of police malfeasance that occurred before David Middleton ever reached Reno. Because of this I knew I could not accurately write this book while still an active member of the law enforcement community. I began writing this book on September 1, 2006—the day I retired from a twenty-four-year law enforcement career.

Research for this book was done by sifting through the voluminous collection of police reports and legal documents available as public record in the states of Nevada, Colorado and Florida. Countless hours of interviews with persons involved in this case were also used to authenticate facts contained in documentation. Names marked with an asterisk are pseudonyms used to protect confidentiality. In all other instances real names are used either with permission or as a matter of public record.

David Middleton was removed from society due to the diligent work of the men and women from the Reno and Sparks Nevada Police Departments, the Washoe County Sherriff's Office and the Washoe County District Attorney's Office. These agencies were very helpful in providing information used to put this story together. Other agencies discussed in this book were not as forthcoming with assistance on this project and I will let the reader formulate their own opinion for their reasons.

Some of the photos contained in this book are graphic in nature, but are necessary to show the killer's degree of dementedness. Crimes such as those described on these pages shock the conscience of a normal person, so photographic evidence of them should be expected to do the same.

TABLE OF CONTENTS

Biography   i

Introduction   ii

Chapter 1   Dumpster Divers   1

Chapter 2   Wheel of Fortune   5

Chapter 3   Death Whispers   12

Chapter 4   Kathy   18

Chapter 5   Beginnings   23

Chapter 6   In Dubio   31

Chapter 7   Warp   36

Chapter 8   Old School   41

Chapter 9   Omicron   51

Chapter 10   Calls Unanswered   58

Chapter 11   The Cable Guy   64

Chapter 12   Sympathy for the Devil   70

Chapter 13   Stupid Crook Tricks   76

Chapter 14   Buffy   88

Chapter 15   Montrose   93

Chapter 16   The Prince of Darkness   99

Chapter 17   The Truth Will Set You Free   110

Chapter 18   Dead Ends   117

Chapter 19   A New Day   123

Chapter 20   Stalker   132

Chapter 21	A Pig in a Poke	138
Chapter 22	Marathon	143
Chapter 23	The End of the Line	153
Chapter 24	The Holy Grail	162
Chapter 25	Chamber of Horrors	166
Chapter 26	Twists	173
Chapter 27	The Ace of Spades	179
Chapter 28	Lines in Time	185
Chapter 29	Sticks and Stones	195
Chapter 30	Thelma	202
Chapter 31	Body Count	209
Chapter 32	Heads of Tails	218
Chapter 33	Task Force	227
Chapter 34	Death of a Cheerleader	235
Chapter 35	Girlfriend-en-stein	242
Chapter 36	True Lies	249
Chapter 37	Your Own Worst Enemy	261
Chapter 38	Welcome to Miami	267
Chapter 39	Seven-and-0	278
Chapter 40	Oedipus	285
Chapter 41	Father Dave	292
Chapter 42	The Arrest	298
Chapter 43	People vs. Middleton	304
Chapter 44	The Black Cloud	310
Chapter 45	Rocky	318
Chapter 46	Great Expectations	325

Chapter 47   Frutiger   332

Chapter 48   Habeas Corpus   337

Chapter 49   For Whom the Bell Tolls   342

Chapter 50   Outside the Box   347

Chapter 51   The Geek Squad   353

Chapter 52   Justice   359

Chapter 53   I'm Ready For'em   364

Chapter 54   Rock and Roll Time   371

Chapter 55   Invisible Victims   377

Chapter 56   Squeak   383

Chapter 57   Don't Cheat the Hangman   389

Chapter 58   Rest   397

Chapter 59   House of Cards   402

Chapter 60   Stringing Pearls   405

Chapter 61   The Knockout Punch   411

Chapter 62   The Old Rag   415

Chapter 63   Going Home   449

Chapter 64   Jabba   425

Chapter 65   The Matron   427

Conclusion   431

Chapter 1

DUMPSTER DIVERS

The radio call sending Reno Police Officer Pat Dreelan to check a report of a dead body found in a dumpster didn't evoke much of a reaction from him when he received it at 9:50 P.M. on Saturday, February 11, 1995. Radio calls were rarely what they seemed to be when initial information was given. The last time he'd checked a supposed body in a dumpster, it turned out to be the remains of a dead deer a poaching hunter had disposed of. He hoped this call was a bogus one too, because standing in the cold at a crime scene wasn't quite as appealing as the warm restaurant he was headed to for his dinner break when the call came out.

The information given to Officer Dreelan was vague. The witness who phoned it in said he was told by a transient leaving the area to call the police because he discovered a body wrapped in a sleeping bag inside of an apartment complex dumpster while searching for discarded aluminum cans. The apartment complex in the southeast section of Reno was in a largely Hispanic area and a gang calling themselves CVC claimed it as their territory. Since the possibility of a gang related crime existed, Officer Dreelan's awareness was heightened as he pulled into the area.

The Southwest Village Apartments were located at 2450 Lymberry Street in Reno, Nevada. This was an older section of the city and the sprawling apartment complex had become quite rundown over the years. The property managers tried their best to spruce things up, but every time they painted a wall or fence it would be covered by gang graffiti the next day.

Officer Dreelan located the dumpster in question in the southeast parking lot of the complex. The sector sergeant was already on scene talking to a witness when Officer Dreelan parked his black and white next to the rusting hulk of a Chevy Impala propped up on cinder blocks. The witness lived in the apartments and had been taking his trash to the dumpster when he encountered the harried homeless person who told him about the dead body. The transient left before the police arrived, but he had told the apartment dweller the sight of the body scared him so badly he wasn't even going back in to retrieve the full pack of cigarettes he dropped while trying to climb out of the dumpster.

The large yellow dumpster was about six feet in height and, like everything else in the area, covered in blue spray painted graffiti. The witness who waited for the police didn't actually see the body, so the inside of the dumpster still had to be checked. Officer Dreelan climbed up the metal ladder attached to the side of the dumpster and peered inside. He could see a brown sleeping bag wrapped in heavy yellow plastic bound in rope lying on top of the trash on the opposite end of the dumpster. Even when he illuminated it with his flashlight he couldn't tell if it was a body or not.

Somebody needed to actually get inside the dumpster and check for the existence of a body in the sleeping bag. Officer

Dreelan was a weight lifter and hoisting his large frame encumbered by an additional forty pounds of police gear over the side of the dumpster would be no easy feat. Since rank does carry some privileges there was no discussion about which officer would be going in.

When relating this story ten years later, Officer Dreelan still remembers it like it was yesterday. "It was my Monday so my uniform just came out of the cleaners that day. Nobody wants to jump into a dumpster in the first place, but doing it in your Monday uniform really sucks. It was darker than hell inside of that dumpster but I couldn't use my flashlight when I was jumping in because I needed both hands to boost myself over the side. The dumpster was half full and I slipped when I landed inside on top of all that garbage. I came down on top of somebody's half-eaten Big Mac and got ketchup all over my pants.

"I was crawling through that dumpster on my hands and knees holding my mini-flashlight in my mouth so I could see where I was going. I tried to remember all the stuff from the academy about crime scene preservation, but all I could think about was a rat the size of Chuck E. Cheese jumping out of the trash at me. That dumpster was only about six feet across, but it seemed like a mile because I had to move so slowly. I kept sinking in the garbage and didn't even want to think about what was getting all over me.

"When I finally got to the sleeping bag the zipper on it was opened a little bit. I shined my light inside and saw what looked like pink skin, but I couldn't tell if it was a body or not. I opened the bag a little further to get a better look, and when I did I saw a pair of little pink hands tied together with rope. I shined my light up a little higher and that's when I saw this big friggin dead eye staring back at me. Right then I didn't care about garbage *or* Chuck the rat anymore. I just wanted to get the hell out of that dumpster. I reached inside of the sleeping bag and grabbed one of the exposed wrists to check for a pulse, but the body was colder than the chills running down my spine. Kneeling there in the dark with mystery meat and ketchup sinking through my pants holding hands with a corpse is still the freakiest thing I've ever had to do. All I could think about was taking the next sergeant's test so I'd be the one on the outside of the dumpster from now on."

Pat Dreelan was visibly shaken when he crawled out of that dumpster and reported what he saw to his sergeant. He forgot about his ruined Monday uniform and even tuned out the jokes the other cops made about him smelling like the alley behind a Chinese restaurant. He busied himself by stringing crime scene tape and wanted nothing more than to finish out his shift and try to drown out the experience with some cold ones.

One of the transients watching the scene gave Officer Dreelan some advice that evening. He said to never go into the *big* dumpsters the night before trash pick up because even aluminum cans weren't worth the risk of drowning in a five-foot pile of trash. That tidbit of dumpster-diver wisdom would be passed on several times before the night was over.

Chapter 2

WHEEL OF FORTUNE

The call out rotation for detectives is known as "the wheel" in police jargon. Detectives Dave Jenkins and John Douglas from the department's Major Crime Unit were at the top of the wheel on the night the body was found in the dumpster and that was the first stroke of luck in the investigation.

As in most modern departments, the position of detective in the Reno Police Department was a temporary one. Officers were generally assigned to a detective slot for a period of four years and then rotated back to uniform patrol. This was done in order to get as many officers as possible investigative training and to eventually have that experience filter back to the street where it could do the most good.

The elite Major Crime Unit was the exception to this process. Detectives assigned there remained as long as they wanted—or until they pissed off the wrong person, as some insiders said. The lead investigators on anything but a "smoking gun" homicide came from the Major Crime Unit and detectives from other units would assist with ancillary investigative tasks. Jenkins and Douglas had both been around the block a couple of times and they swam in the deep end of the pool of experience that existed in the Major Crime Unit.

Jenkins was the most seasoned investigator in the department and there was nobody better to have on a who-done-it homicide. Douglas had a quick-witted sense of humor and easy style of talking to people that made them want to cooperate with the law even if they were guilty. Their investigative skills complimented each other—right down to their nicknames. Jenkins was known as D.J. and Douglas went by J.D. But since Jenkins was *very* white and Douglas was *very* black, and since cops sometimes have *very* sick senses of humor, they were better known in the Detective Division as Ebony and Ivory.

Jenkins received the homicide notification at 10:10 P.M. on Saturday, February 11, 1995, twenty minutes after the original radio dispatch call. Like most nights, he was at home with his wife and two children when he got the call. Being a devoted family man, Jenkins was the type of detective his boss never had to worry about chasing down when he needed him. He was an eighteen-year veteran cop the night of the murder and his wife Terri had been with him since the day he graduated the academy. She was a veteran cop-wife, so even though she hated the late night call outs, she knew there was nobody better responding to a murder than her husband.

Douglas was also at home when he received the phone call describing the homicide scene, but his evening was not quite as relaxing as his partner's. He was in the midst of a quiet romantic soirée with his soon-to-be next wife, and the call came at a particularly inconvenient time. After hanging up the phone and muttering a few expletives, he got out of bed and got dressed.

When his fiancée asked him why he was dressing in old work clothes instead of a suit like he normally would wear to a crime scene, he answered her in his usual stand-up comedic style, "The man just told me there is a dead woman's body inside of a dumpster. I can't even get *live* women to do what I want, so I seriously doubt this one is gonna come out and talk to me if I tell her to."

Jenkins and Douglas arrived at the crime scene almost simultaneously, twenty minutes after the notification. They parked their department-issued cars well away from the yellow crime scene tape, hung their gold badges around their necks, and headed toward the scene together. The parking lot was full of parked cars and a crowd of onlookers had already began to gather. Jenkins made a mental note that the first thing he would need to do was expand the crime scene so the plates on all cars could be run for owner information before they were allowed to be moved. This would be just one of many mundane tasks needed to be done and he hoped his boss had called in enough help.

Jenkins believed a homicide investigator should always dress the part regardless of the circumstances. Tonight he wore a dark woolen overcoat over a grey suit, a crisp white shirt and a blue tie. Were it not for the fact his neatly cut brown hair was matted down in the back, one might have thought he had just left his office instead of his warm bed. At thirty-eight years old Jenkins still had the short powerful frame of a power lifter, but eighteen years in police work—most of them spent as a "corpse cop"—was beginning to take its toll on him. Too many nights spent at crime scenes and too much time spent behind a desk doing follow up investigation was starting to make him a little soft around the edges. The yellow pallor of his skin and dark circles under his eyes attested to the fact that on those nights he was not pulled from his bed for a homicide call out, perhaps ghosts from past investigations came to visit him.

A stark contrast to Jenkins, Douglas was dressed in faded blue jeans, scuffed Nike high-tops, a black hooded sweatshirt and an old olive-drab Air Force field jacket. He looked younger than his forty years and still moved with an athletic grace that made him look like he'd be more at home on the blacktop basketball court across the street than involved in a homicide investigation. He was a Master Sergeant with the Nevada Air National Guard and looked well rested since he just returned from fulfilling his two week yearly obligation. His smooth dark skin was tanned to an even darker shade, attesting to the fact he'd spent the time in a much more exotic climate than Reno. His military buzz cut had already begun growing back to the short afro he normally wore, and the hint of grey beginning to show in his jet black hair was the only thing that hinted at his age.

The local news stations had picked up the call on their scanners and the sector sergeant was busy giving an initial sound bite to a couple of reporters on the outskirts of the crime scene.

Officer Dreelan walked over to the detectives and gave them the initial briefing on what he found inside of the dumpster. When he told them about the warning the transient gave him about dumpster diving the night before trash pick up, both detectives exchanged knowing glances and headed toward the twenty cubic foot yellow metal casket.

Since Officer Dreelan already determined the victim was deceased, there was no need for them to enter the dumpster until the proper resources arrived. They took turns climbing the metal ladder and illuminating the sleeping bag-entombed body with the beams of their flashlights. After seeing enough, they walked to a quiet corner of the lot to compare initial impressions.

Jenkins was the more scholarly of the team and pulled a pen and notebook out of his coat pocket to record their observations. Douglas pulled a pack of gum out of his and put three sticks into his mouth, hoping to cover up any trace odor from the bottle of merlot he had shared with his fiancée over dinner.

The first thing they both noted was there was very little garbage on top of the body, meaning it had been placed into the dumpster fairly recently. They also agreed that the fact that the dumpster was due to be emptied in the morning was probably not a coincidence. There are no coincidences in police work—especially in homicide. Whoever put the body in the dumpster more than likely knew that if it wasn't discovered before morning it would be buried in a landfill forever. They filed that piece of information away in hopes it would help them cull a future list of suspects.

After completing a list of things that needed to be done they headed back to the group of officers standing at the edge of the crime scene waiting for their assignments. The entire apartment complex would have to be canvassed and they'd use the uniformed cops for that. Every scrap of garbage in and around the dumpster would also have to be checked, but the most important pieces of evidence would be on top of or directly underneath the body. They were anxious to get into the dumpster to see exactly what they had, but unfortunately they had to wait for the arrival of the C.S.I. techs before that could be done. The first twenty-four hours of any homicide investigation were the most important, and the clock was ticking.

During the downtime Jenkins headed off to interview the reporting person while Douglas remained at the crime scene to direct the activity. The reporting party was a Mr. James Jansen* who lived in the apartment complex. He was a thirty-eight-year-old single father who lived in an apartment with his two sons, ages ten and twelve. Jansen's statement that he left the apartment only long enough to take out the trash was confirmed by both of his sons. He was visibly shaken and Jenkins viewed his statement as credible.

The transient who had told Jansen about the body was no longer on scene, so he immediately became a person of interest. Jenkins put out an A.P.B. for the man based on the description given to him by Jansen, but unfortunately a dirty-looking homeless white male in his mid-twenties wearing a tattered coat fit the description of a large percentage of Reno's population, so he held little hope of finding him.

The C.S.I. truck was pulling into the lot and the temperature was steadily dropping when Jenkins got back to the dumpster. He hoped they would find some clues when they removed the body from the dumpster, but the sinking feeling he had in his stomach led him to believe they were in for a long night.

Chapter 3

DEATH WHISPERS

It was certainly not a corpse cop who coined the phrase "dead men tell no tales." Any experienced homicide detective knows the evidence recovered from a dead body can be the most significant gathered in the case. That is why the more difficult murders to solve and prosecute are those where the body is never found.

When it came time for someone to crawl back inside of the filthy dumpster and perform the initial examination of the body, there was no question who it would be. Dave Jenkins was a highly religious man who believed in God—not spirits or witchcraft. He also believed he needed to spend time alone with the body of a murder victim in order to let his initial impressions sink in. It was almost like the victim was whispering to him from beyond and if there were any distractions, he might miss a clue that could shape the entire investigation.

Deputy Chuck Lowe from the Forensic Division of the Washoe County Sheriff's Office responded to the scene. After he took photographs of the outside of the dumpster and surrounding area it was time for Jenkins to go inside and check the body. He removed his overcoat and suit jacket, and then donned a white Tyvex jumpsuit, blue paper booties and white latex gloves. Stopping outside of the dumpster, he spoke into a mini-cassette recorder in his shirt pocket in order to record his initial observations.

The large yellow dumpster measured twenty cubic yards and the sides were approximately six feet tall. Jenkins carefully read each letter from the graffiti painted on the dumpster into the recorder so the transcriber would have the proper spelling. He then climbed the metal rungs of the ladder and paused at the top before going over the side.

The inside of the dumpster was now illuminated by the bright Klieg lights hooked up to the generator on the crime scene truck so there was no need for Jenkins to use his flashlight. He could see the trail through the garbage used by Officer Dreelan to get to the body and decided to try and stay as close as possible to that route in order to avoid unnecessary disturbance to the scene. Since both of his hands were free Jenkins was able to lower himself into the dumpster slowly and land on top of the piles of garbage without the messy impact experienced by Officer Dreelan.

Once inside the dumpster Jenkins slowly crawled toward the body, stopping twice to record names and addresses from discarded mail on top of the trash heap. In a homicide investigation one never knew when a scrap of information might be important. Jenkins stopped when he got to the body and knelt in silence on top of the garbage next to it. Douglas and Deputy Lowe watched from above standing on a pair of ladders they had removed from the crime scene truck and set up at the end of the dumpster closest to the body. They were ready to jump in and assist Jenkins if requested, but they quietly watched as the detective performed the ritual they'd witnessed many times before.

Jenkins spoke briefly in hushed tones into his recorder and then quietly knelt motionless next to the body. After a few minutes he slowly nodded his head and began moving trash from on top of the body while Deputy Lowe took photographs from his perch above. The dumpster was about one-third filled, but only a cardboard box and a few small plastic bags of household trash were on top of the sleeping bag. Once they were moved Jenkins was able to get his first clear view of the body contained inside.

The sleeping bag had been wrapped inside of a large semi-transparent yellow plastic bag. This plastic outer covering had been partially pulled away to expose the top part of the sleeping bag, which was unzipped just enough to show a portion of the victim's body. Jenkins surmised the transient who initially found the body had begun removing the plastic covering in order to see what treasures awaited him inside. White-colored rope approximately one-half inch in diameter was tied around the outside of the yellow plastic bag and had been fashioned into a makeshift handle. Jenkins carefully pulled the rope and outer plastic away enough to allow him to better see inside of the sleeping bag.

A small portion of the right side of victim's torso, as well as one eye could be seen through the partially-opened zipper. Jenkins slowly unzipped the sleeping bag further, all the time speaking into his recorder while he worked. The victim's head, neck and shoulders were partially covered by a dark green kitchen-type plastic bag that had apparently been placed over her head, but enough of the face was showing for Jenkins to be able to tell he was dealing with a white female adult.

Bright red discoloration could be seen on the victim's right side, which, to the untrained eye, might appear as bruising. It was actually liver mortis, also referred to as lividity, caused by gravity pulling blood to the lowest parts of the body after death. In and of itself this is not much use in determining time of death, but Jenkins knew he could use it in conjunction with other clues being whispered to him to provide valuable information.

He reached in with a gloved finger and pushed hard against a patch of the victim's reddened skin. If the liver mortis showed a change in color referred to as *blanching*, it would mean the victim had been dead for less then eight hours. There was no blanching, so he knew the liver mortis was *fixed* and the victim had been dead for at least eight hours or longer. The victim was lying on her left side but the liver mortis was on her right. The fact the blood had not drained to the victim's left side told Jenkins she had been positioned on her right side for at least twelve hours after death before being moved to the dumpster. After that amount of time the blood remains where it is, regardless of how often a body is moved.

Jenkins grabbed the exposed fingers of the victim's right hand and checked for rigor mortis, another phenomenon that occurs after death caused by the build up of lactic acid in the musculature of the decedent. It results in stiffening of the body and sets in within six hours of death. What most people don't realize is rigor mortis only lasts twenty-four to thirty-six hours from its onset. After that the muscles begin to degenerate and the rigor mortis completely disappears.

Using the exposed portion of his wrist above the rubber glove, Jenkins felt the victim's skin. It was cold to the touch, but all that told him was the body hadn't been indoors recently. Body temperature drops about three degrees per hour after death, but the cold winter air and the even colder temperature inside the steel dumpster would accelerate that process.

The fact there was fixed liver mortis in the victim told him rigor mortis had already come and gone. That information taken in conjunction with the fact there was not yet any visible decomposition in the victim put his educated guess at time of death to be in the area of forty-eight hours. A more precise time of death would be established by the coroner during the autopsy, but the victim had given Jenkins a ballpark figure to work with.

The last thing Jenkins did was shine his flashlight inside of the sleeping bag in order to get a good look at the body, but he saw nothing to indicate an obvious cause of death. The victim was naked with the exception of a sleeveless black shirt pulled up around her neck and a pair of dark blue socks. The same white rope wrapped around the outside of the sleeping bag had been used to bind the victim. Her hands were tied tightly in front of her and the rope continued between her legs. It was then wrapped around her ankles and the loose end was looped around her neck and cinched tightly so that her feet and legs were pulled behind her. The victim had ended her life the same way it began—naked and in the fetal position. But the look of terror frozen on her face in death attested to the fact something had gone horribly wrong upon her exit into the afterlife.

Chapter 4

KATHY

It was just after midnight when the investigator from the Coroner's office arrived on scene. By that time the sergeant and an additional detective team from the Major Crimes Unit were there to assist. They decided to take the entire body wrapped just as it was found inside the dumpster and zip it into a black plastic body bag. This way they could move it to the controlled environment of the Coroner's examining room without losing any trace evidence.

After several attempts and a few choice words, Jenkins and Douglas were able to lift the body bag out of the dumpster and hand it to the other two detectives standing at the top of the ladder. The victim later weighed in at one-hundred-thirty pounds, but lifting *dead weight* over their heads while standing in two feet of loose garbage was no easy job. Both detectives were exhausted and filthy when they climbed out of the dumpster, but they still had work to do.

Since Jenkins and Douglas were the lead detectives on the case they would follow the body to the Coroner's office and try to get an identity. One of the other detectives would supervise the removal of the dumpster to a secured evidence yard so it could be searched properly in the morning. This job was assigned to Detective Ed Dixon, also known as "Evidence Eddie." He wasn't the sharpest investigator in the unit, but there was no job he wouldn't do and no scrap of evidence that would get by him in an investigation. Dixon's partner would remain on scene to supervise the area canvass and a third two-man team would meet Jenkins and Douglas at the Coroner's office to get their assignments.

Once the body was at the Coroner's office Jenkins pulled back the plastic bag covering the victim's head so he could take Polaroid photographs of her face for purposes of identification. The body itself would not be removed from the sleeping bag until a morning autopsy. One of the Robbery Homicide Detectives who responded to the Coroner's office to assist with the investigation walked in while Jenkins was taking photographs. He immediately noted a similarity between this victim and a photograph he had seen earlier in the day while reading a missing person case assigned to another detective. He could not recall the name of the missing person, but he knew Detective Dave Wood had the case.

It was now two in the morning, but one thing a homicide detective cares nothing about is waking people up in the middle of the night. Jenkins called Detective Wood at home and learned the name of the missing person from the case he was working was Katherine Powell, a forty-five-year-old elementary school teacher who had been missing for eight days.

The adrenal buzz the possible break in the case gave them overcame the fatigue Jenkins and Douglas were starting to feel. They drove the few short blocks to the main police station where the Detective Division was housed and retrieved the missing person case from Detective Wood's desk. Stapled to the inside flap of the file was a photo of Kathy Powell taken in much happier surroundings than the Polaroid photos Jenkins had just taken of her. Although official identification would have to wait until morning, both detectives were certain the body from the dumpster and the missing school teacher were one in the same.

Looking through the file they learned Ms. Powell had last been seen at 3:00 P.M. on Friday, February 3, 1995 when she was leaving her teaching job at Sun Valley Elementary School north of Reno. She was not reported missing until the following Monday when she didn't show up for work, which the report said was out of character for her. The school itself was in the jurisdiction of the Washoe County Sherriff's Office, but Reno P.D. got the call since Powell lived in the city.

Officers got no answer at Powell's northeast Reno apartment when they checked it after the initial report. The doors were locked from the inside, but based on the circumstances, they forced entry into the apartment to check for her. She was not inside and there were no obvious signs of a struggle, but a friend was able to tell police some items were missing from the apartment. Among these were a laptop computer, a fax machine, and a computer printer. The missing items and the no-call-no-show for work raised the investigating officer's suspicions enough to have Powell listed as a missing person.

This was the next stroke of fortune in the investigation, because the quick victim identification would keep the fledgling homicide investigation moving forward. Douglas poured two cups of oily looking black coffee from the coffeemaker in the squad room and brought them back to the desk where Jenkins was busy making a to-do list. The report listed Powell as divorced and living alone in the apartment. A former spouse is always a suspect in a murder investigation until proven otherwise, so one of the first things they needed to do was interview Kathy Powell's ex-husband and get a feel for his involvement. Jenkins and Douglas would take that interview themselves.

Powell's apartment would also need to be thoroughly searched, but since there was no longer an exigency, they would need a search warrant before going back inside. They decided to wait until morning instead of waking up a judge at this late hour to sign the search warrant, so Douglas called Detective Dixon and asked him to go by the apartment and seal it until they obtained the search warrant. Dixon said not only would he do that, he'd arrange for a patrol car to be stationed out front and would personally obtain and execute the search warrant first thing in the morning. Evidence Eddie was on the job.

Powell's apartment complex would have to be canvassed, all of her co-workers and friends would need to be interviewed, and the person who reported her missing in the first place would have to be re-interviewed now that it was a homicide investigation. There is a fine line between people thinking of themselves as a witness or a suspect; waking someone up at 2:30 in the morning to talk could make them think they were on the wrong side of that line. The two detectives were convinced that whatever happened to

Kathy Powell happened at least two days ago, so waiting till the morning in order to get better cooperation from witnesses wouldn't hinder the investigation.

Jenkins called his boss who was still out at the original crime scene and filled him in on the latest details. Reno didn't have the backlog of dead bodies that plague some larger cities so the Coroner's Office would give this case priority and call someone into work on Sunday to perform the autopsy. It was scheduled for 9:30 the next morning, so Jenkins suggested everyone assigned to the case head home for a couple hours of sleep and meet back at the office at 8:00 A.M. They were on a roll, but a little sleep and some clean clothes would be a good start to what would assuredly be a long day.

Chapter 5

BEGINNINGS

The two hours of sleep Jenkins got after returning home from the station actually consisted of a series of several ten minute naps. Thoughts of the ensuing investigation were churning in his head and any semblance of a restful night's sleep was impossible. By 7:00 A.M. he was headed out of his door showered, shaved, wearing a clean black suit, and carrying a travel mug containing his third cup of coffee of that morning.

Another Sunday family day had been interrupted, but at least he'd had time to have breakfast with his wife kids before leaving. His daughter Ali was eleven and his son Adam was nine. It seemed like yesterday they were both babies and sometimes he thought family time for homicide investigators should be measured in dog years. His family was his support system and they understood the importance of his job. Somebody needed to speak for the dead and that's what he hoped to do today.

Jenkins started a pot of coffee when he arrived at the Detective Division and then sat down at his desk to go over the original missing person report taken on Kathy Powell. There were five detectives and one sergeant in the Major Crime Unit. Each man had a standard gunmetal grey desk in the small cubicle that separated the unit from the other detectives in the division. The cubicle itself was made of grey six-foot tall portable partitions placed next to each other to form a square. It did little to keep out noise or provide privacy, so Jenkins was thankful for the quiet time the early hour and off day afforded him as he started reading the report.

Officer Bob Bennett initially responded to the missing person call and did an excellent job of writing a detailed report of his preliminary investigation. Powell was a third grade school teacher and left work at 3:15 in the afternoon on Friday, February 3, 1995. Not only did she fail to show up for work the following Monday morning, she did not call and arrange to have a substitute teacher take her place. Powell was described as a dependable and caring teacher who would sooner drag herself out of a sickbed than leave her students without a teacher. It was this uncharacteristic behavior that caused the school principal to be concerned enough to call the police.

Powell's townhouse apartment was located at 3484 Terrace Knolls Court and Officer Bennett was met there by the school janitor at 10:30 in the morning on Monday, February 6, 1995. The janitor, Stephen Mizzen, said he was not only a co-worker of Ms. Powell's but also a friend of hers. He said he had been an invited guest in Powell's home on prior occasions and that he knew her well enough to be certain she never would miss work under these conditions unless something was wrong.

The only entrances leading into the apartment were the front door and the overhead garage door. Both were locked, but Officer Bennett could see inside of the apartment through a partially opened curtain on the front window. There did not appear to be any sign of a struggle and two rolled up newspapers were on the kitchen counter. There were also two newspapers delivered that morning still in the driveway as well as mail in the mailbox and a note from T.C.I. Cable Company on the door. The note said a repairman had been there at 1:30, but there was no date. Officer Bennett surmised this would have been 1:30 the previous Friday since cable company repairmen routinely don't work weekends.

After knocking on the door several times Officer Bennett contacted his sergeant and requested permission to force entry into the apartment to check for Powell. Powell drove a small pickup truck, which was not in the driveway. Since her car was not there the sergeant denied the request for forced entry and told Officer Bennett to have Mizzen go to the police station to make a missing person report if Powell did not show up for work by the next morning.

Jenkins had been around long enough to be able to read between the lines in a police report and Officer Bennett was obviously not happy with the sergeant's response. In his report he wrote that he next told his sergeant he could not be sure Powell's car was not there because he could not see into the garage. The sergeant again denied the request for forced entry, but fortunately Bennett took good notes on his initial response and even performed a brief canvass of the neighboring apartments.

Jenkins sipped coffee and silently wondered if Kathy Powell had still been alive during this encounter, and if so would things have turned out differently for her if Officer Bennett had been allowed to listen to his cop instincts. Forced entry into the apartment would entail the sergeant writing a report to detail the event. He despised sloppy police work and hoped it was more than avoidance of paperwork that influenced the sergeant's decision.

Reading on, Jenkins saw that Officer Bennett contacted three of Kathy Powell's neighbors before leaving the apartment complex. None of them knew her well nor did they remember seeing her over the weekend. One of the neighbors did recall seeing an older model car parked in front of Powell's apartment early Saturday morning, but she did not remember anything about it except that it was a *beater*.

The next morning, Tuesday, February 7, 1995, the police were summoned again when Powell did not show up for school. Officer Bennett responded to the school and took the missing person report from the school principal. The school nurse, Grace Johns*, was a friend of Powell's and accompanied Officer Bennett back to Powell's apartment. The apartment looked the same as it had the day before with the exception of another newspaper in the driveway and more mail in the mailbox.

Officer Bennett's sergeant showed up at the apartment and this time they *did* force entry in order to get inside. Ms. Powell was not there and there were no obvious signs of foul play. Her pickup truck *was* located inside of the closed garage. Ms. Johns had been to the apartment several times before and looked around to see if there was anything amiss. It was she who noticed the laptop, printer, and combination fax/answering machine were missing. In addition, Powell's backpack-style purse was on her desk in her bedroom. Ms. Johns said Powell never went anywhere without it and that she rarely accepted rides from anyone. The fact her car and purse were there and she wasn't were even more cause for concern than her not showing up for work.

Ms. Johns said she was aware Powell had suffered bouts of depression in the past, most recently over her deteriorating relationship with a boyfriend who had moved to Pittsburg, Pennsylvania. She said she knew Powell had a prescription for lithium, but did not think she was currently taking the drug and did not consider her to be suicidal. She based that opinion on her personal *and* professional knowledge of Powell.

Officer Bennett found a note next to the two rolled up newspapers on the kitchen counter. The note said, "Kathy, I came by to get the pets but you weren't here. I let myself in and locked up behind me. Thanks for watching them and call me when you get home."

The note was dated Sunday, February 5, 1995 and signed by a man named Jerry Brown. Ms. Johns said she knew Brown to be a friend of Powell's and that Powell had been watching his pets for him while he was out of town. Officer Bennett found Powell's phone book in her purse and located both home and work numbers for Brown. He used his cell phone so as not to disturb any potential evidence in the apartment and located Brown at his office.

The last page of the report said Brown stated he had returned from a two week business trip in Arizona on Sunday, February 5th and went straight to Powell's apartment from the airport to pick up his pets. Powell had been watching his dog and ferret for him while he was out of town and she told him she would be home grading papers Sunday when he returned. He said he was surprised when he got to Powell's apartment and she was not there, but used a key she had given him to retrieve his pets. He found his dog in the garage and judging from the mess it didn't look like he'd been let outside for a while. Powell had mentioned she had plans to go skiing the day before so he assumed she must have spent the night away from home.

The follow up reports from Detective Wood were next in the file. He was assigned the case in the late afternoon of Tuesday, February 7th. The first thing he did was re-interview Jerry Brown since he had been inside of the apartment over the weekend. Brown showed Detective Wood his airline ticket receipt showing he had returned to Reno from Phoenix at 5:50 P.M. on Sunday, February 5th. He said when he got to Powell's apartment he found newspapers from Saturday and Sunday in the driveway. He picked them up and brought them inside. That accounted for the two rolled up newspapers Officer Bennett had found on Powell's kitchen counter.

Brown said he had a key to Powell's apartment because he would take care of her plants when she traveled. Brown had known Powell for about five years and their relationship was friendly but not of a romantic nature. He said he thought it odd that Powell was not home when he went to her apartment and it was totally out of character for her to not show up for work. The only other thing of interest Jenkins found in Brown's statement was he said Powell always went in and out of the apartment through the garage door and used her electronic door opener to open and close the overhead door. The opener was not in her truck in the garage and Detective Wood had not located it inside of her apartment during a later search.

Detective Wood conducted telephone interviews with Powell's mother and brother who lived in Southern California. Neither of them had heard from her in the past week. Powell's ex-husband Roy Robbins lived roughly five miles from the school where she taught. Robbins hadn't talked to Powell all weekend and he also said it wasn't like her not show up for work. He was able to supply the name of Powell's cousin in San Francisco that she was supposed to meet for a ski outing in Lake Tahoe on Saturday, February 4th. The man's name was listed as Russ Davis and although he had not been formally interviewed yet, he did tell Detective Wood during a phone call that Powell did not show up for the trip as planned.

A phone call to Powell's boyfriend in Pittsburg, Pennsylvania also netted no valuable information. Mr. Don Barley told Detective Wood he could account for his whereabouts in Pennsylvania all weekend. He said although his relationship with Powell is long distance they still remain close and talk by phone every night. He most recently spoke to her on the evening of Friday, February 3rd, and tried to call her several times since but got no answer. He did say he thought it strange that Powell's answering machine did not pick up when he called her as she always kept it turned on.

Jenkins had four pages of notes scribbled on a yellow legal pad by the time the rest of the detectives arrived at 8:00 A.M. He ripped the pages from the pad and placed them and the copy of the missing person report into a brand new black three-ring binder which was now the official murder book. Jenkins had started more than his share of murder books over the years and his handwritten notes were just the beginning of the story of Kathy Powell's death. It was now up to him and the other detectives assigned to the case to make sure the story had a proper ending.

Chapter 6

IN DUBIO

Latin phraseology is heavily used in the medical and legal fields, and forensic science is no exception. The word forensics itself is derived from the Latin *forēnsis,* meaning public knowledge. In 1100 A.D. the King of England commissioned doctors to examine the dead and they became known as *Crowners,* since they answered to the crowned heads. The Latin word for crown is *corona,* and over the years the examiners of the dead became known in the English language as Coroners.

In the state of Nevada any suspicious or non-clinical deaths are investigated by a coroner, so the autopsy of Kathy Powell would be done by the Washoe County Coroners Office. It is the job of the coroner to establish not only the *cause* of death, but the *mechanism* and *manner* of death as well. The difference between these terms is widely misunderstood by the general public.

Cause of death is simply the reason the person died. Some say the cause of every death is the same—stoppage of the heart. The mechanism of death is the actual physiological change or variation in the body's inner workings that causes the cessation of life. A heart attack and a bullet will both cause the heart to stop functioning, but the evidence to tell the difference can only be obtained through an autopsy.

Perhaps the most important evidence discovered through autopsy from an investigative viewpoint is the manner of death. The four main manners of death are natural, accidental, suicidal and homicidal. The Latin term for the fifth and less often used category is *in dubio,* which translates to *undetermined.* This is used when the coroner cannot accurately determine the appropriate manner of death. Since homicides are deaths that occur by the hand of someone other than the deceased, a finding of undetermined manner of death is the one most feared by a homicide detective.

The job of attending the autopsy of Kathy Powell fell upon Jenkins and Douglas since they were the lead detectives on the case. The other three Major Crimes Unit detectives, with the assistance of Detective Wood, were already busy working other aspects of the investigation when Jenkins and Douglas arrived at the coroner's office at 9:00 A.M.

Deputy Chuck Lowe was waiting for them in the dressing area outside of the autopsy room. Since he performed the initial crime scene investigation it was his job to follow through with evidence collection at the autopsy and fingerprint the victim for positive identification. The mood was somber in the room as the three men exchanged greetings. Some cops used *black humor* to mask the atrocities they witnessed on a daily basis, but not these cops. Working homicides taught them respect for the dead and none of them looked forward to the task ahead. Witnessing the autopsy was a necessity, but a cop who said he enjoyed it was a good person to keep at a distance.

The three men pulled on green surgical scrubs complete with booties, caps and masks over their clothing. In most medical procedures protective garments are worn to shield the patient from germs, but the opposite is true in an autopsy. All autopsies were considered potentially infectious, so universal precautions were required before entering the examining room. The last thing they did was pull on white latex gloves before pushing through the door to Autopsy Room One.

The room was large and well ventilated. Seeing the doctor and his assistant pulling the body bag containing the remains of Kathy Powell off the large scale in the corner and onto a stainless steel cadaver table gave Jenkins a chill that added to the cool air temperature in the room. The stark walls, light colored floor tiles and bright white overhead florescent lighting made the room seem even colder. The interior smelled slightly antiseptic, but even the scent of Pine-Sol couldn't cover the smell of death that had seeped into the walls over the years.

Dr. Roger Ritzlin would be performing the autopsy. Jenkins hadn't had any bad experiences with him, but he hadn't had any really good ones either. The only cases he'd worked with the man so far had obvious causes of death and judging from what Jenkins saw during his initial inspection of Powell this one might be a bit different. Corpse cops always shared autopsy horror stories when they got together, and as Jenkins watched the doctor wheel the table with Powell's body on it toward the center of the room, two of these came to mind.

Both autopsies were from the Las Vegas Coroner's Office and the doctor who had performed them was fortunately no longer with the Coroner's Office. In the first case the doctor would not rule a homicide in a death where the victim was shot in the heart with an arrow from a crossbow, even though the weapon was never found. His reason was the victim might have accidentally discharged the arrow while loading the crossbow, and vandals might have stolen the weapon before the body was discovered.

In the second case the victim was bludgeoned to death with a ball-peen hammer. The victim had been despondent over a divorce and the coroner ruled the death a suicide. Even though the man had been struck in the head six times, only one of the blows was severe enough to cause death. The coroner said the first five blows must have been hesitation strikes since the victim's fingerprints were among those found on the hammer. The fact his wife's fingerprints were also found on the hammer didn't play into his decision because the hammer was taken from the garage, so they both would have had access to it over time.

Both of these cases were eventually cleared by arrest as homicides, but investigation and prosecution was made much more difficult due to the reluctance of the coroner to make a firm decision as to manner of death. Jenkins and Douglas exchanged sideways glances over their surgical masks as they watched Dr. Ritzlin arrange his instruments, both silently hoping for the same thing. Some cops loved to clear their case load in any way possible, but not these ones. The old adage says if it looks like a duck, walks like a duck, and quacks like a duck—it's probably a duck. The same could be said for a homicide, and both felt that was exactly what they were dealing with. All they needed now was for the man unzipping the body bag to confirm their gut feelings.

Chapter 7

WARP

Once the body was removed from the body bag, the black bag itself was folded and sealed inside a clear plastic bag to be examined by the crime lab later. The body was still enclosed in the sleeping bag and yellow plastic bag just as it was when removed from the dumpster. It was the outer plastic bag that drew their attention now that they could see it much clearer under the bright lights. The two homicide detectives along with the crime scene detective and corpse doctor all agreed on one thing. None of them had ever seen a plastic bag quite like this one.

The doctor carefully removed the bag and Deputy Lowe stretched it out on a work table. The bag was bright yellow and a heavy enough grade of plastic to be able to hold the body without tearing. It measured sixty inches by one-hundred-eight inches, making it much larger than the standard thirty-three gallon trash bag covering Powell's head. After the bag was photographed Lowe left it stretched out on the table so the remaining condensation on it could dry before he packaged it. They then turned their attention back to the cadaver table.

The sleeping bag had been hand-sewn closed at the top with black thread. The stitching was sloppy, making it appear that whoever did it was in a hurry. Dr. Ritzlin was able to unzip the bag and pull it away from the body without cutting the threads in case they had evidentiary value. Once the sleeping bag was removed from the body, it was photographed, folded toward the inside to preserve any potential evidence, and sealed in plastic by Deputy Lowe.

Dr. Ritzlin next removed the black plastic bag that was partially covering the victim's head and handed it to Deputy Lowe for processing. The victim's eyes appeared to be ready to bulge out of her head and her tongue was protruding from her mouth. Dr. Ritzlin explained this was the result of bacteria in the decomposing body creating gasses that were trying to escape. He then pointed to an olive-green colored patch of skin on the right side of the victim's lower belly and said that was further sign that internal decomposition had begun. His educated guess was the victim had been dead for at least five days, but he'd be able to narrow that down after a complete examination.

The knots in the rope binding the victim's body were tight, but the ropes themselves were loose enough to allow Deputy Lowe to freely move the right hand in order to obtain fingerprints. He inked each finger and rolled the prints onto a white laminated fingerprint card. He then stepped over to a lighted table and used a magnifying glass to compare the victim's prints to Kathy Powell's fingerprints on the card Jenkins had brought with him. After a minute he returned to the cadaver table and informed the rest of the group the prints matched. Additional DNA and dental record comparisons would be done at a later time, but the photograph and fingerprint match would be enough for the coroner to say this victim was definitely Kathy Powell.

Dr. Ritzlin began carefully cutting the ropes off of Powell's body under the watchful eyes of both detectives—cutting between the knots so they could be preserved. As each section of rope was removed it was picked up and packaged separately by Deputy Lowe. The manner in which the killer had looped the rope from Powell's ankles around her neck would have caused the rope to tighten if she tried moving her legs too much. It appeared to the detectives that Powell's death had resulted from ligature strangulation caused by the rope, so they were shocked when Dr. Ritzlin voiced his disagreement with their observations.

When the last piece of rope was removed from Powell's neck Dr. Ritzlin pointed out that although the rope had left a mark in the skin, it wasn't deep enough to have been caused by the force necessary for strangulation. He also pointed out the absence of petechiae—small red conjunctival dots—in the whites of Powell's eyes. Dr. Ritzlin said it was his belief that petechiae are present in all deaths related to strangulation or asphyxiation. Jenkins knew from his research on the subject that Dr. Ritzlin's opinion on this was not accurate, but he decided not to voice his opinion until all the facts of the autopsy were in. Nevertheless, his opinion of Dr. Ritzlin had been formed.

Powell's body was stretched out on the table and the autopsy room attendant flipped a wall switch to turn on the overhead fan so the escaping gasses could be ventilated. This was one of the parts of the procedure that sometimes caused onlookers to vomit, but the men in the room continued working without making mention of the odors of death. Dr. Ritzlin removed Powell's black tank top and blue socks from her body and handed them to Deputy Lowe. He then performed a visual examination of the body.

There was heavy bruising on Powell's knees and elbows. After examining them Dr. Ritzlin determined they had been caused antemortem. There was also a discernable human bite mark on Powell's left breast which was likewise caused while she was still alive. Using a special blue light to examine the body, a semen stain was located on Powell's right thigh. Deputy Lowe gathered evidence from the bite mark and semen stain, and then Dr. Ritzlin continued his examination.

Rolling the body over on its side, Dr. Ritzlin pointed out the absence of fecal staining which would also be present along with the petechiae if the death resulted from strangulation or asphyxiation. He did see enough tearing and discoloration to lead him to believe Powell had been engaged in vaginal and anal sex shortly before her death—possibly not as a willing participant.

When Dr. Ritzlin began cutting into Powell's body to examine her organs Douglas walked over to the table where Deputy Lowe had laid out the evidence gathered so far. He knew the drill well enough by now. Each organ would be taken out of the body, examined and weighed, then placed back inside of the body before the doctor sewed it back up. It wasn't squeamishness that caused him to step away from the cadaver table, but the yellow plastic bag that caught his eye.

Using a gloved hand he lifted the bag and examined the writing etched into the lower corner of it. There were a series of numbers, and underneath them in large letters was the word "WARP." Douglas smiled his toothy grin under his surgical mask as he transcribed the letters and numbers the manufacturer had put on the bag into his notes. Every detective loved clues, and he'd just found his first.

Chapter 8

OLD SCHOOL

Signs of frustration showed on the faces of Jenkins and Douglas when they walked into the Detective Division at 1:00 that afternoon. The other detectives assigned to the case were at their desks and the unit's sergeant was on the phone inside of his glass-walled cubicle. They all looked up when Douglas loudly said, "Man, that was bullshit!"

Sergeant Matt Toliver* hurriedly finished his conversation and hung up his phone. He was fifty-five years old, a twenty-five year veteran, and it was rumored he was only in the Detective Division to pad his salary with overtime to boost his retirement rate. Since his retirement was close at hand he rarely left the safe confines of his office. The detectives said it had been so long since he'd been outside during daylight he was paler than Count Dracula jonesing for a blood fix.

Toliver stepped out of his office and said, "Does that mean things didn't go well at the autopsy?"

Douglas said, "The autopsy was *perfect,* but that lame-dick doctor is gonna say the death could have been an accident."

Jenkins cleared his throat and said, "What my esteemed partner is trying to say is the doctor performed professionally, but in his opinion he is not entirely certain this death occurred at the hands of another person."

Douglas gave a sideways glance and added, "No, what I meant was that lame-dick doctor is gonna say the death could have been an accident."

"How could it be an accidental death?" Toliver asked. "She was tied up and dumped into a trash dumpster!"

Jenkins briefed them on the antemortem injuries, the bites marks and the semen stain found on her thigh. He then looked at his notes and said, "Preliminary lab tests show a non-toxic amount of lithium in the victim's blood. This isn't out of the ordinary because the initial police report shows a prescription for lithium was found inside of Ms. Powell's apartment. The lithium *could* have caused some judgmental problems or slowing of other bodily functions."

Toliver asked, "So if the lithium was in a non-lethal dose, what does it have to do with the cause of death?"

"The doctor is basing his entire theory on lack of petechiae, which he says is present in all deaths related to strangulation of forced asphyxiation. This is where he and I disagree, but he's the doctor and I'm just a homicide detective.

"He located some fibrosis and acute cell death in the left ventricle of the victim's heart. It appears the cell death occurred a couple of days before her death. Naturally, the cause of death in this case is stoppage of the heart. The doctor is not prepared to say the circumstances causing the heart to stop fit the description of a homicide since other contributing factors are not present.   "There is evidence of sexual activity shortly before death, albeit rather rough sexual activity. It is the doctor's opinion the victim *might* have had a heart attack during some type of auto-erotic sexual encounter. The lithium might have masked the symptoms of a possible heart attack until it was too late for the victim to do anything about it."

Douglas remarked, "The way he's describing it is worse than the old joke about having a heart attack during a game of charades. You're writhing in pain and the other people think you're just really getting into the game."

"So, the ruling from the coroner is accidental death?" Toliver asked.

"No," Jenkins answered. "There were enough inconsistencies with what we found on the body to keep the coroner from saying it was definitely accidental. I got him to commit to the fact there was no way she could have tied herself up like that without help, and there were a couple of other things that looked out of place. The one visible bite mark on the victim's breast occurred before death and it was so deep it most assuredly would have been very painful. There were also blue fibers and trace amounts of some type of metal—probably aluminum—located around the victim's neck. We got a ruling of *undetermined* cause of death, but we're still investigating it as a homicide until we rule out foul play."

"Accidental death would be a lot easier," Toliver said.

In an annoyed voice, Jenkins said, "If you want a quick-fix to this you're going to have to assign it elsewhere."

"Relax," Toliver cautioned. "You know I want this thing investigated properly. I'm just saying don't rule out the accidental thing all the way yet. For now I'll leave the whole team assigned to this, but if you don't get some evidence pointing away from what the coroner said I might have to pull some manpower off of it. Things are slow right now, so let's just see what happens."

"Fair enough," Jenkins said. "What did the rest of you come up with?"

"We finished the search of the condo," Detective Dixon replied. "The friend of Ms. Powell's who reported her missing met us there to see if she could help identify the missing items. So far we know the missing items are a Brother brand combination fax and answering machine, a Sony cordless phone, a Texas Instrument computer printer and a Macintosh laptop computer. I got the brand names and serial numbers from a file I found in Ms. Powell's desk.

"We combed the place pretty good and the evidence tech took a ton of fingerprints, but she said almost all of them match so they're probably from the victim herself. I did find a rolled-up ball of used duct tape and two unopened packages of Trojan condoms behind the garbage can under the kitchen sink. It looks like somebody tried to throw them in the garbage can but missed, so that's why the cops didn't see them when they originally went through the place. The lab says it's kind of tough to get DNA off of tape, but they'll see what they can do. When they unrolled the tape it was a single strip just about big enough to be used as a gag too."

Jenkins nodded and commented, "An excellent job as usual, Eddie. Who's next?"

Detective Joe Dypsynski had assisted Dixon on the search. He replied, "I found Powell's banking and credit card records in her desk. She banks at First Interstate Bank and only has one credit card issued through Chemical Bank MasterCard. Banking information is tough to get on a Sunday, but the head of F.I.B. security is an ex-cop buddy of mine. I called in some favors and found out the only banking activity done on Powell's account is a check she cashed at their Sun Valley branch 3:15 P.M. the Friday she was last seen. The check was only for sixty dollars and her account has been dormant since."

"Well that begins to establish her movements after she left school that day," Jenkins said. "Are they able to retrieve any video of the transaction so we can be sure it was actually her that cashed the check?"

"Yeah, but we're gonna have to wait till tomorrow to look at them. I need to get a subpoena for the video so my guy doesn't get his ass in a jam for releasing the information, but he's already gone to the bank and looked at them. I faxed him a photo of Powell and he says it's definitely her who cashed the check. Woody has the credit card information from his original case, so I'll let him cover that."

Detective Wood looked at his notes and said, "I just pulled this stuff up on Friday and haven't really had a chance to get into it because I was on my days off. Kathy Powell's credit card was used for a telephone purchase from the Good Guys Electronics Store at 2:36 P.M. on Sunday, February 5th. That was two days after she was last seen, but it was also two days *before* she was reported missing, so it didn't raise any red flags at the time.

"I called down there and talked the guy who took the order." Wood stopped to flip through his notes and then added, "Here it is. His name is Gary Cable and he was just about to get off work when I called. He said a person identifying herself as Kathy Powell called the store and placed an order for a Yamaha stereo amplifier valued at about two thousand dollars. The caller said it was going to be a gift and that it would be picked up the next day. The charge went through OK, so the sale was approved.

"The same person called Cable the next morning and said a courier service would be by in the afternoon to pick up the stereo equipment. Later that afternoon a white female with blonde hair wearing a yellow windbreaker with some type of logo on it came to the store and picked up the merchandise. Cable didn't actually help the lady, but he remembers her because he said she was wearing so much make up she looked like a clown. He also said the person who called the store saying they were Kathy Powell sounded like a man trying to disguise his voice to sound like a woman."

Jenkins asked, "Did this guy get a look at the logo on the courier's jacket or the car she was driving?"

"Nah, but he said the kid who helped her must have. I was planning on talking to him on Monday, but I can call down there today to see if he's working."

Toliver said, "Well if he's not, find out where he is and get his ass down here for a statement. It might be nothing, but he also might have dealt with our killer. Didn't you think that lead would be worth following up on when you got it? Powell had been missing for at least five days by then!"

"Of course I did," Wood replied disgustedly. "Like I said, it was Friday afternoon and I was about to get off duty for the weekend. The lieutenant wouldn't approve the overtime, so my boss told me to follow it up on Monday. I didn't like it, but I can't overrule the lieutenant."

Detective *Bruce Hunt had been quietly listening to this exchange. The square-jawed former Army Ranger didn't speak often, but when he did people usually listened. At this moment he spoke up, using the term of endearment he reserved for people who irked him. "The lieutenant's a fuckin *clam*! We could've had a lead on the suspect last night if we had that information."

Toliver said, "Give the guy a break. The lieutenant has to answer to the Deputy Chief if his O.T. budget goes overboard so he has to be careful with it."

Hunt's face was red with anger when he said, "The Deputy Chief is an even *bigger* clam than the lieutenant. You don't solve murders worrying about budgets. Anyway, me and Woody will head over to the Good Guys as soon as we finish up with this other interview we have scheduled."

"What interview is that?" Jenkins asked.

Hunt looked at his notes and said, "According to Powell's date planner she was supposed to meet a friend of hers for coffee right after school the Friday she was last seen. The guy's name is Royal Alexander* and he lives up in north Reno. What kind of clam names their kid Royal? Anyway, I called him and he said Powell and him had coffee at that French place *Deux Gros Nez* Friday evening at about 5:30.

"So this guy Alexander is the last person we know of right now who saw Powell alive. He's meeting us here at 2:00 for an interview, but he don't feel right to be a suspect. He's been in San Francisco all week on business, and from the sound of his voice he don't seem like the type to be too interested in kinky sex with a woman. I guess you predestine a kid to go that way when you name him Royal."

Jenkins said, "Your powers of perception never fail to amaze me. John and I stayed at the Coroner's office while they made the death notifications to the next of kin. Powell's mother and brother are driving up from California in the morning and they asked that the ex-husband be notified since he and Powell were still quite close. I made that call myself and he sounded legitimately upset. We're heading up to his house as soon as we break here to interview him, but my gut feeling is he's not going to be a suspect. When we finish with him we're going to stop by the evidence yard to complete the search of the dumpster. Who said homicide work isn't glamorous?"

Dixon said, "Joe and I are heading back to Powell's complex to re-interview the neighbors. We'll swing by the evidence yard and meet you when we're done. There was a lot of garbage in that dumpster so it'll go faster with four of us working on it."

Douglas had been working on his computer throughout the entire meeting. He sat back and exclaimed, "I found it! Our mystery yellow plastic bag is called a Warp's Brothers Banana Bag and they're manufactured in Chicago. They only list two local outlets here in Reno. One is up in the north valley and the other one is downtown. The number on the bag is a tracking number, so we should be able to tell which store sold it."

"That's *if* our suspect is a local," Toliver said.

"He's a local," Douglas said. "I checked with the trash company and they said the apartment manager pays extra for the additional Sunday pickup at that complex because of the rat problem they get if the garbage piles up too high. I think whoever dumped Powell knew the trash schedule and picked that place so her body would end up in the landfill while they had a skeleton crew working there."

"I concur," said Jenkins.

Douglas stood up and said, "Then let's get off our asses and start knocking on doors. It's old school, but it always worked for Joe Friday on Dragnet."

Chapter 9

OMICRON

The buzzing noises made by the overhead fluorescent lights were the only sounds in the detective's conference room as Jenkins sat alone going through his notes. The main squad room was empty at 10:00 on a Sunday night, but the private conference room shielded him from the occasional inquisitive uniformed officer who wandered into the detective division to see what was going on.

The other detectives had completed follow up reports on their activities before heading home for some well deserved sleep an hour earlier. Jenkins decided to stay after they were gone so he could review all the reports before their morning briefing. Deciding to save his own notes till last, he pushed them to the side and grabbed the top report off of the pile stacked next to him.

It was Detective Hunt's report detailing his interview with Royal Alexander. Mr. Alexander described himself as a close friend of Powell's, but not in a dating capacity. He said he had met Powell for coffee at the *Deux Gros Nez* restaurant on California St. in Reno at 5:30 P.M. on Friday, February 3rd.

Powell told Alexander she was planning to go on a ski trip the next morning and had just cashed a check at her bank to cover the expenses for it. He was certain she had her backpack-style purse and her checkbook with her because she wrote him a check for some business products she had purchased from him. She left in her truck at about 6:30 P.M. and Alexander said this was the last he saw of her as he left for San Francisco later that night. He still had Powell's check with him and gave it to Detective Hunt to be placed into evidence.

Detective Hunt's case notes said he had ruled Alexander out as a suspect based on his alibi for his whereabouts during the days following his meeting with Powell, as well as "other contributing factors." Jenkins knew they were Hunt's gut feeling that Alexander wasn't the type to engage in sexual activity with Powell, but that isn't the kind of thing a detective writes into his police report.

The second report was written by Detective Douglas. It was short and to the point, but did little to describe the agonizing hours four detectives had spent wading through trash in the police evidence yard. The last line of the report read "nothing of evidentiary value was discovered, but a good time was had by all."

The next report was six pages long and listed the names and addresses of everyone Detectives Dixon and Dypsynski had spoken to in Powell's apartment complex. Two of her neighbors had seen an older model pickup truck parked in front of Powell's condo when they came home at about 4:00 A.M. on Saturday, February 4th.

The truck stood out because it had household belongings in the back. It was dark outside, but they both described the truck as being faded red with a light colored license plate on the back. They didn't notice what state the license plate was from, but both were certain it wasn't Nevada. Neither neighbor knew Powell well, but they said she often had visitors so they didn't think anything was amiss when they saw the truck. Their description of the truck seen outside Powell's apartment made the next report seem even more important.

This one detailed the interviews Detectives Hunt and Wood conducted with the employees at the Good Guys electronics store. Two employees had spoken to the person identifying herself as Kathy Powell on the phone and they both described the caller's voice as deep and husky. They were almost certain the caller was a male, but since Reno has a large transsexual population, neither of them gave this much thought.

The caller told the store manager they were buying the stereo equipment as a gift for a family member in Lake Tahoe. They also said arrangements had been made with a local courier service to pick up the equipment at the store and deliver it to Lake Tahoe. The Lake Tahoe connection wasn't given when Detective Wood first contacted the store. Since he'd already confirmed Powell had no relatives in the area, this might have made the transaction seem more suspicious if he'd had the information two days earlier.

The courier arrived at the Good Guys store at 2:45 P.M. on Monday, February 6th. She was assisted by a store clerk named Mike Sarratea, and Detectives Hunt and Wood took a detailed statement from him. Sarratea described the courier as a heavyset white woman in her mid-forties with frizzy blonde hair. He said her face was heavily made up and she was wearing a yellow windbreaker with some type of logo on it. He couldn't remember the exact logo, but he did remember it was a company name with the word "Messenger" in it.

Sarratea said the woman had a clipboard with papers on it and had the proper customer I.D. number with her for the order placed by the caller. She loaded the stereo receiver onto a red hand truck she brought with her and wheeled the merchandise out to her truck which was parked in the customer loading zone. Sarratea helped her load the large box into the bed of the truck and she left after he gave her a receipt for the merchandise. She was not required to sign anything and the copy of the receipt included with the report had the words "phone order" handwritten on the signature line.

Sarratea said the courier's voice was neither deep nor husky as the caller's voice was described. When Hunt asked him to describe the courier's vehicle, Sarratea said it was an early 70's model International Harvester open bed pickup truck, faded orange in color, with plywood covering the bed and a green and white license plate. When Hunt asked him how he could be certain the truck was an International Harvester, Sarratea told him he was helping his father restore the exact type of truck. He said he might be off by a year in either direction, but it was definitely in the right time frame because that style of truck was only used between 1970 and 1975.

Jenkins smiled when he read the last paragraph, thinking about this next stroke of luck in the investigation. Since the witness had personal experience with the exact brand of truck the courier was driving, his statement was credible enough to use on a nationwide law enforcement B.O.L.O. to try and locate it.

There were five courier services with the word "Messenger" in their names listed in the phone book and he was reasonably certain none of them would be using an early 70's International Harvester truck. He'd have to wait till morning to check with them to be certain though. It would be an incredibly stupid move for the suspect to use a distinctive vehicle like that if it was actually theirs, but Jenkins' instincts told him the two crimes were related.

The last report Jenkins read was the one he had written describing the interview he and Douglas had done with Kathy Powell's ex-husband, Rick Hughes*. Jenkins eliminated Hughes as a suspect not more than a minute into his conversation with him. It wasn't what Hughes said, it was how he said it that gave both Jenkins and Douglas the gut feeling they were dealing with an honest man.

Hughes was a fifty-one-year-old electrician. He was a big man, bulked up like a construction worker, not like a weightlifter. When he met the detectives at the door to his house his eyes were red-rimmed and the telltale salt stains from tears streaked his face. With a meaty paw he shook hands with both detectives and invited them into his home.

They sat at the kitchen table and Hughes poured them coffee from a glass coffeemaker on the counter. Next to the coffeemaker was a mason jar filled with Tennessee Moonshine, homebrewed by relatives of Hughes' current wife. He said he held off on opening the white lightning as a show of respect for the detectives, but he intended to put a dent in it as soon as they left.

Hughes had been a cop in a central California city for twelve years when he met Kathy Powell, and by that time he was frustrated with the trials and tribulations of police work. He said Kathy brought out the good in him and turned his life around. He got out of law enforcement, married Kathy and moved to Reno to be with her. Hughes described Powell as a good and trusting person, but it was her trust in people that brought about their divorce in 1989.

Shortly after they were married Powell became involved in a cultish-style set of beliefs called the Trust Theory, also known as *omicron* for the Greek letter *o* which signifies unity. Hughes explained that people involved in the Trust Theory were called *seekers,* believing there was good inside of everyone if you looked hard enough. She once told him even a genocidal butcher like Hitler had a kernel of sweetness at his core—it was just never brought out into plain sight.

Eventually *trust* became the driving force behind all of Kathy's thinking. She distained monogamy and promoted openness and experimentation in everything—including sexual relations. Her credo became "life is short and death is long, so why not be passionate and see the potential in everyone."

The last statement Hughes made in his interview was that he never stopped loving his ex-wife—he just couldn't live that type of life with her. His cop senses made him too cynical to trust people and he told Kathy that someday her beliefs would get her hurt. His tears flowed freely as he wondered out loud if that had been a self-fulfilling prophecy, and the detectives set the jar of white lightning on the table in front of him before they silently let themselves out of his house.

Chapter 10

CALLS UNANSWERED

The detectives were back at it by 7:00 A.M. Monday morning and the day brought with it a flurry of activity for them. At their morning briefing each man was given a list of persons to contact. By 4:00 in the afternoon they were back in the Detective Division seated around the oval conference room table comparing notes on their progress.

The conference room had become the temporary headquarters for the ad hoc task force and a timeline based on what they knew so far was written in black marker on the white dry-erase board at the front of the room. The timeline was sparse, but enough room had been left between entries to add on as more information was obtained.

Jenkins started the afternoon meeting by going over what he'd learned about Kathy Powell thus far. Besides the interview with her ex-husband, Jenkins and Douglas had also spoken to several of Kathy Powell's co-workers in addition to her brother and mother who were now in town. They all painted the same picture of Kathy Powell—a caring and trusting person who looked for good in everyone.

The Trust Theory was continually mentioned as a rudder that Kathy Powell used to guide her life, so Jenkins researched the philosophical belief and learned it had quite a large following. The

Trust Theory was started in San Diego in the early 1970's by a psychologist named Jack R. Gibb. Interestingly enough, Powell's brother told the detectives Kathy had actually taken Gibb into her home for a short time and cared for him until he succumbed to terminal cancer just a month before her own death. The two deaths appeared unrelated, but the fact she brought the man into her home went along with everything they heard about Kathy Powell. She took in strays that had nowhere to go and tried her best to make life comfortable for them.

Kathy Powell had no serious medical problems other than having had a hysterectomy at an early age. Perhaps the fact she couldn't have children of her own was the reason she was so loved by the underprivileged children she taught. Her co-workers said she was the student's favorite teacher and that she allowed them to call her Kathy instead of Ms. Powell. She cited developing trust within her students as the reason for the lack of formality.

Trust is also what brought Kathy Powell into her long distance relationship with her fiancé, Pittsburg attorney Don Barley. She met Barley at a Trust Theory meeting six years earlier while she was still married to Hughes and the two started a relationship almost immediately. Powell's brother said she dove headfirst into a fascination with everything about Pittsburg from its sports teams to its history, and she planned to move there to be with Barley after she retired from teaching.

Powell's family never approved of her relationship with Barley and suggested this might be a good place for detectives to focus their investigation. It seems she spent five weeks with him in Pittsburg a year earlier while he was recovering from an aneurysm. While she was there he made her sole beneficiary of his will. In turn she did the same with him. Powell's assets included her condo, a modest life insurance policy and a small savings account. Everything combined equaled just under $100,000 which was not a staggering figure, but Jenkins had seen murders committed for far less monetary gain.

Jenkins and Douglas had done a taped telephone interview with Barley earlier in the day and he seemed legitimately upset by Powell's death. Barley was fifteen years older than Powell but he said their mutual beliefs in the Trust Theory gave them something in common and kept them together. He said they visited as often as possible given the distance between them, but when they were not together they spoke by phone nightly.

Barley said the last time Powell called him was about 7:30 P.M. P.S.T. and they spoke for about thirty minutes. He knew about her ski trip the next morning, but became concerned when he did not hear from her the following night. He made several calls to her apartment over the next two days, but they all went unanswered. He found it strange that her answering machine did not pick up his calls since she religiously kept the machine turned on and checked her messages frequently. After Detective Wood contacted Barley during the initial missing person investigation he stopped trying to call Powell. He said he and Powell shared a mental connection and deep inside knew something had happened to her.

Barley was able to substantiate the fact he had not left the Pittsburg area during the time frame of Powell's disappearance. Even though murder for hire was always a possibility, Jenkins and Douglas ruled him out as a suspect. They made their living listening to their instincts and decided to focus their efforts locally.

A detailed telephone interview was also done with Russ Davis, the cousin of Kathy Powell she was supposed to ski with on Saturday, February 4th. Davis said he was supposed to meet Powell in Truckee, California thirty miles west of Reno and drive from there to a Lake Tahoe ski resort. He got a late start leaving his San Francisco area home and began calling Powell from his car phone at about 6:30 A.M. to let her know. He made several calls to her home over the next couple of hours, but they all went unanswered. He made the same statements as Barley about it being out of the ordinary for Powell not to have her answering machine on.

Powell was not at their pre-arranged meeting place when Davis arrived in Truckee. He waited for a short while and then drove to the ski area in case she had gone there without him. He did not find her there and Powell did not have a cell phone for him to call her on. He spent part of the day skiing and then drove back to the Bay Area without having contact with her. He had his punched ski pass to confirm his story and his whereabouts before and after skiing could be confirmed by family members.

The detectives had also contacted every courier service in the Reno-Lake Tahoe area—even those without the words "Messenger" in their names. None of them used a 70's model International Harvester pickup truck for deliveries, so the truck was now listed as used by a person of interest in the case. A nationwide teletype was sent out and the information was passed on to all local departments.

Several sightings of similar vehicles had already come in locally. Detectives went to Good Guys and picked up Mike Sarratea to look at two possible matches. A 1972 model parked on a street in south Reno was an exact match for the style, but Sarratea said it was too clean looking and did not have the plywood in the truck bed. Regardless of the false sightings, the detectives were certain the truck was one of their best clues.

The other solid clue was the Warp's Brothers Banana Bag, and Douglas spent a better part of the day tracking that down. Using the tracking number he was able to determine the bag had been purchased at the Commercial Hardware Store in downtown Reno at 3:32 P.M. on Thursday, February 8, 1995. When Douglas went to the store he learned they had a copy of the receipt for the sale on file, but no one remembered who made the purchase and there was no video of the sale. The $9.36 transaction had been done in cash so there was no credit card paper trail to chase, and the ten-dollar bill used for the purchase was long gone.

According to the receipt, a fifteen-count box of heavy duty 33-gallon black plastic garbage bags had also been purchased at the same time as the four-bag package of Warp's Brothers Banana Bags. Douglas purchased these two exact items from the store in order to compare them with the bags taken from Kathy Powell's discarded body. The black plastic bags and the Banana Bags both matched exactly in brand, color and size. Since coincidences rarely exist in police work, Douglas' theory about the killer being local was bolstered with this discovery.

Jenkins used a black marker to update the timeline with the new information from this afternoon's discussion. He then picked up a red marker and drew brackets around the time frame between Powell's last call to Barley at 7:30 P.M. Friday, February 3rd and Russ Davis' first call to her at 6:30 A.M. Saturday, February 4th. Whatever hell Kathy Powell had gone through had already begun before that unanswered phone call, because whoever took her also took her telephone answering machine.

There was only one entry between the two times bracketed on the timeline chart. It read, "Feb. 4, 1995 0400 hours: Faded red beater pickup truck seen in front of victim's condo." Their investigation now had a focus...

Chapter 11

THE CABLE GUY

During the next morning's briefing it was decided the Good Guys transaction would become the focus of the investigation as this was by far the most active lead in the case. The department's civilian statistical analyst was brought on board and tasked with compiling a list from Department of Motor Vehicle records of trucks matching the description of the one used by the courier at Good Guys. They would start out with Nevada registered vehicles and branch out to other states from there as needed.

The registered owners of each matching vehicle would have to be checked for criminal history and the likelihood they might have crossed paths with Kathy Powell. This would be a time consuming job and their resources had already begun to dwindle. Since the official Coroner's ruling on cause of death was now "undetermined," the division lieutenant decided to lessen the priority of the case and moved Detective Wood back to his unit. He also said further manpower would be removed from the case if progress wasn't shown in the near future. This decision brought on one of Detective Hunt's infamous tirades, which of course ended in the words *"that fuckin clam!"*

A computerized data base was created and Toliver was able to get two clerical employees to assist with logging vehicle and owner information into it. This alleviated some of the workload on the detectives, but there was still a lot to be done. In addition to looking for the vehicle through records and putting the word out to patrol, they decided to go public with the information and put out a press release with the description of the truck and the courier from Good Guy's. This would generate a lot of tips—mostly false—but every one would need to be checked.

By the end of the day sightings of matching vehicles already had started coming in from law enforcement agencies—one of them from as far away as Navajo County, Arizona. They were all logged into the data bank, but it would take time to run checks on the registered owners. Eventually none of these initial sightings proved useful to the investigation.

The detectives also had a chance to review the video surveillance tapes from the F.I.B Bank. Not only did they confirm it was Powell who cashed the check the date she was last seen, but that she was also wearing the same black shirt that was found on her body when she was discarded in the dumpster. In addition, she had her backpack purse and the outside camera captured her coming and going alone in her pickup truck. Besides adding credibility to Royal Alexander's story, this also told the detectives they were working within the right timeframe. Kathy Powell went home that evening, but she never had the chance to change out of the clothes she was wearing the last time she was seen alive.

The first twenty-four to forty-eight hours in a homicide case are the most important, after that incoming information starts to fade. Unfortunately, the investigation into Kathy Powell's death was no different. Within days the detectives were at a virtual standstill and all of them except Jenkins and Douglas were assigned to different cases. The command center set up in the detective's conference room was disassembled and the timeframe once written on the large whiteboard was now condensed to a page on a yellow legal pad.

On Wednesday, February 22, 1995 Jenkins and Douglas decided to go back to square one in the investigation and pour over everything they had accumulated. They both had the nagging feeling they'd missed something, and even the most minute, overlooked detail might give them the direction they needed. They were slogging through their notes when the phone on Jenkins desk rang at 10:40 in the morning.

A young patrol officer named Reed Thomas had located an International Harvester pickup truck matching the description put out by Jenkins. The truck was parked in the employee parking lot of the T.C.I. Cable Company on Vassar Street in south Reno. The officer was watching the truck from a distance and didn't want to get too close to it in his black and white in case it belonged to the suspect, so he was requesting detectives come to his location to check it out.

Jenkins hung up the phone and told his partner about the truck. Douglas asked, "Didn't we have something about T.C.I. Cable in the reports somewhere?"

"I think you're right," Jenkins said. Flipping the murder book open, he said, "Here it is. The original missing person report from Bob Bennett says there was a note from T.C.I. Cable on Powell's front door saying an installer had been there but she wasn't home."

Douglas said, "That's it! We assumed since the note was still on the front door that it was left there *after* Powell went M.I.A., because she would have taken it off the door if it was left there before. That's why we never followed up on it! But remember what the dude with the ferret told us about Powell never using the front door?"

Jenkins excitedly paged through the murder book until he found the statement given by Powell's friend, Jerry Brown. "I've got it," he said. "It says here that Powell always used the garage entry to go in and out of her house. That note could have been on the front door for a while and she never would have seen it."

"Bingo!" exclaimed Douglas. "So we've got a note from T.C.I. Cable Company on the front door and a beater International pickup in their employee parking lot. There ain't any coincidences in this job, baby! You get down to T.C.I. and I'll get over to Good Guys to pick up the witness and see if it's the right truck."

Before heading out of the office Jenkins stopped by Detective Ed Dixon's desk and asked for some unofficial help. Powell's records were in a box underneath Jenkins' desk. Somebody needed to go through them to see if she was a customer of T.C.I. Cable Company, and if so, make a discreet inquiry about the service call to her condo. Even though he'd been pulled off the case, there was nobody better suited for the job than Evidence Eddie.

Jenkins met Officer Thomas across the street from the lot the truck was parked in. The young officer had been keeping a vigil on the truck and Jenkins borrowed his binoculars to look at it. The truck was parked with its rear end facing the street and Jenkins' heart began beating faster with excitement when he looked at it.

There was no tailgate on the truck, so Jenkins could see into the bed even from this distance. It matched the description given by the witness right down to the plywood and spare tire in the truck bed. The green and white license plate was from Colorado, and Jenkins wrote the plate numbers 7861-WC into his notebook. Officer Thomas had already run the plate and found out the truck was registered to a David Middleton with a listed address in Montrose, Colorado.

Witness Mike Sarratea wasn't working when Douglas got to the Good Guys store, but the other employee who had assisted the courier with the transaction was. Douglas brought him to look at the truck in the T.C.I. lot, but he hadn't gotten as good of a look at it as Sarratea had. The witness said he was almost certain it was the same truck, and almost certain was more than they'd gotten so far.

Since the truck was parked in the secure employee lot at the cable company, Jenkins wasn't concerned about leaving anyone to watch it. If it was there today it would be there again tomorrow, so he pulled Officer Thomas off the surveillance and headed back to the station to run a background check on David Middleton. Douglas said he would meet him back there to help after he dropped the witness off at Good Guys.

Ed Dixon was at his desk talking on the phone and taking notes when Jenkins walked into the Detective Division. Jenkins heard him say, "So your technician Dave made the service call on January 28th at 3:30 in the afternoon, and his last name is spelled M-I-D-D-L-E-T-O-N? Thank you very much. You've been a big help."

Jenkins was smiling when Dixon hung up his phone. He said, "Eddie, if you weren't so big and ugly I'd hug you."

Dixon said, "Then I'm glad I'm big and ugly because you're not my type. Does that mean I'm back on the case?"

Chapter 12

SYMPATHY FOR THE DEVIL

The detectives were like sharks on the scent of fresh blood after discovering Middleton's link to the case, except it was information feeding their frenzy. All five Major Crimes detectives were back on the case and by 8:00 that night they had compiled enough information to convince them Middleton was involved with the disappearance and murder of Kathy Powell. What they had on Middleton thus far was only the tip of the iceberg, but that wasn't the part that had sunk the Titanic. The detectives now needed to see what lurked below the waterline in David Middleton's life.

The only thing the Reno P.D. had on file for Middleton was a burglary report he'd filed when his truck had been broken into in front of his apartment in November of 1994, but this was enough for a start. In the report he listed his address as 1425 Carlin St. in northeast Reno, his place of employment as T.C.I. Cable Company and the red International Harvester pickup as his vehicle that had been burglarized. Besides giving the detectives points of reference, this also established Middleton as a Nevada resident since he'd been living in the state for longer than sixty days. His truck registration and driver's license were both still from Colorado, so this would give them built-in probable cause if they needed leverage to stop and detain him at a later time.

The other interesting information gleaned from the report was a statement taken from Middleton's live-in girlfriend, Evonne Haley. She'd also had property taken in the burglary and said she often drove Middleton's truck with his permission. Haley's photo was on file with the Reno P.D. Records section since she had a work card for employment with a local casino. When the detectives looked at the photo they agreed her heavily made up face actually *did* make her look like a clown, and they'd have to write a thank you note to the Good Guys employees for their accurate description if they ever made a case on her.

Since all of Middleton's personal information was listed on the police report, the detectives didn't have to risk tipping their hand by going through the personnel department at T.C.I. Cable Company to start their investigation on him. When the records clerk who was helping them ran Middleton through the National Crime Information Center's computer program she got an instant hit. Jenkins and Douglas huddled around the computer and read Middleton's arrest record over the clerk's shoulder.

David Stephen Middleton was a convicted sex offender—arrested and convicted in Miami, Florida in 1990. His original charges were kidnap and sexual assault, and the arrest date showed to be November 19, 1989. According to the N.C.I.C. readout he was convicted on the charges of false imprisonment and aggravated battery in June of 1990. He was sentenced to two concurrent five year prison terms, but was released in 1993 after serving a little more than two years of this sentence.

Middleton was no longer on parole, but since he was an ex-felon he still needed to register his local address with the police department within forty-eight hours of moving. It was a misdemeanor crime for him not to do so, but they needed to be careful about arresting him prematurely.

The best way to interview Middleton about the Kathy Powell case was to do it while he was not in custody. This way they would avoid any Miranda issues regarding the right to an attorney during custodial interrogations, because those rights only kicked in after he was under arrest. If they had a valid charge for him being an ex-felon who failed to register, then his attorney could later argue the only reason they didn't arrest him was to deny him his rights. They decided to wait until after they talked to Middleton to contact the Records section of the Miami Metro-Dade Police Department to confirm his ex-felon status. This way they could say in all honesty they didn't have probable cause for an arrest when they talked to him. The Miranda decision had been around since 1963 and both sides of the law have been trying to figure out how to use it to their advantage ever since.

Detectives equate building a case against a suspect to erecting a brick wall. You start with a strong foundation and work your way up from there. Middleton's obvious involvement in the fraudulent use of Kathy Powell's credit card was their foundation. The connection with his installing her cable and now the fact he was a convicted sex offender were the first two bricks in the wall.

The records clerk pointed out something else interesting on Middleton's rap sheet. Included in the N.C.I.C. information bank is a program called Criminal Justice Information Services, or C.J.I.S. More secure information was contained in this program and Middleton's records had a C.J.I.S. number attached to them. The clerk could not access the information without security clearance, but all Major Crimes detectives were issued control numbers to access secure files. Jenkins typed his security number into the computer program, and he and Douglas stared at the screen in disbelief when the following information popped up:

MIDDLETON, DAVID STEPHEN: B/M/A D.O.B. 25 JUNE 1961
P.O.B.: BOSTON, MASS.
LAW ENFORCEMENT AFFILIATION:
1) <u>BOSTON POLICE DEPT</u>: 01/15/80-01/20/82
RANK: POLICE CADET
STATUS: RESIGNED
2) <u>MIAMI METRO-DADE POLICE:</u> 01/25/82-
12/12/90 RANK: OFFICER
STATUS: RESIGNED

It didn't take them long to notice the sequence in dates contained in the printout. Middleton had been a cop with the Miami Metro-Dade Police Department for eight years when he was arrested for kidnap and rape in Florida. His arrest date was in November of 1989, but his date of resignation from the department was December 12, 1990. That meant he was still actively employed as a cop when he'd committed the crimes he'd been convicted of. Based on what they knew about cops who are convicted of sex crimes—two years in prison seemed light.

The fact his employment status read *resigned* instead of *terminated* was important too. Police departments—their own included—were notorious for cutting deals to avoid embarrassing publicity. Officers were sometimes allowed to resign in lieu of termination if they promised to go away quietly. This way they could save some of their benefits and employment prospects, while the department avoided public scandal. It was a win-win situation—except for the public they were sworn to protect. If one deal had been involved when Middleton was arrested in Miami then there was a possibility there were others too. It rankled the detectives when the other anomaly in the dates on the computer printout jumped out at them. If Middleton was still serving time for his Miami crimes, might Kathy Powell still be alive?

With copies of the computer printouts in hand, Jenkins and Douglas headed back to the conference room to share the news with the other detectives that their main murder suspect was an ex-cop. One of a cop's worst nightmares is to have to investigate another cop. One reason is the suspect's knowledge of police procedures can severely limit the investigative tools used against them. The bigger rationale is that cops are idealistic, and none of them like to face the reality that there are bad members in the brotherhood of the badge.

A fraud detective working late had a stereo on his desk tuned to a classic rock station and the Rolling Stones *Sympathy For The Devil* was playing. Mick Jagger belted out the line, "Every cop is a criminal, and all the sinners are saints," just as Jenkins and Douglas walked into the Detective Division office. The déjà vu experience caused them to stop and exchange wide-eyed looks, because neither one of them liked the dimension the investigation had just taken on.

Chapter 13

STUPID CROOK TRICKS

After a roundtable discussion, the detectives unanimously agreed to keep their cards close to their chests for now when it came to Middleton's involvement in the case. The Miami connection needed to be checked, but there was no way to know if Middleton still had friends in the department there. Cops were notorious gossips and if word got out Middleton was being investigated in Reno, it could get back to him. He'd only been out of the department for five years, so there was a good chance he still spoke to people there.

The arrest of a cop usually generates publicity, so they booted up the computer in the conference room and logged into the archives of the *Miami Herald*. Jenkins typed the words "arrest of David Middleton" into the archive search box and hit the enter button. Six articles popped up, which didn't seem like a lot for a case that sent a cop to prison. They were dealing with Miami though, so events like that were a bit more commonplace than in a small town like Reno. Jenkins used the cursor to scroll through the articles while the other detectives pulled up chairs to see what he came up with.

The first article they looked at was dated October 12, 1990 and the bold-face title jumped out at them from the computer screen. It read:

METRO COP CHARGED WITH RAPING
TEEN ELUDES ARREST

Carlos Harrison Herald Staff Writer

A Metro-Dade Police detective was charged Thursday night with kidnapping and raping a 16-year-old girl handcuffed inside of his unmarked police car-but officers who went to arrest him at his home found he had vanished. Metro detective David Middleton, 29, a seven-year member of the department's Warrants section had been absent without leave since he found out that investigators suspected him of sexually assaulting the girl, sources in the department said.

Police went to arrest Middleton at his home Thursday evening after a warrant was issued but couldn't find him.

The girl was raped Saturday, September 29, 1990 between 1:30 and 4:30 A.M., detective Lizette Williams said.

Investigators said Middleton allegedly found the unidentified girl wandering near the Metro Justice Building. Middleton was off-duty but dressed in his police uniform and driving his unmarked car at the time of the incident. Williams said Middleton questioned the girl, who said she was waiting for a friend, then ordered her into his unmarked car. He told her he was taking her to Juvenile Hall, but then drove her to a South Dade parking lot where he handcuffed her and raped her. Then he drove to North Dade where he dropped her off.

Police sources say the victim picked Middleton out of a lineup as her rapist. Middleton's unmarked police car was impounded after the incident, sources said, presumably so investigators could check the car for evidence. The Dade State Attorney's Office declined comment. "I just can't comment at all," said Chief Assistant Attorney John Hogan.

Jenkins pushed his chair back and said, "I don't want to read too much into this because we all know newspapers can sometimes be slightly jaded in their publications. But if this article is even half true, what does it tell us?"

Dixon answered, "It tells us we were right about him still being a cop when he committed the crime."

"Right," Jenkins said. "But look at the part where the article says he was off-duty but in uniform. He was a detective, so what's he doing out on the street in uniform at four in the morning?"

Dixon shrugged and replied, "Maybe he was working some O.T."

"Or maybe he's out trolling the streets like Jack The Ripper," Dypsynski said.

"I like that idea better," said Douglas. "And the article says he was gone when the cops got to his house, so that means the brother runs when he gets spooked."

Hunt shook his head and said, "And *that* tells me I'm being discriminated against. If I use the words 'run,' 'brother' and 'spook' in the same sentence when I'm talking about a black suspect, I'll be up in front of some clam in I.A. for making racial statements."

Douglas smiled and said, "And don't you forget it either, cracker. But it still means we've got to be careful about him bolting if he finds out we're looking at him. The fact he split before the cops got to him also means he probably got tipped off from the inside, so I say we stay clear of Metro P.D. till we get our shit together. Bring up the next article so we can decide what we're gonna do with this dude. My ass is draggin so bad even this plastic chair is startin to feel good on it."

The next article was dated November 21, 1990, almost one month to the day of the first one. It read:

FUGITIVE COP IN RAPE CASE FOUND IN MISISISSPPI

David Hancock Herald Staff Writer

A Metro-Dade police officer who disappeared after he was charged with raping a 16-year-old girl in his police car was returned to Miami Tuesday night, a month after he fled to a small city in western Mississippi. Metro-Dade officer David Middleton, 29, was arrested Monday morning at his new apartment in Greenville, Miss., population 50,000. He had been laying low with his two children and his common-law wife, Evonne Haley, who joined him after he fled Miami last month, police said. Middleton, an eight year veteran of the department, was arrested without incident when Metro-Dade and Greenville police knocked on the door to his apartment, Greenville Police Chief Ken winter said.

"He was somewhat surprised," Winter said.

After being tipped off that Middleton was in Greenville, police were able to locate his apartment, Winter said. Middleton is black and his wife is white. "That drew attention to them in these parts," Winter said. Middleton's wife was not arrested.

Middleton is accused of picking up a 16-year-old girl in Northwest Dade County on September 29, 1989. He told her he was taking her to Juvenile Hall, but instead handcuffed her and allegedly raped her in the front seat of his unmarked police car. Middleton, who worked in Metro's Warrants section, called in sick for three days before officers went to his home to arrest him and discovered he had left.

Winter said Middleton and his wife didn't explain after being arrested why they stopped in Greenville. "We asked why they came to Greenville, and they said they didn't know," Winter said. "They'd would've fit in a lot better in some other places I can think of if they was trying to lay low."

Middleton faces charges of kidnapping and sexual assault. He waived his rights to fight extradition and was flown to Miami Tuesday.

Douglas whistled and then said, "Too bad homeboy wasn't being tried in Greenville instead of Miami, cause a brother ain't getting a *fair* trial in that town. I'm picturing that cop Buford Justice from those old *Smoky and the Bandit* movies givin that interview while banjo music is playin in the background. You just *know* there's a pillow case with some eye holes in it and a rope-noose hanging in that dude's locker next to his deputy chief uniform."

When the laughter subsided, Jenkins said, "So, our girl Evonne was with Middleton way back then. That means she waited for him to get out of prison on top of running away with him when he was trying to avoid arrest. It also means she must have been with him if he was living in Colorado before he got to Reno too. It's interesting the article refers to her as his *common law wife.* Maybe there's more to our prom queen than meets the eye."

"Her meeting my eyes isn't something I'm looking forward to," Douglas said. "Read on."

Jenkins said, "I looked ahead while you were making your astute observations about our esteemed law enforcement colleague in Mississippi. You're gonna love this one, because it proves the theory that if crooks were smart, we'd probably never catch them"

The next article was dated March 14, 1991 and it read:

OFFICERS USE OF TOLL CARD LEADS TO HIS ARREST
Don Van Natta Jr. Herald Staff Writer

Police may never have pinned kidnapping and rape charges on a former Metro-Dade detective if he had paid his own way at a toll booth on State Road 874. Instead, then-cop David Middleton charged the fare to Dade County by handing the attendant a county-issued credit card. The toll was 25 cents.

"If it wasn't for that toll, we never would have traced the car and found our suspect," Assistant State Attorney Kathleen Hoague said Wednesday.

The victim told detectives she saw the police officer who had just raped her hand a credit card to a toll-taker. The girl remembered the card was cracked and "the toll booth lady put tape on it."

That night, only two unmarked Metro patrol cars used county-issued cards at the Southwest Dade toll plaza. Only one matched the victim's description of the officer's car: a 1988 grey Dodge Aries, vehicle number 10871.

And only one of four officers with keys to car 10871 matched the description of her attacker: a black male, around 30, over six feet tall, heavyset, with a distinctive under bite. That description fits David Middleton, 29, an eight-year veteran in Metro's Warrants section.

"The toll booth record was good luck for us, and bad luck for him," Hoague said.

The next three articles covered the court proceedings against Middleton. Victim testimony—often quoted as being tearful—was given by the 16-year-old female the papers referred to as "A.C." This was damning testimony because she said the only reason she willingly went along with Middleton was because he was a police officer, so she *trusted* him.

Middleton never took the stand in his defense, but twenty-three witnesses testified throughout the court proceedings. Some defense witnesses testified that Middleton was an excellent and respected officer who would never break the law, but this was overshadowed by a personnel record that showed him being disciplined for charges of consorting with known criminals.

At the end of the trial the sequestered jury deadlocked after twelve hours of deliberation. They agreed to find Middleton guilty of the amended charges of false imprisonment and sexual battery. Since the most serious charges had been dropped, so was the cap for prison sentencing. Instead of life in prison he was now facing a maximum of five years on each charge.

The prosecutor was quoted as being disappointed with the verdict and pointed to the fact that the trial judge, Philip Davis, was forced to drop out of the case during deliberations because he was being investigated for bribery charges. She said this very well might have contributed to the hasty verdict, but there were no plans for re-filing.

Jenkins rubbed his eyes with the back of his hands. He said, "Something's not right here, but I'm too tired to see it. What are we missing?"

They were all silent in thought, and then Douglas snapped his fingers and exclaimed, "Rodney King! That's what we're missing!"

"What in the hell are you talking about?" asked Hunt. "Every case involving a black crook don't have to be racial."

"I ain't talking about the black crook, I'm talking about the white cops. When the State jury came back with the not guilty verdict on the cops involved in the Rodney King thing the prosecution went federal with it. They charged the cops under the Oppression Under Color Of Authority statutes and they all got federal jail time for violating King's rights while they were on duty."

"I'm with you," Jenkins said excitedly. "Even though Middleton was off duty when he snatched that girl, he was in uniform and driving a police car. That puts him *on* duty when he committed the crime no matter how you look at it."

Douglas stood up and said, "Exactly! And you can't violate a persons rights much more than committing sexual battery on them while you've got them falsely imprisoned. So why didn't the Florida people file federally after Middleton got his charges reduced?"

"That ain't our investigation," Hunt said. "Who the hell knows what goes on in places like Miami?"

"Well somebody has to ask that question," Jenkins said. "John raises a legitimate point. If you put a cop in front of a federal jury they're going to find him guilty of *something.* And in a case like this it would be a slam-dunk. Double jeopardy doesn't come into play because the oppression charge is completely separate from the other charges. Middleton would have gotten at *least* ten years federal time if they would have pushed this."

"And ten years federal is ten *real* years," Douglas added. "There ain't no early release program in Club Fed, so Middleton would have been off the street till about the year 2000 if they'd have done things properly!"

"We can't go back and undo what's been done," Jenkins said. "The ball is in our court now, so what are we going to do with it?"

"I say we pick this clam up and sweat him on the Good Guys case," Hunt said. "At least that way we can get him off the street for a while till we look into the murder."

"That's plausible," Jenkins said. "I'd like to give some thought to how we go about picking him up though."

Dixon said, "It should be easy getting to this guy. First he uses his city credit card while he's kidnapping a girl, and then he sends his girlfriend down to pick up a stereo charged on a dead lady's credit card using his own truck, which is so distinctive looking even *we* found it. My son watches some T.V. show called

Stupid Pet Tricks. Maybe we should make a show called Stupid Crook Tricks and feature our guy Middleton on it."

"I'm not seeing stupidity here, Eddie," Jenkins said. "I'm seeing complacency, and that only shows in crooks who have done things so many times they feel confident they will never get caught. Unfortunately, it's my opinion the 16-year-old girl Middleton got caught raping in Florida was not his first victim. That's why he was comfortable enough to use his city credit card. It was just business as usual. Do you know what that means?"

"Yeah," answered Dixon. "He was complacent after Kathy Powell too, so she's probably not his first. I gotta get out of here and get some sleep. This investigation is getting way too complicated for my simple mind."

Everyone stood up to leave, but Jenkins continued, "There is a link at the bottom of the Miami Herald page saying to go to the archives of the Rocky Mountain Press for additional information on Middleton. Let's see what they've got to say about our friend."

Jenkins used the computer mouse to click on the link. After a few seconds an article from the Colorado paper filled the screen. Douglas summed it up in two words. "Holy shit!"

"I couldn't have said it better," said Jenkins. "Sit down gentlemen, we've got work to do."

Chapter 14

BUFFY

Five bleary-eyed detectives read the article from the *Rocky Mountain News* describing the disappearance of 18-year-old Buffy Rice Donohue from Montrose, Colorado on November 21, 1993. The article was dated December 24, 1993 and the title read:

DISAPPEARANCE DARKENS CHRISTMAS;
MONTROSE MAN TELLS STORY IN DENVER IN HOPES
OF FINDING HIS DAUGHTER
Robert Jackson, Rocky Mountain News Staff Writer

The story was an interview of Walt Rice—the father of the missing girl. Buffy Rice had married her high school sweetheart Mason Donohue five months before her disappearance. Walt Rice and his wife Bonnie were letting the couple live at their Montrose, Colorado home until they raised enough money to rent a place of their own. Buffy worked at a local Sizzler Restaurant and her husband worked construction.

Buffy was last seen when she left the family home at 1:30 in the afternoon to get her car washed and go to a Wal-Mart two miles away. Her husband and father went out looking for her when she had not returned home four hours later. They found her car in the Wal-Mart parking lot with the doors locked and her wallet inside. There were no keys and Buffy was nowhere to be found.

Montrose is not a big town, so Rice and Donohue started checking to see if anyone had seen Buffy. They located two of Buffy's friends who had seen her getting into a red Mazda RX-7 in the Wal-Mart parking lot at about 2:30 that afternoon. The car was driven by one of Buffy's co-workers at Sizzler, Evonne Haley. The witnesses knew the car was owned by Haley's boyfriend, David Middleton.

Both Rice and Donohue were familiar with Haley and Middleton. Middleton was employed by an aluminum siding contractor and Donohue had befriended him after meeting him at a job site. Buffy worked with Haley at Sizzler and the two couples had socialized on several occasions. Their friendship deteriorated after Buffy admitted to her husband and father that she had started experimenting with cocaine and that Middleton was her supplier. Buffy told her husband she wanted to get away from the drugs and that being around Middleton scared her. They decided to stay away from Middleton from that point forward.

Middleton and Haley had moved to Montrose about six months earlier and Walt Rice was familiar with them. He knew Middleton was an ex-cop from Florida who had done some prison time and Haley was an ex-stripper. When Buffy confessed her drug use to him, Walt went to the Colorado Bureau of Investigations with the information to ask agents if they could do something about it. He told reporters he felt that because of the drug connection, Montrose Police didn't take the investigation of his missing daughter seriously when he and Donohue reported it the night of November 21, 1993.

Rice and Donohue had gone to the apartment Middleton and Haley shared to check for Buffy before calling police. The RX-7 was gone and they were told by Haley's daughter that Buffy had been there, but Middleton left to take her home. Haley was not at the apartment either and this did not make sense to them since the car was a two-seater. If they had both left with Buffy, where would she sit in the car? It was this inconsistency that caused them to go to the police.

The police took the report from Rice and Donohue, but said since Buffy was over 18-years–old, an active investigation could not be done until she was missing for over twenty-four hours. Even though she was last seen getting into a car with Haley, she did so of her own free will. They were told if she was still with Middleton and Haley it was most probably by choice, so officers would not go out to the residence to speak with them until the twenty-four hour time frame had elapsed.

The frustration Rice and Donohue felt that night was compounded the next day when a friend of Buffy's who works at a convenience store directly across from Middleton's apartment called to tell them she had seen suspicious activity the night before. She had a clear view of Middleton's apartment through the plate glass store window and around midnight she saw Middleton and Haley loading plastic bags into the trunk of Haley's car. She said

Middleton was struggling with one of the bags because of its weight and he needed to wrap both of his arms around it in order to carry it. She said the bag was easily big enough to conceal a body.

The friend was aware of Buffy's disappearance and Middleton's involvement, so she telephoned the police with the information. She was told by the dispatcher that the police were not taking calls on that case for at least twenty-four hours. It was two days later when the police finally contacted Middleton and Haley and by then Buffy was nowhere to be found.

Rice said the reason he'd come to Denver from Montrose was to try and generate public interest in the case and to put pressure on the Montrose Police Department to investigate Buffy's disappearance more aggressively. Buffy had never left home for an extended period of time before and there was no reason to believe she had left of her own volition this time. Rice was certain David Middleton was responsible for his daughter's disappearance, but so far the Montrose Police were treating Rice himself as more of a suspect than Middleton.

The last line of the article was a quote from Walt Rice. It read, "We will have no Christmas this year. Christmas was Buffy's favorite part of the year, and we won't have another one until Buffy returns home."

All five detectives reading the article had children of their own. It was silent in the room for a moment before Douglas said, "That poor bastard. His daughter ain't coming home."

"I'm afraid you're right," commented Jenkins. "Look at this other article from the *Colorado Springs Gazette* a month later. It says Buffy's not the first girl to go missing from that area. There was a 14-year-old girl named Cindy Booth who disappeared from a town called Delta about twenty miles from Montrose. She was last seen riding her bicycle on August 4, 1993.

"The reporter draws a very interesting timeline here. Middleton moved to Montrose on June 25, 1993 just after he got out of prison. Haley was already living there because she has relatives in Grand Junction, Colorado, so Middleton moved in with her and her two kids. The 14-year-old girl disappeared on August 4, 1993—just a little over a month after Middleton got to town. Then Buffy Rice goes missing on November 21, 1993. The reporter says that area didn't have a suspicious missing female case for ten years before Middleton arrived and there hasn't been one since he left. And my guess is they won't have another one, because their nightmare is now ours."

Chapter 15

MONTROSE

As Jenkins scrolled down the screen, Douglas said, "Some of those articles are pretty recent so I'm guessing Buffy's never been found. Judging from the titles of the news stories, it looks to me like her family has gone on a press campaign against the police department too. Click on the article that says charges were brought against her parents. I wonder what in the hell that's about."

The detectives took their time reading the *Denver Post* article because none of them could actually believe what had been written. The article began with an incident on November 27, 1993, six days after Buffy disappeared. Walt Rice had received a tip that Middleton and Haley might be holding his daughter in a cabin in an area called Waterdog Mountain. He gave this information to a Lieutenant Chinn at Montrose P.D., but since this was out of their jurisdiction Rice was told the police would not investigate the tip.

The distraught father and husband took it upon themselves to check the information. Rice, Mason Donohue and two friends went to the Waterdog Mountain cabin at 11:00 P.M. that night to see if there was any sign of Buffy. A blacked-out truck was driving down the dirt road leading away from the cabin in question when they got there. When the driver spotted the four men he attempted to make a u-turn but got stuck in a ditch. The men surrounded the truck, but it turned out to be a hunter poaching game after hours.

Rice and his friends detained the driver until they were satisfied he wasn't involved in Buffy's disappearance. They left the area after finding no trace of her.

In January of 1994 Walt and Bonnie Rice were told by someone within the Montrose Police Department that investigators had found a roll of undeveloped film while searching the trailer Buffy and her husband lived in just after they were married. The investigators developed the film and found it contained nude photographs of Buffy that her husband took on their honeymoon. The police source told the Rices he had walked by Lieutenant Chinn's office and the nude photos of Buffy were spread out on his desk. Chinn and several officers were laughing and making crude comments about the photos. The officer came forward with the information because he thought the conduct was inappropriate.

When Walt Rice began checking the information he discovered a female employee at the local Sheriff's Department had also seen the photographs of Buffy. She told Walt that two Montrose P.D. officers had come to the Sheriff's Department to see a co-worker of hers and they had nude photographs of Buffy with them. She said they showed the photographs to several male officers like they were pornography and made disparaging remarks about Buffy's character.

Walt Rice was incensed and went to Lieutenant Chinn to ask about the photographs. Chinn said they did in fact have nude photographs of Buffy and they were part of the investigation. He could not offer a reason why these photographs were important to the investigation or why they were not placed into evidence. He refused to give the photographs to Rice, who left after threatening to sue the department over this incident and their inept investigation.

Shortly after this confrontation charges of felony menacing and false imprisonment resulting from the Waterdog Mountain incident were filed against Walt Rice and Mason Donohue.

One week after Walt Rice was criminally charged, Bonnie Rice also had a run in with the Montrose P.D. She and a male friend went to Haley's apartment on February 21, 1994 to confront her about Buffy's disappearance. While Bonnie and her friend stood outside Haley's doorway in a heated discussion, David Middleton came out of the apartment and threatened them with what Bonnie described as a .12 gauge shotgun.

The police were summoned but by the time they got there Middleton had put the shotgun inside the house. Instead of investigating Middleton for being an ex-felon in possession of a firearm, the police cited Bonnie Rice for trespassing. Only *she* was cited, even though the friend who accompanied her had been standing right next to her during the confrontation.

David Middleton and Evonne Haley left Montrose in April of 1994. Bonnie Rice told reporters that Haley said the Montrose Police had advised Middleton that leaving town might be a good idea because they were getting public pressure to arrest him for Buffy's disappearance. A police spokesperson would neither confirm nor deny that allegation.

In May of 1994 the charges of trespass were dismissed against Bonnie Rice. Walt Rice and Mason Donohue pled no contest during that same month to the charges against them stemming from the Waterdog Mountain incident.

The article ended by saying the animosity between the Rices and the Montrose Police Department continued even after Middleton and Haley moved from this sleepy bedroom community of 12,000. The Rices are preparing a lawsuit naming Montrose Police Chief Gerald Hoey and Lieutenant Thomas Chinn as principles.

The Rices also filed charges against a Colorado State patrolman for calling their home and making threats. They recorded the conversation unbeknownst to the caller, identified as Patrolman Jack Charlton. During the phone call the officer expressed his displeasure with the Rices criticism of the local police, and is heard saying, "You're a dead S.O.B." Charlton pleaded no contest to the charges.

After reading the article, Hunt remarked, "What kind of bullshit is this? Instead of jamming this guy up on the missing girl, these fucking yahoos tell him to get out of Dodge? First Florida gives him the boot, then Colorado throws him out of their state, and now we're stuck with him in our backyard."

"Let's remember we're only dealing with news articles here," Jenkins said. "We won't be able to sort out the mistakes in the investigation from journalistic sensationalism until we talk to the cops themselves. There is a much shorter article here where the police say they gave Middleton a polygraph test before they allowed him to leave their jurisdiction. The results were inconclusive, which really doesn't mean anything, but I'm sure they still felt confident they didn't have anything to hold him on."

"Any cop who's been around a polygraph can beat the test," Dypsynski said. "Especially one who is a sociopath, and that's what this guy sounds like."

Douglas shook his head and asked, "The local cops can't nail Middleton, so they figure they'll go out and arrest the victim's parents instead? That's always good for P.R. The mother said Middleton pulled a gauge on her. An ex-felon in possession of a firearm is a felony in all 50 states, so they could have at least held him on that. I've only been reading about this guy for two hours, but I've already seen about a half dozen times he could have been stopped before getting to Reno. If he really *is* our killer then I'm gonna be asking some questions."

"All I know is we've got to do something with this asshole quick," exclaimed Hunt. "If he gets away there's gonna be a bunch of slob cops like us in another city sitting around bashing us the way we're bashing these other guys."

'You're right," said Jenkins. "We don't have nearly enough for an arrest, but based on the truck and Haley's physical match of the courier at Good Guys we certainly have enough to pick him up and question him about that case. I'm sure I can get search warrants for his truck and apartment too, especially if I bring copies of these articles to show the D.A. There's no exigency for a nighttime search warrant though, so I'd like to set up surveillance on Middleton at his apartment right now and stay on him until we have the search warrants in hand. I'll call Toliver at home and see if he can get some people from the Street Crimes Unit to help out with that so we can get some sleep."

"Sleep's highly overrated," Hunt said. "I'll head out there now and get an eyeball on Middleton's place while you're setting things up with Toliver."

"I'll go with you," said Dixon. "But you might want to show this to the D.A. too. I scratched out some notes on the physical descriptions the news articles gave of the victims we think are related to Middleton so far. They are all petite in height and weight, they're all white, and they all have long hair. Kathy Powell fits into that category too. Middleton's driver's license information puts him at six-two and two hundred and forty pounds, so that all matches the profile of a dominant sociopath who is into kidnap and bondage."

Douglas smiled and exclaimed, "I'll be damned! And here I thought you were just another pretty face, Eddie. That's one more brick in the wall."

Chapter 16

THE PRINCE OF DARKNESS

Within an hour a five-man team of undercover detectives from the department's Repeat Offender Unit were set up on Middleton and Haley's apartment to assist Hunt and Dixon with the surveillance. Middleton's International Harvester truck was parked in the lot in front of his apartment building. An older model red Mazda RX-7 with Colorado license plate UUB811 on it was parked in the space next to the truck. This car was registered to Middleton and Haley and the detectives recognized the description from the article they had read about the disappearance of Buffy Rice Donohue.

Jenkins, Douglas and Depsynski had initially remained at the station to prepare the search warrant affidavits, but by 1:00 A.M. they joined the other detectives watching Middleton's apartment. Accompanying them was Detective Sergeant *Steve Burns who had taken over the supervision of the investigation. Toliver was preparing to leave for a vacation so he asked Burns to take over for him. Burns was a hard charger and well liked by the detectives so they welcomed the change in supervision.

After a brief strategy session held in a darkened grocery store parking lot it was decided the Major Crimes detectives would turn the surveillance over to the undercover cops so they could get some rest. Jenkins planned to meet with the on-call Assistant

District Attorney at 8:00 in the morning to review the search warrant affidavit, so there was not much to do until then. If Middleton made any suspicious moves before that, the surveillance teams would detain him for the driver's license and vehicle registration violations until the detectives could respond. One of the benefits of dealing with a hardcore criminal was there was usually *something* they could be held on.

By 9:00 the next morning, Thursday, February 23, 1995, Jenkins had search warrants for Middleton's apartment and truck signed by Washoe County Justice of the Peace Fidel Salcedo. The warrants covered only evidence related to the crimes stemming from the Good Guys' case. Since there was nothing yet to tie Middleton or Haley to the murder of Kathy Powell the warrant would not cover a search for evidence related to that crime. But if the cops discovered something linking Middleton or Haley to the death of Kathy Powell while searching for credit cards or stereo equipment, it was fair game.

The surveillance teams followed Middleton to work at T.C.I. Cable Company at 8:00 that morning. He drove his International Harvester truck to work and parked it in the employee lot. A short time later he emerged from the building and began loading equipment into a T.C.I. Cable Company truck. When he was through, he drove out of the lot in the company truck and the surveillance team followed him to his first service call of the day.

Since Jenkins had a court appearance on another case scheduled that morning he gave the search warrants to Douglas to execute. Detectives Douglas, Depsynski and Dixon went to Middleton's apartment to serve the search warrant. They borrowed Detective Mike Whan from another unit to watch the outside of the apartment while they were searching since Detective Hunt had gone to T.C.I. Cable Company to photograph and search Middleton's truck.

Evonne Haley was at the apartment when detectives arrived to execute the search warrant. After they advised her of the reason for the search she denied any knowledge of the crime or possession of any new stereo equipment. She also said she never heard of Kathy Powell and had never seen her credit card. Haley remained at the apartment while detectives searched and she was less than cooperative. She made a phone call and they assumed it was to Middleton as the surveillance team had him moving immediately after the call.

Fifteen minutes after they started searching the apartment one of the detectives following Middleton called Douglas to tell him he was pulling into the area of the apartment in his T.C.I. truck. Douglas went outside and with the assistance of Detective Whan intercepted Middleton before he got to the apartment. The detectives advised Middleton the reason they were searching his apartment and also told him Detective Hunt was in the process of searching his truck at T.C.I. Cable Company. They told him about the Good Guys' case, but made no mention of Kathy Powell's death. When they were through explaining, Middleton agreed to accompany the detectives to the station for an interview. He rode to the station with Douglas and Whan and left his T.C.I. truck parked at the apartment.

When they got to the station Detective Hunt called in to advise he had photographed and searched Middleton's truck, but no evidence relating to the Good Guys' case was found. He did note the inside of the truck had recently been cleaned. The truck was left at T.C.I. Cable Company and Hunt said he was going to track down Powell's two neighbors who saw the truck outside of her apartment to show them the photos. One detective from the surveillance team was left with the truck in case Middleton or Haley went to get it.

When Jenkins returned from court Middleton was in an interview room being watched by Detective Whan. They had decided Jenkins would handle the initial interview of Middleton and Douglas would watch over closed circuit T.V. from an adjacent room. This way if something started going wrong in the interview or if the chemistry was wrong between Jenkins and Middleton, Douglas could come in and take over the interview from a different angle without being tainted by whatever went wrong with Jenkins. Detective Whan would act only as a witness to the interview and would not ask any questions.

Jenkins started the interview at 11:00 A.M. by first obtaining basic personal information from Middleton and then telling him the interview would be recorded. The next thing he did was tell Middleton he was not under arrest and that he was free to get up and leave at any time. Jenkins was the most skilled interviewer in the department, and, in fact, taught interview techniques to other departments. Just from what he'd read thus far about Middleton he knew he was the type of person who would welcome the interview—not walk away from it. A sociopath always thought he could lie his way out of a situation, and Jenkins knew he was looking into the eyes of a true sociopath as he stared at the man across the table from him.

True to form Middleton consented to stay for the interview, so Jenkins told him he first wanted to talk to him about a cable installation he did at 3484 Terrace Knolls Court in Reno. Jenkins did not initially mention Kathy Powell's name, but Middleton said he remembered the installation. He said he had given the female resident a cable converter box and she had also asked him to install an additional two outlets in her home.

Jenkins then asked Middleton if the resident's name was Kathy Powell. After a brief hesitation Middleton said that name did sound familiar. Jenkins next told Middleton that Kathy Powell had recently been found dead and her credit card had been used for a telephone transaction at Good Guys store. He then told Middleton that he strongly believed his International Harvester pickup truck had been used to collect the stereo equipment purchased with Kathy Powell's credit card.

Middleton denied any knowledge of the credit card transaction or of Kathy Powell's death. He said his girlfriend often uses his truck when he is at work and perhaps she had been at Good Guys when the person had picked up the stereo equipment.

That could have been what caused the confusion with the salespeople who saw the truck.

When Jenkins asked Middleton if he had ever been to the Southwest Village Apartments, Middleton said the apartment complex is on his route and he responds there often for service calls. When Middleton asked why Jenkins wanted to know about the Southwest Village complex, Jenkins let the question hang in the air unanswered while he pretended to be studying his notes.

Middleton appeared to be very nervous and apprehensive during these beginning stages of the interview, so Jenkins asked him about this instead of answering his question. Middleton said he was nervous because the other detectives told him they were in the process of searching his apartment. He said his wife had a small amount of methamphetamine in the apartment and he was afraid she would get in trouble if they found it. Middleton admitted to using methamphetamine on a recreational basis, but said he hadn't used any in a couple of days.

Jenkins asked Middleton if he and Haley were legally married, and Middleton said she was his common law wife. Jenkins told him Nevada didn't recognize common law marriages, so for the purpose of the interview he would refer to Haley as his girlfriend. He then asked Middleton if it was possible Haley might have picked up the stereo equipment from Good Guys, to which Middleton said if she did then it was without his knowledge.

Jenkins then switched the line of questioning to Commercial Hardware store. Middleton initially denied knowing where the store was, but then said he had been in there a few times to buy tools and drill bits. He said he had no checking account or credit cards and always paid cash for purchases. Jenkins asked him specifically if he had gone to Commercial Hardware store on February 8, 1995 and bought some 33-gallon plastic trash bags and some plastic wrap. Middleton said he had definitely not made those purchases.

Middleton's key ring was on the table in front of him and Jenkins noted there were several smaller keys on it. He asked Middleton to describe what each key was for. Middleton identified his truck key, the key for the Mazda RX-7 and his house key. He said the other keys were just for miscellaneous locks. Jenkins thought one of the keys looked like the type for security padlocks like those utilized on storage sheds. He asked Middleton if he had a storage shed and Middleton replied he did not.

Throughout the interview Middleton mentioned several times that he used to be a cop and he wanted to help the detectives any way he could, because he was *one of them.* Jenkins asked him if he would voluntarily supply samples of his blood and fingerprints if he really did want to help. It was at that point Middleton said he wanted to consult with an attorney before doing that or going any further with the investigation. Jenkins terminated the interview at that time, but asked Middleton if he would remain at the station for a couple of minutes while he cleared up some minor details. Middleton agreed and Jenkins left the room to confer with the other detectives.

Douglas had the same gut feeling as Jenkins that Middleton was lying and trying to ingratiate himself with them by continually saying he was *one of them.* They decided right then that Middleton might himself be a skilled interviewer so they would have to incorporate a system of checks and balances for themselves into any further interviews. A skilled crook could turn an interviewer into an interviewee without the cop even realizing it if he wasn't careful.

While Jenkins was interviewing Middleton, Detective Hunt had returned from showing the Polaroid photos of Middleton's truck to Kathy Powell's neighbors. One of them said the truck looked about right and the other said she was almost positive it was the same truck. It wasn't a positive identification, but it was another brick in the wall.

At the same time Detective Dixon had been on the phone with the Records section of the Miami Metro-Dade Police Department. He'd confirmed that Middleton was an ex-felon out of their jurisdiction, so now the detectives knew he met the criteria for registration with the Reno Police Department. Part of that registration process was fingerprinting and he had no right to consult an attorney prior to doing it.

Jenkins went back into the interview room and asked Middleton if he had registered with the Reno Police Department as a convicted person. Middleton said he was not aware of the requirement so he had never registered. Jenkins told Middleton since he had been so cooperative with the investigation he would help Middleton register so he wouldn't get into any trouble. Jenkins then made arrangements for a clerk to meet them in the Records room during the time it was closed to the public for lunch so Middleton could complete the registration process in private and avoid embarrassment—since he was *one of them.*

Idle conversation is not considered questioning, so even though Middleton invoked his right to an attorney Jenkins kept talking to him as they made their way to the Records division. He told Middleton that he realized he was afraid, but all the detectives were interested in was getting to the truth. He also said he was aware there could be circumstances involved in Kathy Powell's death that might make it something other than a murder. Jenkins said if it was not a murder then he didn't want Middleton held for such a crime. He mentioned nothing about what they knew of Middleton's criminal involvement in Florida and Colorado.

Jenkins then threw out the bait. He said, "I can tell you were a good cop at one time, and you know how cops work off of their instincts. I don't have all the answers, but I know in my heart you were associated with Kathy Powell's death. You were *one of us,* so you know what I'm talking about."

Middleton took the bait, and Jenkins silently cursed himself for leaving his cassette recorder in the interview room. Middleton stopped and said, "Well…it's not a murder, but I think I need to talk with an attorney before I tell you anything else about it."

Jenkins considered that statement to be an admission by Middleton that he was somehow involved in Kathy Powell's death, but there were no witnesses and it was not recorded. When Douglas joined them after the ex-felon registration process was completed Jenkins tried to get Middleton to repeat the statement. Middleton denied making any statement, and said even is he had, it would be inadmissible because he'd already asked for an attorney.

Middleton smiled and said, "So am I free to go now, detective? If so then I'd appreciate a ride back to my truck. I don't want to keep my other customers waiting too long."

An equally disingenuous smile spread across Jenkins face as he tried his best to hide his anger. He said, "Not recording your statement was a mistake on my part, David. It won't be the last mistake I make in my life, but I will guarantee it will be the last one I make as far as you're concerned. Now by all means let's get you back to your truck.. I said you were free to go and I'm a man of my word. Remember that."

Douglas drove the unmarked detective car with Jenkins in the front passenger seat and Middleton in the back as they made their way to Middleton's apartment. A cassette recorder hidden under a newspaper was running throughout the ride, but Middleton only made small talk about police work and the difference in crime rates between Miami and Reno. When they got to his apartment he thanked them for the ride, got out of their car and drove away in his T.C.I. Cable truck without going into the apartment. Two unmarked surveillance cars followed him from a safe distance. Jenkins was reasonably certain the key on Middleton's ring was to a storage shed and he hoped he'd lead the surveillance team to it.

When they were alone in the detective car, Jenkins asked, "So what do you think?"

Douglas shook his head and replied, "If I didn't know better I'd think we were talking to another cop when we were with that guy—*most* of the time. He seems like a regular guy and looks like he used to be an athlete, but then when he gave you that wicked grin in the hallway after he said you couldn't use his statement it was like I saw little horns sprout out of the front of his head. I had to check his nametag to make sure it didn't change from Dave to *Lucifer*! That dude's evil man—I can feel it!"

Jenkins said, "I get the same vibes from him—and we can't both be wrong. He played us this time, but that won't happen again. Let's go check with the boys in the apartment and see what they came up with inside the Prince of Darkness's lair."

Chapter 17

THE TRUTH WILL SET YOU FREE

Evonne Haley was seated on the living room couch when Douglas and Jenkins walked into the apartment. This was their first exposure to her and she silently glared at the two detectives when they introduced themselves. Dixon was kneeling next to the couch looking through some drawers in an end table. He said, "Ms. Haley isn't very happy with us at the moment."

Detective Depsynski called Jenkins into the kitchen and showed him a black plastic garbage can liner he'd found in the kitchen cabinet. It was a 33-gallon size with the same grey block-lettered suffocation warning label printed in the corner as the bag used to cover Kathy Powell's head had bore on it. This bag was distinctively different from the variety of trash bags routinely sold in grocery stores. The only place he'd seen this type of bag other than on Kathy Powell was at the Commercial Hardware store when he and Douglas had purchased a box of them.

The four detectives gathered in the kitchen for a brief conference. They now had Middleton's statement to Jenkins about having knowledge of the murder, his recorded statement that there might be drugs in the apartment and the garbage bag that was possible evidence linking him to Powell's death. They could also now bring in what they knew about Middleton's past criminal history. It wasn't nearly enough to arrest him on, but it was certainly enough to go back to the judge and request the scope of their search warrant be widened to include evidence linked to the murder and narcotics activity. That would virtually open up every inch of the apartment and the couple's two vehicles to their search.

When Jenkins told Haley they would be remaining at the apartment while he met with the judge to get a new search warrant, she flew off the couch and unleashed a stream of profanities at him. It was then he noticed the telltale signs of methamphetamine use on her. After calming her down somewhat he asked her about the drugs Middleton said might be in the apartment and if she had been using them. She admitted using methamphetamine just before the detectives got to the apartment that morning and said there was none left in the apartment.

The next decision was a no-brainer. Detective Whan had just pulled up in front of the apartment and Jenkins told him to take Haley up to the County Jail, have a drug recognition test done on her and then book her for being under the influence of methamphetamine. Haley struggled with the detectives at first, but then became somewhat cooperative when they said she could call some friends and arrange to have her twelve-year-old daughter picked up from school before they took her to jail.

Arresting Haley would benefit them in three ways. First, it would get her out of the way while they completed their search of the apartment. Second, it would get her on file and they would now have her fingerprints and photo to use to further their investigation.

And third, it would show both Haley *and* Middleton the investigation was about more than just credit card fraud.

After Haley was gone Jenkins and Douglas drove to the District Attorney's office to get help with updating the search warrant. The attorney who worked on the original warrant with Jenkins was busy, but a young attorney named Thomas Viloria volunteered to assist them.

The thirty-year-old prosecutor was fairly new to the Washoe County District Attorney's office, but he'd already earned the reputation of having a bulldog mentality and the tenaciousness of a pit bull when he was prosecuting a case he believed in. Vilonia's handsome Mediterranean features coupled with the build of a middleweight boxer earned him the nickname *Italian Stallion,* since his co-workers said his courtroom demeanor mimicked Sylvester Stallone's character Rocky Balboa in the ring.

After Jenkins laid the case out for him, Viloria was fascinated by it. Not only did he help update the search warrant, he cornered Judge Salcedo who had signed the original warrant and had him personally read and sign this one. Before they left the courthouse Viloria told the detectives he would like to stay involved in the case and for them to call him if they ever needed further assistance. The young bulldog attorney had no idea at the time how drastically that one statement would change his career *and* his life.

At 3:30 in the afternoon Jenkins radioed Depsynski and told him he and Douglas were on their way back to the apartment with an updated and signed search warrant. The scope of this new warrant expanded their search to any items associated with Kathy Powell's body as well as evidence of narcotics possession. The warrant covered Middleton's truck and the red RX-7 in addition to the apartment. They would have to call in a crime scene team to collect trace and fingerprint evidence, but Jenkins gave the go-ahead for Depsynski and Dixon to start the search in the interim.

Thirty minutes later Jenkins and Douglas walked into Middleton's apartment and found two smiling detectives standing in the dining room. Depsynski and Dixon were both wearing white latex gloves, and lying on the table in front of them was a Remington 870 Wingmaster .12 gauge pump shotgun. This is the kind of shotgun used by most police departments, but it was also exactly like the one Bonnie Rice said Middleton pointed at her the night she went to confront Haley about her missing daughter in Montrose, Colorado. Although this brand of shotgun is mass-produced and a big seller amongst gun enthusiasts, the old adage about there not being any coincidences in police work ran through all the detective's minds.

Depsynski had discovered the shotgun hidden under the covers of the bed Middleton shared with Evonne Haley. Since the gun was in that close of a proximity to Middleton's everyday living area there was no way he could deny knowledge of its presence in the apartment. The law said as long as they could show that a convicted ex-felon had that knowledge, they did not have to prove actual ownership of the gun.

The discovery of the shotgun gave validity to the Montrose news article, and they were now more convinced than ever that Middleton was involved in Kathy Powell's murder. Unfortunately they could not arrest him based on their gut instincts, but they now had a valid felony charge to arrest him on if they chose to do so.

The state of Nevada took the crime of ex-felon in possession of a firearm seriously. A high bail was set for persons arrested for the charge and a minimum mandatory sentence of one year in prison was given if convicted of it. The next decision was another no-brainer for the detectives. They would take the extra step the Montrose cops didn't and remove David Middleton from society while they continued their investigation into Kathy Powell's murder. With Middleton in jail at least they could be sure he wouldn't rack up any more victims while they put their case together against him.

A slamming car door got their attention and when they looked out the front window they saw Middleton walking toward the front door from his International Harvester pickup truck. Jenkins and Douglas met him outside of the front door and this time the smiles on their faces were anything *but* disingenuous.

Jenkins explained the updated search warrant and the discovery of the shotgun to Middleton. He looked almost relieved, saying the shotgun actually belonged to Haley and that it couldn't be fired since it was unloaded. For those two reasons he said the detectives couldn't arrest him for possessing the shotgun.

Jenkins said, "That may be true to a jailhouse lawyer, but let me explain the way the law really works. The statute says 'possession of a firearm—constructive or physical—by a convicted felon is a felony and shall be punished by a minimum of one year in a State institution.' You see, David, there are no exceptions in the law based on whose side of the bed the gun was on or whether you loaded it before you went to sleep last night."

Douglas said, "And like my grandma used to say, '*once burnt, twice lernt.*' I think she used to say *boy* first too, but that was socially acceptable back in those days."

"What my partner is trying to say in his own way," Jenkins added, "is you are under arrest for being an ex-felon in possession of a firearm."

"No, I *said* what I was trying to say," Douglas said. "You burned the cops once with that gauge and you *ain't* gonna do it again. Now put your hands behind your back so I can put these nice silver bracelets on you."

Jenkins searched Middleton after he was handcuffed and removed the large key ring he'd seen earlier at the police station from his pants pocket. He said, "We'll need your keys, David. We're going to be towing your truck to the crime lab for processing and it will be much easier for the driver to hook it up if he can back it out onto the street. We also need to search the RX-7 and I'd like to have a key to the house so we can lock up when we're through here. It seems Evonne won't be back for a few hours."

After Jenkins explained Haley's arrest, Middleton said, "You can take the ignition key for the truck off the ring, but I want the rest of the keys kept with me in my property. The RX-7 is unlocked and you can use the handle lock on the front door to lock up the apartment when you leave."

The keys felt like they were on fire as Jenkins held them in his hand. He knew in his heart they were somehow involved in the case, but as hard as he tried he couldn't think of a reason to put them into evidence. If he kept the keys without cause and they later proved pertinent to the case, anything he discovered by using them would be thrown out of court as fruits of the poisonous tree since Middleton was specifically asking they be returned to him.

Jenkins took the truck key off the ring and put the remaining keys back into Middleton's pocket. He said, "As you wish, David. I'll know where to find them if I need them. I'm going to drive you to jail myself and I'd like you to remember something. From this day forward if there is anything at all you want to discuss with us, we're always available."

Douglas added, "All we're after is the truth, and like my grandma *also* used to say—'*the truth will set you free.*'"

Jenkins gave a tug on the handcuff chains and said, "Of course, his grandma spoke in metaphorical terms. Let's go."

Chapter 18

DEAD ENDS

Nothing was found during the search of Middleton's apartment and vehicles to tie him or Haley to the Good Guys' case or to Kathy Powell's murder. As a matter of fact, with the exception of some drug paraphernalia and the shotgun, nothing was found to tie them to *any* type of criminal behavior. This made the detectives even more certain Middleton had a storage shed somewhere, because as Douglas put it, "nobody *that* dirty can be *that* clean."

Evonne Haley was released from jail on her own recognizance later that evening. The detectives did not charge her with anything related to the Good Guys crime because they felt they didn't have enough yet. All they had was the fact she matched the description of the courier and Middleton owned a truck matching the one used to pick up the stereo equipment.

There were several sightings of similar trucks since the start of the investigation and Reno had more than it's share of overweight blondes who wore too much make up. To say Haley was the courier and Middleton's truck was the same as the one used at Good Guys wouldn't hold up in court without additional evidence. They didn't want to do a photo lineup to see if the witnesses from Good Guys could pick out Haley since if even one of them didn't pick her out, it would ruin the chance of filing charges against her later. Even if they *did* identify her, they wouldn't be able to prove she knew she was picking up merchandise that had been fraudulently obtained. They needed to keep building their wall, but at least Middleton was off the street while they were doing it.

By Friday, February 24th the investigation appeared to be once again coming to a standstill. It had been thirteen days since Kathy Powell's body was discovered and although they had zeroed in on a suspect, they weren't even close to making a case against him. Motive was a key clue in any homicide investigation, but they had none. They didn't even have a viable cause of death to work with and the only evidence they did have was circumstantial at best. Without any new leads, overtime to work the case over the weekend certainly would not be approved, and everyone but Jenkins and Douglas were pulled from the case to help with the mounting case load.

The detectives were still convinced Middleton had a storage shed and finding it would give the investigation the boost it needed. They began calling storage facilities and by noon had contacted every one in a fifty mile radius. None of them had a storage unit rented to Middleton or Haley and they all said they required identification from their renters. It looked like another dead end, so they treated themselves to a sit-down lunch and spent the rest of the day organizing their case notes.

Jenkins made a phone call to Montrose, Colorado that day and spoke with Lieutenant Chinn from the Montrose P.D. As they suspected, Buffy Rice Donohue still had not been found—dead *or* alive. The case was still listed as open and both Middleton and Haley were persons of interest in Buffy's disappearance.

When Jenkins told Chinn about Middleton's arrest for being an ex-felon in possession of a firearm he was told a story that may have contributed to the reason the same thing wasn't done in Colorado. Most people in Montrose didn't know Middleton was an ex-felon, and that may also have been true of the officers who had responded to the disturbance. Middleton told people that he was an ex-cop from Miami and had been put in prison as part of an undercover sting operation targeting drug dealers. He alluded to the fact that he ended up in Montrose as some type of Witness Protection Program.

Shortly before Buffy's disappearance she told her parents she found out Middleton had actually been in prison as a prisoner and not as an undercover cop. Walt Rice came forward with that information after Buffy's disappearance. Nobody believed it at first because by then Middleton had a lot of friends in the community—local cops included. As a routine part of the investigation Chinn ran Middleton's criminal history a few days after the missing person report was filed. He learned Middleton was in fact an ex-felon, but he wasn't certain if that information ever filtered down to the rank and file officers.

Jenkins had researched the Montrose Police Department through their web site before making the call and learned it was a forty-three man department with a five-man detective division.

How information that important could not *filter down* in a department that small was beyond him, but it was not his job to second guess, so he kept quiet. He also didn't ask whether the officers who responded to Middleton's apartment during the shotgun incident were among the group he had befriended. He could picture Middleton standing on the steps of his apartment saying, "Come on, I was *one of you* once. I'd never pull a gun on a lady."

Chinn did not know how Buffy had learned Middleton was an ex-felon and he would not be able to ask Walt or Bonnie Rice about it. Due to the hostility between the Rice's and the police department, the City's attorney had advised against any unsupervised contact between the two parties. Jenkins again kept silent about his knowledge of the pending lawsuit and the allegations of misconduct regarding the nude photos of Buffy.

Chinn surprised Jenkins when he told him he had traveled to Reno in October of 1994 to interview Middleton about the Buffy Rice case. He said he notified Reno P.D. that he was in town to interview Middleton, but when questioned about the notification he said he called police dispatch and advised them. The fact this information never made its way to the Detective Division did not surprise Jenkins. The Dispatch Center was sometimes referred to as the "Black Hole," among other things. Sometimes information went in there and just never came out. It was water under the bridge now, but it would have been nice to have Middleton on their radar screen five months before Kathy Powell was killed.

After Jenkins got off the phone he discussed the conversation with Douglas. His handwritten notes confirmed most of what they'd read in the newspaper articles, and it seemed to them like Middleton did in fact slip through some very large cracks in order to get to Reno. They decided right then and there that the focus of their investigation would remain on what Middleton did in Reno—not what could have been done to prevent him from getting to Reno in the first place. Their job was to bring to justice the murderer of Kathy Powell and dragging investigations from other jurisdictions into their investigation would only muddy the waters. If mistakes were made, the people they were made by would have to live with them.

Before leaving for the day Jenkins made one more telephone call. This one went to Assistant Attorney Tom Viloria who Jenkins had called earlier to ask assistance in getting Middleton's bail amount raised. Viloria talked to the judge and Middleton's bail was raised from $25,000 to $750,000 cash-only based on his flight from justice when he was a fugitive in Florida. Jenkins thanked him and smiled as he hung up the phone.

Middleton did not even have a checking account and his most valuable possession was the 1972 International Harvester pickup truck which was still in police custody. There was no way he could raise $75—never mind $750,000. They decided to let him sit in jail over the weekend and try an interview with him on Monday. A few days in jail might jar his memory, and two days away from the investigation might help them blast through their dead ends.

Chapter 19

A NEW DAY

Monday morning came around all too soon for Jenkins. He managed to spend a rare two-day weekend devoid of any detective call outs, but his days off still flew by. He was able to spend some quality time with his family, hit the gym twice and sip some good red wine for the purpose of relaxation instead of memory obliteration for a change. But the weekend was over, and he had his game face on when he walked into the Major Crimes Unit office at 7:00 in the morning February 27, 1995.

It had now been sixteen days since the discovery of Kathy Powell's body. Even though he had time for relaxation over the weekend, his mind often drifted back to the investigation and how to get things moving. He was convinced they were focused on the right suspect, but getting to David Middleton was now the problem.

The new day brought with it one of the Sierra Nevada's bigger winter storms of the year. Although large accumulations of snow usually fell only in the high mountains surrounding Reno, this storm threatened to dump six inches in the valley before it moved on. As a result of the storm, the morning commuter traffic was a nightmare. There was a pink telephone message slip on Jenkins' desk when he got to it informing him Douglas would be late. He lived in a community thirty-five miles east of Reno and a wreck on I-80 currently had the road closed. The message said he'd catch up with him when he got there.

Crime had been relatively slow in Reno over the weekend, so the Kathy Powell case was all that was discussed in the morning detective staff meeting. Even though they were convinced that they already had their suspect identified, other leads had to be followed up on and eliminated. It was a common defense technique for an attorney to go in front of a jury and say the police focused only on his client from the beginning of the investigation, so the *real* killer went free. This was especially true when the suspect was black, the victim was white and there were other possible suspects who also happened to be white that were not properly eliminated as suspects.

Sergeant Burns dedicated the rest of the unit to the case to help Jenkins and Douglas as long as things remained slow. Follow up interviews needed to be done with everyone involved, but especially with Powell's boyfriend in Pittsburg. He would be the one a defense attorney would focus on since he stood to gain monetarily from Powell's death. Depsynski volunteered to interview Don Barley and said he hoped he could nail everything down over the phone. If somebody had to fly to Pittsburg in the winter for a face-to-face interview, he would not be volunteering.

Other interviews and tasks were assigned, but Jenkins said his first stop was going to be 911 Parr Boulevard—the Washoe County Jail. He'd given a lot of thought over the weekend as to how he was going to handle Middleton, and it was time to play his first card. Since Douglas hadn't arrived yet Hunt volunteered to accompany Jenkins. Keeping Douglas out of the interview process while it was still in its infancy was also still a good ploy, because he could always come in and play the good cop if things went bad with Jenkins.

The Washoe County Jail complex was located in the foothills overlooking north Reno. The Sheriff's Department, crime lab and the jail intake were housed in the main building and the inmate facilities were located in pods that extended from that building like fingers from a hand. The section of the complex that faced the main road consisted of modern looking buildings constructed of clean white brick and an abundance of tinted glass. At first glance one would think it was a modern office complex—until they drove to the rear of the building. Located there was the telltale ten-foot chain link fence topped by concertina wire that surrounded every jail in America. It was *this* section of the complex that the detectives entered when they arrived.

It was 8:35 in the morning by the time they got to the jail and all of the inmate interview rooms were already filled. Mornings were the busiest times at the jail and they'd wanted to arrive earlier, but the drive took them twice the usual time because of the inclement weather. After a brief conversation with the jail intake personnel Jenkins got approval for Middleton to be brought out to the jail corridor for a short conversation. Since Middleton had already invoked his right to an attorney the detectives would not be able to ask him any questions, but that wasn't the purpose of this meeting.

Middleton was brought out into the jail corridor wearing jail garb consisting of an orange jumpsuit and blue plastic sandals over white socks. The outfit made him appear smaller than he did in his civilian clothing. He also appeared less confident than he had during their last meeting. The dejected look on his face reminded Jenkins of a dog who had just been disciplined with a rolled-up newspaper.

Jenkins introduced Middleton to Detective Hunt and told him they were just stopping by to see how he was doing. He told Middleton that since he was an ex-cop they were worried about his physical and mental well being now that he was behind bars again. When asked if he'd like to be placed into protective custody Middleton replied he was fine for the time being. Jenkins was trying to establish some type of rapport with Middleton, and it seemed to be working.

Middleton told the detectives he wanted to speak to them and tell them what happened, but before he did that he wanted to talk to an attorney to ask a couple of legal questions. He said no matter what his attorney told him he would still speak to the detectives—he just wanted to make sure he had the right understanding of the law before he did.

Middleton said he knew the detectives weren't there to talk about the gun charge, so that's why he wanted to talk to an attorney first. He said he'd called Haley over the weekend and she said she'd called a local attorney for him, but he hadn't been contacted by anyone yet. Middleton said as soon as the attorney contacted him he'd have the jail deputies call the detectives to set up an interview.

Jenkins told Middleton he was eligible for representation by the Public Defender's office and to send him a "kite" if he would like that arranged. A "kite" is jailhouse language for a written note inmates can send through the interdepartmental mail inside of the jail. Middleton thanked Jenkins for the offer and said he'd be in touch. He was then led back inside of the jail by his escort deputy.

Before leaving the jail the detectives stopped at the intake desk and checked Middleton's property and visitor log sheet. He'd had no visitors since he was booked, but he had released his cash and key ring to Evonne Haley. Jenkins was now more certain than ever that the keys were somehow related to Kathy Powell's murder.

Detective Depsynski called Jenkins as he and Hunt were leaving the jail. An operator from T.C.I. Cable Company had heard about Middleton's arrest and contacted the police with some information she thought might be pertinent. The operator had received a call two weeks ago from a female who identified herself only as Suzy. The female said she had been getting threatening phone calls from Middleton's girlfriend and she wanted it to stop. The caller said Middleton's girlfriend was calling her place of employment to make the threats and she was about to get fired over it. She said she wanted T.C.I. Cable to put pressure on Middleton for this to stop.

Jenkins looked up Evonne Haley's phone number from his notes and called her to see if she would speak to him. He didn't tell her the exact reason, and she said the detectives could come to her apartment to talk to her. The weather and the roads had begun to clear, so thirty minutes later Hunt was pulling the unmarked detective car into the spot Middleton's truck usually occupied.

Haley looked disheveled and exhausted when she let the detectives into her apartment. The inside was in the same state of disarray as they had left it after their search, and traces of black fingerprint powder could still be seen on the white paint on the door jambs around the front door. She apologized for the appearance of the apartment, but said she felt as if her whole world was crashing down around her since Middleton's arrest. She said even though she worked at a local casino, Middleton's check paid for most of their living expenses and now she was afraid he'd lose his job. She then quickly switched gears and asked if what she'd heard on the news was true—that the police thought Middleton killed Kathy Powell.

Jenkins' tone of voice was sympathetic when he explained that the police were looking at Middleton as being involved, but they hadn't narrowed their investigation into Kathy Powell's death to any one suspect. He told her that of course the police needed to look into Middleton's possible involvement since his truck had been identified as being used in the fraudulent use of the deceased woman's credit card. He then told her they were somewhat familiar with Middleton's problems in Colorado and Florida, so it was only natural the police needed to look into his possible involvement in Kathy Powell's death.

Haley crossed her arms in front of her chest and stepped away from the detectives when Jenkins mentioned Colorado and Florida. There was so much Jenkins wanted to ask her, but based on her body language he decided to keep this interview focused on the present. There would be time for the other questions later.

Jenkins moved the conversation to Haley's daughter and asked if she had been picked up from school alright the day she was arrested. Haley seemed to calm down at the mention of her daughter and said she had been taken care of. She then thanked Jenkins for allowing her to make those arrangements before going to jail.

Haley sat down on the living room couch and Jenkins took a seat on a worn-out arm chair across from her. Hunt remained standing by the door since they'd already decided Jenkins would take the lead on the interview. Now that the mood was more amicable Jenkins asked Haley about the female caller to T.C.I. Cable.

Haley's face blushed and she wrung her hands together as she spoke. She said she knew Middleton cheated on her with other women over the years, but she loved him and didn't want to leave him. She said she was an extremely jealous person and when she found Suzy's phone number in the pocket of Middleton's workpants she became incensed. She began calling the woman and making threats to hurt her if she didn't stay away from Middleton, and even confronted her in person one night as she was leaving the bar she worked at.

Jenkins asked Haley the name of the bar and she said it was The Brew Pub on Victorian Square in Sparks. He then asked Haley to describe Suzy, and the description she gave caused the two detectives to exchange quizzical looks while Haley was staring down at the table in front of her. With the exception of the weight, Suzy's description closely matched the description of the courier seen at Good Guys. This threw their investigation into that crime in an unexpected direction.

Jenkins changed the subject and asked Haley if she had retained an attorney for Middleton. She said she had left a message for one but he hadn't gotten back to her yet. Jenkins told her that if he didn't hear from her by the end of the day he would contact the Public Defender's office and arrange representation for Middleton. She thanked him and he stood to leave.

As an afterthought he asked her about Middleton's keys. She said Middleton got a message to her through the deputies as she was being discharged from jail and asked her to take his keys and cash out of his property. She said she needed the cash, and figured he wanted her to have the extra house and car keys with her.

Jenkins asked if she would mind giving him the keys in case they could somehow help in the investigation. Haley's mind seemed to be in another place, but she took the key ring out of her purse and handed it to Jenkins without questioning his reason for wanting it. Jenkins looked at the key ring and saw it was the one he had seen Middleton with. He now had legal possession of the keys and slipped them into his coat pocket without making further mention of them.

When they were back in the car, Hunt said, "That's just great. If you shave forty pounds off that broad she could have been describing herself instead of that bartender. Do you think there really *is* a bartender or do you think she's blowing smoke to throw us off?"

"I don't think she's smart enough to throw up that kind of smokescreen," Jenkins replied. "We've got the phone number and name of the bar, so tracking the girl down can't be too difficult for a couple of super sleuths like us. You're right about this other girl matching the description of the courier, but there is one other troubling possibility."

"What's that?"

Jenkins turned in his seat and said, "If you shave forty pounds off of Evonne Haley, she would be about the same height and weight as Kathy Powell. That means this bartender Suzy fits into the same list that Eddie put together of the physical characteristics of Middleton's known victims. When we find her we might just be looking at Middleton's next victim. That is *if* we don't do our jobs before he does his."

Chapter 20

STALKER

By 3:00 that afternoon the detectives had Suzy identified as forty-two–year-old Suzanne Atkinson*. Jenkins and Douglas had gone to The Brew Pub and spoken to the owners who supplied them with Atkinson's information. She no longer worked at the bar, as the owners fired her just after the first of the year. They said the reason they fired her was that a person named Evonne had been constantly calling the bar and making disturbing threats towards her. They also heard rumors that Atkinson was selling methamphetamine to bar patrons.

The mention of methamphetamine sales interested the detectives and they began thinking maybe it *was* her instead of Haley who had been involved in the Good Guys crime. They went to Atkinson's Sparks apartment and when she answered the door the detectives were surprised by her appearance. Hunt was right—she looked like Evonne Haley with forty pounds shaved off.

When Jenkins told Atkinson they were there to ask her questions about David Middleton, she said, "That creep?"

She then invited them into her apartment but told them she had to leave for work shortly. Since being fired from The Brew Pub she had taken a job tending bar at one of the local casinos and she was currently working the night shift.

When Jenkins asked how she knew Middleton she said she first met him about three months ago in a Sparks' bar called Sierra Stix. She had gone there with friends one night and noticed Middleton sitting at the bar by himself. She sat down next to him and struck up a conversation. She told him he looked athletic, at which point he told her he used to play football for the Washington Redskins until an injury ended his career.

At some point in the evening Atkinson invited Middleton to go into the ladies room with her and do some methamphetamine. Atkinson said the methamphetamine was hers, and while they were doing the drugs Middleton told her he used to be a Miami cop. She said she was about to run from the ladies room because she though he was going to arrest her, but then he assured her he was no longer in police work.

He told her he worked for T.C.I. Cable Company, and later that night he asked her if she would be interested in getting cable installed in her apartment for free. She said she would like that and gave Middleton her address and phone number. She also told him the name of the bar where she worked and said she would buy him drinks there if he ever did install the free cable.

Atkinson said she left the bar with her friends and had no further contact with Middleton that night. About two weeks later she came home and found a note from T.C.I. Cable Company on her front door saying cable had been installed in her apartment. The note was not signed, but since she never ordered the cable service and never received a bill she knew it was Middleton who hooked it up.

A couple of days later Middleton began coming into her bar and she would buy him drinks each time. He asked her out several times, but she continually declined his offers. She said there was something about him that gave her an odd feeling, but she couldn't say exactly what it was. Middleton eventually stopped coming into the bar, and shortly after that Atkinson began receiving threatening and obscene phone calls at her home and work. The caller identified herself as Middleton's wife and told Atkinson to stay away from Middleton. She described the woman who eventually confronted her at the bar, and the description matched Evonne Haley. It was right after that incident that Atkinson got fired from the bar.

Jenkins asked Atkinson when the last time she saw Middleton was, and she said this whole thing happened in late December 1994, right before Christmas. She said the calls from Middleton's wife stopped right after she complained to T.C.I. Cable Company and she hadn't seen Middleton or his wife since.

When questioned about Middleton's truck she said she had no idea what type of vehicle he drove. When asked about her whereabouts on Monday, February 6th—the date of the Good Guys transaction—Atkinson consulted her date planner and said she had worked a day shift at her new job on that date. She gave the detectives the name of her boss who could confirm her whereabouts, but they both already knew what they'd be told when they called him.

As the detectives were leaving, Atkinson said, "You know, I've been in this business a long time so I'm a pretty good judge of character. I can tell a stalker a mile away, and that guy Dave is stalker material."

As Jenkins started the car, he said, "When Hunt and I left Haley's apartment I told him when we found Suzy we would probably be looking at Middleton's next intended victim. I was wrong. He moved from her to Kathy Powell, and Suzy Atkinson will never know how lucky she was."

Douglas said, "Kathy Powell might still be alive too if she got into a cult run by a bartender instead of a psychologist. Bartenders and cops are a lot alike. We don't *trust* nobody."

"And I believe they call that a blessing and a curse," Jenkins said. "Let's round up the rest of the cynics and compare notes before we call it a day."

The detectives met in their conference room at 4:30 in the afternoon and Douglas briefed the rest of the unit about their interview with Suzanne Atkinson. After he was through, Depsynski told them another female had called the detective squad earlier in the afternoon to recount her experiences with David Middleton.

A forty-year-old female named Tina Bronson* who lived in the Smithridge Condominiums was referred to detectives when she called in information to T.C.I. Cable Company. Her condominium complex was about two miles from where Kathy Powell's body was discovered and was on Middleton's route. Ms. Bronson told Depsynski that Middleton installed cable service in her condominium in early November 1994 and made arrangements to return after hours to provide additional service at no cost.

In addition to the cable services, Middleton spent the night at Bronson's condominium to provide services of a different sort. Bronson said she and Middleton engaged in consensual sex that evening and he left early in the morning. He told her he was divorced and lived alone on Carlin Street in Reno, but had to leave in order to get to work in the morning. She had since spoken to him on the phone several times, and always called him at T.C.I. Cable since he told her he did not have a home phone. They had planned to get together again, but never did due to scheduling conflicts. Bronson said she became concerned for her safety after seeing the news story about Middleton's arrest and that is why she called T.C.I. Cable Company.

Bronson said there was nothing unusual about her sexual activities with Middleton in the way of violence or bondage, but one thing did stand out in her mind as being out of the ordinary. After they had begun getting romantic, Bronson told Middleton she would like him to use a condom. She offered him one from a box she had in her nightstand, but he refused saying it was not his brand. He got dressed and went to his truck to retrieve a condom, telling her he prefered Trojan condoms because of a reaction he has to some of the other brands on the market. Bronson described herself as five-three and one-hundred-fifteen pounds with shoulder-length brown hair.

They now had an established pattern of behavior relating to Middleton becoming involved in romantic encounters with female customers, his interest in another female fitting the victim profile and Middleton stating his preference in condoms was the same brand found in Kathy Powell's apartment. The wall was becoming taller, and it was time to find Middleton a lawyer.

Chapter 21

A PIG IN A POKE

Jenkins received a phone call from the Public Defender's office at 10:30 in the morning on Wednesday, March 1, 1995. The head Public Defender, Michael Specchio, had gone to the jail the day before to interview Middleton since all of his deputies were busy with other cases. Mr. Specchio said he did not believe the police had a murder. He had advised Middleton not to talk to them about the case, but Middleton told him he wanted to do so anyway. The attorney ended the conversation by saying, "I guess he's all yours."

As soon as Jenkins hung up the phone, he and Douglas drove to the County Jail to do a second interview with Middleton. They secured an interview room in the Sheriff's Detective Division and Dixon set up in the adjacent room to record the proceedings.

The first thing Middleton did when he was brought into the room was complain that one of the detectives involved in the case had told his twelve-year-old step-daughter that he was a rapist and a murderer, and would be going to the electric chair. Because of that he now had his doubts about whether or not he wanted to cooperate with the police.

Jenkins smoothed things over by telling Middleton none of the detectives had yet spoken to the child and perhaps she had misinterpreted something she heard on one of the news stories about his arrest. The department had not put out any type of press release regarding his possible involvement in Kathy Powell's death, but some parts of the investigation such as the search warrant affidavits were public information routinely examined by the press. This seemed to placate Middleton and he agreed to talk to the detectives without his attorney present.

In answer to Middleton's concern about the death penalty, Jenkins explained to him that was only an option in first degree murder cases. He told him about his conversation with Mr. Specchio and that the attorney represented it was his opinion there was not a murder involved in Kathy Powell's death. Jenkins told Middleton Kathy Powell's death was shrouded in unanswered questions, and the only promise he would make was to fairly and accurately record what he said in an effort to determine the truth about what happened.

Middleton told the detectives he wanted to negotiate some type of cap on his prison sentence in exchange for giving his statement. He said he could provide information on his drug use, involvement with the fraudulent use of Kathy Powell's credit card, grand larceny and unlawful disposal of human remains.

Both detectives perked up when Middleton mentioned disposal of human remains, but tried not to show their excitement. It appeared Middleton was getting ready to talk about what happened to Kathy Powell and they did not want to shut him down by appearing overanxious. Jenkins told Middleton he was not in a position to talk about any potential sentencing deals, but he would call the District Attorney and ask for assistance. Jenkins and Douglas left Middleton alone in the room while they made that call and discussed their next move.

Washoe County District Attorney Richard Gammick had been voted into office in January of 1995. Because this had the potential of being the first major case prosecuted by his office since he took control, the District Attorney personally responded to Jenkins' request for assistance with Middleton.

Gammick was a short, wiry, bald-headed man in his fifties who had been a prosecutor with the D.A.'s office for ten years before being elected to the top job. His country drawl and the cowboy boots he routinely wore with his business suits were remnants of his upbringing in Elko, Nevada. Since Gammick had been a Reno cop before becoming an attorney he was familiar with both Jenkins and Douglas. He listened intently as they briefed him on the case before going into the interview room to speak to Middleton.

After making sure Middleton understood his rights and the information his attorney discussed with him, Gammick let Middleton talk. Much to the detective's disappointment, Middleton made no concrete statements regarding Kathy Powell's death while he spoke to Gammick. He reiterated that this was not a murder and said he would give detailed accounts on the entire incident if they could reach an agreement.

What Middleton wanted in return was a promise of a limited amount of jail time based on the property crimes he was willing to admit to. He would name the crimes he thought he was guilty of and wanted to know how much time each carried as a penalty before he admitted to them.

Gammick was a hardnosed prosecutor and he listened patiently as Middleton described the deal he wanted. When he was through talking, Gammick said, "So what you're asking me to do here, Mr. Middleton, is buy a pig in a poke. Well I don't buy pigs in pokes, because that's just plain stupid. The deal I have for you is that you come clean with everything you've done in this case and then we'll talk about the penalties. If this investigation determines you've only been involved in property crimes, then I'm sure there'll be room for negotiation between your attorney and my office."

After Gammick left the room Middleton gave Douglas a quizzical look and asked him what buying a pig had to do with anything. Since Douglas grew up in an inner city he had no idea what the saying meant either. Not wanting to appear uninformed in front of the prisoner, he said, "Everybody knows what that pig in a poke thing means. Tell him, Dave."

Being astute in the old English language, Jenkins knew exactly where the phrase came from. A burlap sack was referred to as a poke on the English countryside in the 1800's, and it eventually evolved into the word pocket in modern language. The advice from one farmer to another was to never buy a pig concealed in a burlap sack, because you just didn't know what you were getting. This sound advice was the segue into our modern saying, "let the buyer beware."

Knowing that the history lesson would be lost on Middleton, Jenkins said, "It's like the reason dope dealers wrap rock cocaine up in cellophane instead of aluminum foil. There is so much bunk out there that the person buying it wants to see he's getting the real thing before he closes the deal. Mr. Gammick just wants a little transparency to your deal before he commits to anything."

This seemed to make perfect sense to Middleton. He said, "Come back to see me in twenty-four hours. I need time to think about what I'm gonna say."

Chapter 22

MARATHON

On Thursday, March 2, 1995 at 3:00 in the afternoon Jenkins and Douglas drove to the Washoe County Jail and had Middleton released into their custody so they could take him to the Reno Police Detective Division to complete their third interview with him. They wanted him on their turf in order to demonstrate to him who was in control of the interview.

After they arrived at the police station Middleton was placed into an unoccupied office and allowed to use the telephone to contact his attorney, Mr. Specchio. The two detectives waited outside the closed office and after twenty minutes Middleton opened the door and told them he was through. He was then moved to an interview room where Jenkins and Douglas read him his Miranda rights and had him sign the waiver agreeing to talk to them. Dixon was recording the interview from the video surveillance room.

What followed next was certainly not the longest police interview in the history of law enforcement—but it was the longest any of the three men seated in the interrogation room had ever been through. In later appeals Middleton's attorney would refer to it as the *Marathon Interrogation* and seek to have statements made by Middleton quashed because of the duration. Since Middleton was treated humanely, and he never actually *asked* to leave, what was said over the next nine and a half hours would remain on record.

The interview started at 4:45 in the afternoon with Middleton making statements about his relationship with Kathy Powell. He said he first met Kathy Powell when he made a cable service call to her apartment on January 28, 1995. He said he installed a cable converter box for her and afterwards she requested he provide two additional cable outlets in the apartment. He told her he could not do that at the time, and then heard her on the phone with the cable company setting up an appointment to get the additional work done.

Middleton struck up a conversation with Powell and told her it would be much easier and cheaper for her if he came back after hours and did the additional work. She agreed to this and gave him her phone number so he could contact her when he had time to do the work.

Middleton said he next went to Kathy Powell's apartment on Wednesday, February 1, 1995. He went there at her invitation and performed the additional cable service for her. He said he spent a couple of hours with Kathy Powell and the two of them conversed at length. He said it was during that conversation that the two of them discussed beginning a sexual relationship. He claimed Kathy Powell told him she had a serious love relationship in Pittsburgh and she planned to eventually marry that person. According to Middleton she then told him she was open to sexual experimentation, but had no interest in anything other than that with him. He left that evening without having any type of relations with her, but they agreed to get together again soon.

Middleton said he next saw Kathy Powell on Friday, February 3, 1995 when he once again was an invited guest at her apartment. Middleton also said he drove to Powell's apartment in his International Harvester pickup truck and parked on the street in front of her building. This was consistent with Powell's neighbors' recollection of seeing his truck parked there.

According to Middleton, he and Kathy Powell spent at least two hours after his arrival talking and drinking vodka. He said they then engaged in consensual sex in her bedroom. He described the sex as normal and in the missionary position. The detectives asked Middleton no questions, electing to let him tell the story in his own words and get it on record without interruption. Middleton stopped at this point and drank half of the bottle of water on the table in front of him before continuing.

When Middleton continued, he told the detectives that after he and Powell were through having sex he got dressed and went out to the store to get them more vodka. He said when he returned from the store approximately one hour later he found Kathy Powell had died while he was gone.

At this point Jenkins sat forward and asked Middleton how Kathy Powell had come to be bound in rope. Middleton calmly said that she was into some different kinds of sex and had apparently bound herself while he was gone. He said the rope was hers and she must have died while she was waiting for him to get back to her apartment. He said he panicked when he found her dead and disposed of her body.

Jenkins pressed Middleton for more details on the claimed sexual activity and to explain how Kathy Powell's property had come to be missing from her apartment. Middleton maintained his calm façade and steadfastly declined to provide any further information. The detectives spent the next several hours trying to pick apart Middleton's story without giving up what information they had, but Middleton stuck to his story. The only thing he did do was ask for something to eat at 8:00 P.M.

Jenkins and Douglas huddled in the outer office to discuss Middleton's statement while Dixon went out to get pizzas and sodas. The most glaring inconsistencies were the time of death, the date Powell had been placed into the dumpster and the fact the Warp's Brothers Banana Bags were not purchased until February 8th—five full days after Middleton said Kathy Powell had died. There was also the fact that the Coroner's report said Powell had been brutally raped prior to her death.

In spite of all that, both detectives agreed on one thing. David Middleton was good at holding his own in an interview—perhaps the best either one of them had come up against. They said he was the master of the Jedi mind trick and they both felt him getting inside their heads during the interview. There were times *they* even began doubting the evidence they possessed and began imagining Kathy Powell wrapping herself up in rope while poor David Middleton was out fetching more booze.

The frequent breaks they took during the interview were used to get their own heads straight—not to try and figure out how to get inside of Middleton's.

So there they sat at a crossroads in the investigation. They were now more convinced than ever that Middleton was a textbook sociopath. One of the qualities possessed by a sociopath is an above average intellect, and Middleton certainly had that. He had just laid the groundwork for his own defense, and when the detectives tried to pick apart his story they could see how it could actually work in court.

Since Middleton admitted being inside of Kathy Powell's apartment lawfully on at least three occasions, any fingerprint or trace evidence associated with him found inside the apartment could be explained away. Likewise, any DNA evidence resulting from the consensual sex he admitted to having with Powell could not be used against him.

He admitted to disposing of her body after finding her dead, but would not commit to where or when he did so. Even though Powell's body had not been in the dumpster for longer than a day, the possibility that someone other than Middleton had placed her in there not knowing the bags contained a body could be raised in court. The bags bought on February 8th could not actually be traced to Middleton, so the fact the purchase was made five days after he allegedly disposed of her was a moot issue.

The only evidence in their favor at this point were the time of death and the signs of sexual trauma found on Kathy Powell during the autopsy, but the D.A. would never prosecute based solely on those two facts. Time of death could be easily challenged, and Middleton left himself an out for the rape allegations.

Middleton made a point of saying the front door was unlocked when he returned to Kathy Powell's apartment. That left open the allegation that an unknown person entered the apartment during his absence and it was actually *that* person who tied up and raped Kathy Powell. As far fetched as that seemed, the burden of *proof beyond a reasonable doubt* was often difficult to achieve in front of juries who were not always made up of reasonable persons.

The detectives needed more from Middleton, so they went back into the interview room after their dinner break to pick apart his lies. As hard as they tried to trip him up and get him to admit what actually happened to Kathy Powell, they could not get him to budge from his story. By midnight the two exhausted detectives stood in the hallway actually thinking it was possible Kathy Powell *hadn't* been murdered.

They'd been collectively dealing with hardcore criminals for almost forty years, but Middleton was unlike any other person they'd ever met. Were it not for Eddie Dixon pointing out that anyone short of a contortionist couldn't tie themselves up like Kathy Powell had been, they might have actually begun to believe Middleton. He was inside their heads, and he was good.

Jenkins and Douglas went back inside the interview room and tried to crack Middleton one more time. This is when he laid his trump card on them. The following excerpt is from the transcripts dealing with the final stages of this interview:

MIDDLETON: "I laid this all out for Specchio before I said I'd talk to you. I put it in a little more detail for you, but I laid in all out for him too."

DOUGLAS: "I'll bet it was more detailed for us. Eight hours worth."

MIDDLETON: "Anyway, Specchio says it ain't a murder, but you're gonna charge me with first degree murder anyway and make me prove otherwise."

JENKINS: "Well I hate to disappoint him, but from the story you've told us I don't see a murder or sexual assault either."

MIDDLETON: "Then why would he say that?"

JENKINS: "Because he has to. He's covering himself to avoid a malpractice suit. If somewhere down the road you get three days or three hundred days and you think it's too much, you can't go back and say he didn't warn you."

MIDDLETON: "Why can't lawyers just do like other people?"

JENKINS: "Because they can't. It's the system we work in. I'd rather have my kid grow up to sell cocaine than be a lawyer. I say that in jest, of course."

MIDDLETON: "Well it don't matter anyway, cause I can't get a fair trial in this town. You might as well just book me for first degree murder and get it over with."

JENKINS: "Why do you say that?"

MIDDLETON: "Because of the publicity! I mean, this has been told to me since I was arrested. I have no chance of winning because I'm black, and because of the town I'm in. You said it yourself when you got, when you arrested me. You said this is the Mississippi of the west!"

JENKINS:	"No, that isn't what I said. I remember talking to you about racism and agreeing with you that racism is alive and well in some places today."
MIDDLETON:	"No, you might have forgot what you told me, but I didn't. When you jumped me and had me in the front of your car in front of my house, you said this is the Mississippi of the west and that was a white school teacher. You don't stand a chance." (little laugh from Middleton)
JENKINS:	"No, I never tied those two together."
MIDDLETON:	"Whatever you say. I need some sleep."
DOUGLAS:	"This is silly. This is ludicrous. I'm tired and cranky, and I don't want to be here anymore. I need out."
JENKINS:	"Yes, we've gone too long. Transcriber, the time now is 1:10 A.M. on Friday, March 3, 1995. This interview is terminated."

They left Middleton inside of the interview room while they waited for a uniformed officer to take him back up to jail. Douglas said, "Tell me you didn't really say that Mississippi of the west shit to him. He just played the race card and now his whole defense is gonna head in that direction."

"Of course I didn't say that," Jenkins said. "Didn't you hear that sick laugh after he made that accusation? He knows exactly what he's doing. He knew we were recording that interview and his statements are on record. Now it doesn't matter whether I said those things or not. He's said I did, so that's going to go down as his mindset if we go in front of a jury."

Douglas exclaimed, "That's just perfect! We don't have shit on him as it is, and now it's gonna look like us rednecks are persecuting the poor innocent black dude because he screwed the white school marm."

Dixon had joined them and asked, "Do you want me to back up the tape a little bit?"

Jenkins smiled and replied, "Thanks, but no thanks, Eddie. Middleton's game is the act of a guilty man, but fortunately for us—my partner's neck is anything but red."

Chapter 23

THE END OF THE LINE

By 9:00 the next morning the local news reporters were hovering around the station like buzzards over carrion. They were already asking questions about the all-night interview of Middleton and if an arrest for the Kathy Powell case was on the horizon. One reporter even made mention of the racial undertones and the alleged "Mississippi of the west" statement made by a lead investigator in the case. This same reporter asked the department spokesperson if it was true a detective said he'd rather see his kids dealing crack than becoming an attorney.

Since the only law enforcement personnel who had witnessed the interview were people Jenkins trusted, he was reasonably certain the information had been leaked to the press by the Middleton defense camp. Fortunately the higher-ups in the department trusted Jenkins' investigative and interview techniques enough to stand behind him. The department's official comment to the allegations was no comment at all. The P.I.O. told the morning gathering of reporters that Middleton had been questioned in the Kathy Powell case and the investigation was continuing. This investigation—like *all* Reno Police investigations—would remain unbiased in regard to race or ethnicity of all involved parties.

This boilerplate answer did little to appease the press buzzards. They left the station, but Jenkins had been around long enough to know they would now ad lib with information from their own sources since they smelled a story. He attended the morning administrative staff meeting and assured the department heads he would come up with something concrete on the case soon. How he was going to do that was the unanswered question of the day.

The Friday after payday Thursday is usually very quiet at a police station, since civil servants often developed vision problems after cashing their checks – some of them just couldn't see coming into work when they had money in their pockets. This Friday was no different and even Douglas called in to say he was taking the day off. It was his weekend to fulfill his monthly training obligation with the Air Guard and the all-night interview had left him drained. He said he wanted to be well rested in case a foreign country decided to take over Arkansas while he was training there.

One of the things on Jenkins' to-do list for the case was to build a suspect profile on David Middleton, so he decided to use the quiet time in the office to do just that. He spent the next several hours on the phone with police departments in Boston, Montrose and Miami.

David Middleton was born in Boston, Massachusetts on June 25, 1961. Coincidently, his father was a police officer at Tufts University in the suburban Boston area. Middleton's mother was a stay-at-home mom who raised him in their home in a town called Tucksbury, just outside of Boston.

His parents divorced when he was eleven-years-old, but his mother re-married two years later. He had a step-father, a step-brother and a step-sister, but didn't associate with them after his mother's death from cancer in 1988.

Middleton attended Boston Tech High—a school for academically superior students. Upon graduation in 1979 he earned a full-ride scholarship for basketball and academics at Suffolk University. He attended Suffolk for one year and then transferred to the University of Massachusetts. He quit school in December of 1981 and never completed his degree.

When Middleton was eighteen-years-old he attended the Boston Police Department's Police Cadet Academy. He served as a police cadet from 1979 through 1981 while attending college classes. Although this was a non-sworn position, it was considered a prerequisite for persons wishing to get hired on the Boston Police Department.

A Boston P.D. lieutenant named Frank Armstrong was still working at the department and remembered Middleton from his cadet years. Armstrong went through the Cadet Academy with Middleton and the two became friends while serving as cadets together. The police cadets performed clerical desk duties and were often used to run errands for the brass. Times were tight in Boston in the early 80's and the only way to get hired onto the department was by performing well as a cadet.

Armstrong had vivid memories of Middleton. Since he grew up in a predominantly white Irish-Catholic Boston neighborhood he said it was out of the ordinary to have a black person come to your house. Middleton had been to his home several times for dinner, but Armstrong said he had to do some fast talking to convince his old-school mother that he was OK.

He described Middleton as a well-liked and charismatic young man who quickly became earmarked as a future rising star in the department. He said Middleton was very athletic, and at the time minority hiring was being pushed in the department. It was said Middleton would be able to write his own ticket in the Boston P.D., but then a chance happening changed all of that.

It seems Boston's mayor in the early 80's was a corrupt individual who was keeping two sets of books on the city's budget. In 1981 the Boston P.D. experienced its first and last layoffs in the history of the city. A hiring freeze was initiated and no new police officers would be hired until all officers who had been laid off were re-hired. It was said that would take at least three years.

At the same time Miami Metro-Dade Police Department sent fliers to Boston soliciting applicants from the officers who had been laid off. An estimated 125,000 Cuban refugees from the Mariel Boatlift had been dumped on the shores of south Florida within a six-month period in 1980. A good deal of these refugees had been released from prison by Fidel Castro before making the journey to Florida, so Miami was experiencing an unprecedented surge in crime. They were begging for police officer candidates, and anyone with a police background stood an excellent chance of getting hired.

By then both Middleton and Armstrong were strapping young twenty-one-year-old men with their sights set on careers in law enforcement. Since prospects looked bleak to fulfill that dream in Boston they both headed to Florida and took the test for the Metro-Dade Police Department. They both passed, but before they were hired the police union in Boston uncovered the second set of books the mayor had been keeping. The laid off officers were put back on the payroll and the police hiring freeze was lifted.

Armstrong had family roots in Boston so he elected to stay there and eventually got hired by the police department. Middleton, on the other hand, found Miami to his liking. The warm weather was a definite plus after spending twenty-one long cold winters in Boston, but there were two other things that attracted him. The girls on the beach and the Miami nightlife were unequaled anywhere else in the world. He packed his belongings and took the position with the Miami Metro-Dade Police Department in January of 1982.

Armstrong hadn't heard from Middleton since then and was surprised to learn he'd been in trouble. Armstrong said he was the last person anyone would have expected to be suspected of rape and murder, although he did have an almost macabre fascination with the Boston Strangler case. He used his father's police connections to research the case in the Boston P.D. records section for a college paper and he spoke about the infamous murders often.

The information went a long way to explain how Middleton ended up in Florida, and the Boston Strangler story was also an interesting twist. Jenkins sat at his desk and wondered how many lives had been adversely affected by one corrupt Boston politician

who set that chain of events in motion. At least three that he knew
of—an eighteen-year-old girl in Montrose, a school teacher in
Reno, and a sixteen-year-old girl in Miami. Had Middleton
remained in Boston chances are he never would have crossed paths
with *any* of his victims.

In speaking with the Montrose P.D. Jenkins learned there
was nothing new with the Buffy Rice Donohue investigation.
Detectives from Montrose and Delta, Colorado were interested in
coming to Reno to question Middleton in the near future. In
addition to the Buffy Rice case there was the missing fourteen-
year-old girl from Delta and the remains of an unidentified woman
in her forties that were found in a shallow grave in the area. All of
these crimes coincided with the time Middleton was in Colorado. It
was agreed between the detectives that keeping the lines of
communication open during the investigation was important.

Jenkins' phone call to the Miami P.D. was met with a bit
more apprehension. He was told that several of Middleton's former
coworkers were still with the department, but phone interviews
with them would not be allowed. Also, any information included in
Middleton's personnel file had already been sealed, so an
administrative subpoena from the Dade County Court would be
needed to access it. After completing the call it appeared a road
trip to Florida might be necessary before the investigation was
over.

Jenkins was able to get through to the attorney who
prosecuted Middleton in Florida, Kathleen Hoague. She was able

to confirm most of the information the detectives had read in the Internet news articles, but also gave her own opinion of Middleton.

She described him as a bad cop, twisted enough to use his badge and uniform to hunt down women and sexually abuse them. She used the words "smug" and "cocky" to describe Middleton, adding that he used his job as a warrants detective to prey on the most defenseless women he could find. It was her opinion Middleton had problems that centered around control and dominance of women, and although she doesn't think he killed anyone in Florida—he was definitely headed in that direction.

Ms. Hoague said when they arrested Middleton they confiscated two videotapes from his police locker. One tape was of him and a civilian Metro-Dade secretary having sex in an empty department D.U.I. room. Middleton told this lady he was a Santeria priest and having sex with him would act as a natural anti-depressant for her. As if that wasn't bad enough, her husband was also a Metro-Dade cop.

The other tape was even more disturbing. It showed Middleton having sex with several women who were obviously prostitutes. Some of the women were in handcuffs and at least one of them appeared to be in a great deal of pain. The tapes were shot in a room at Middleton's house and in some other unidentified locations—possibly a storage shed. In the tapes Middleton didn't appear to be enjoying himself, but looked more like he just wanted to tape himself doing sadomasochistic stuff. Since the tapes couldn't be introduced as evidence at his trial, the origin and filming locations were never explored. The Internal Affairs Division never investigated the civilian employee's claims against Middleton, so they never looked into the tapes either.

Ms. Hoague was also familiar with Evonne Haley and said she was working as a topless dancer in a club Middleton frequented when the couple first met. Middleton was married, but he began an affair with Haley long before his arrest in Miami. Ms. Hoague described Haley as being supportive of Middleton's kinky passions and said she believes this is actually what helped them develop a steadfast bond. Although she thinks Haley shot at least some of the video footage of Middleton, she was never able to prove it. It was her theory that Haley actually got women for Middleton, but she was never able to prove that either.

The last thing the prosecutor told Jenkins was that Middleton scared her to death and she would have buried him under the courthouse if she could have. A bureaucratic snafu with a rape crisis center employee prevented evidence needed to convict Middleton from being introduced at his rape trial. She said the victim was credible and there was no doubt in her mind Middleton was guilty. When she tried to press for additional federal charges against him, she was shut down by her boss, Janet Reno. She was forced to watch Middleton plead to the lesser charges and take his five-year sentence. Ms. Hoague seemed reluctant to get into more detail and Jenkins didn't push. He thanked her for her help and said he would keep her updated on the Middleton case in Reno.

Jenkins now had a much better understanding of his adversary and was glad he'd taken the time to put together the profile. Before leaving for the weekend he briefed Sergeant Burns on his progress and made copies of his notes to give to the other detectives at their Monday morning briefing.

Everything he'd heard throughout the day from people who knew or had dealings with David Middleton confirmed what Jenkins already knew; he was a sociopath career criminal who had spent his life slipping through the cracks. It was now time to make Reno the end of the line for him.

Chapter 24

THE HOLY GRAIL

At 7:00 P.M. on Saturday, March 4, 1995 Dave Jenkins was standing at his kitchen sink helping his wife with the dinner dishes. When the phone rang his wife gave him the sideways, squinty-eyed look that all married cops who are subject to callouts have grown to know and fear. Since he was not the on-call Major Crimes detective that weekend he was not obligated to answer the call, but his theory was that when you took the job you took the baggage that came along with it.

Dodging his wife's mad-dog stare he stepped around her and picked up the phone. The call was from a police records clerk named Lynn Austin who had just received a secret witness call regarding the Kathy Powell case she thought Jenkins would want to know about. Most secret witness reports coming in this long after a crime occurs are routinely filed away for the detectives to go through when time permits. But like the detectives handling the Powell case, Ms. Austin was also a veteran at her job, and her gut instincts told her this secret witness report was different.

A male caller had telephoned the secret witness line and said he had read about Powell's death in the local newspaper. In one of the press releases put out about the case, information was included about detectives looking for leads regarding Middleton possibly renting a storage shed. This caller said Middleton and

Haley were associated with a company named Hal-Data and the detectives should check local storage facilities under that name.

The caller was vague with his information, but Ms. Austin pressed him for the reason he knew this in order to establish his credibility. He finally told her he worked for the Post Office and delivered the mail to Middleton and Haley at their Carlin Street apartment. He said that in addition to mail addressed to them personally, he remembered the company name of Hal-Data Research with their address on some of the mail.

The caller gave his name so detectives could contact him if they had to, but said he could get in trouble at work if it was learned he released this type of information. He then told Ms. Austin he had delivered mail to Middleton's address the day before addressed to Hal-Data Research and the return address was from a business called Sierra Royal Mini Storage in Sparks, Nevada.

After thanking Ms. Austin for the call Jenkins hung up the phone and found the listing for Sierra Royal Mini Storage in the yellow pages. The address was 450 Howard Drive in Sparks, but when Jenkins called the number listed for the business he got the after hours recording. He decided to wait until the morning to check out the lead and called Sergeant Burns to fill him in. Since Douglas was still out of town he called Eddie Dixon and made arrangements to meet at the station in the morning to assist him.

Before heading to the storage facility in the morning Jenkins had an evidence custodian meet him at the station. He checked Middleton's key ring out of evidence and took it with him

on the off chance he might locate a storage shed. At 11:00 A.M.
Jenkins and Dixon met with the resident managers of the facility,
Verrel and Freddie Tucker. The Tucker's had recently moved to
the area and took over management of the facility sometime after
the canvass of the local storage units had been done by Douglas
and Jenkins. They were not familiar with the Kathy Powell case,
but said they would be more than happy to help the detectives.

Mrs. Tucker checked her computer for a storage shed
registered to either David Middleton or Evonne Haley and came up
with no results. Dixon gave her the name of Hal-Data Research
and when she checked under that she got a hit for unit #16-28. The
actual name of the renter was not in the computer and both
detectives waited anxiously as Mrs. Tucker hand-searched the
rental applications.

After a long two minutes, Mrs. Tucker walked back to the
counter looking pleased with herself and handed the rental
application to Jenkins. He and Dixon both experienced the kid on
Christmas feeling when they read it. The owner of Hal-Date
Research and the renter of the storage shed was David Stephen
Middleton. He listed his social security number on the application
and 1425 Carlin Street #3 in Reno, Nevada as his business address.
He even had his sister in Milton, Massachusetts listed as the
emergency contact.

Middleton had rented the ten-by-ten foot storage unit on
August 8, 1994. Prior to that he had a smaller unit in the same
facility, but he listed the reason for the move as a need for more

storage space. Mrs. Tucker made a copy of the rental agreement and Jenkins tried to hide his excitement as he folded it and placed under the clip in his notebook. Mrs. Tucker then walked the detectives down to storage unit #16-28.

They stood outside the roll-up door to the unit for a moment before Jenkins removed Middleton's key ring from the pocket of his suit coat. He moved the keys around the ring until he came to the one that had attracted his attention during his first interview with David Middleton. Bending down he inserted the key into the keyhole on the security lock and turned it to the right. When the lock opened with a metallic snap, Detective Dave Jenkins experienced the euphoric feeling King Arthur *never* got to experience in his lifetime quest to find the Holy Grail. It was now time to call a judge.

Chapter 25

CHAMBER OF HORRORS

At 2:45 in the afternoon on Sunday, March 5, 1995
Detective Jenkins returned to the Sierra Royal Mini Storage
facility carrying a signed search warrant authorizing the search of
unit #16-28. The warrant listed the scope of the search to include
anything related to the murder of Kathy Powell as well as any
evidence related to the Good Guys crime.

Eddie Dixon had remained behind to guard the storage shed
and was waiting when Jenkins returned with the warrant. In
addition to him, Sergeant Burns, Detective Hunt and a detective
from the Robbery Homicide Unit named Mike Cleveland were
there to assist. Cleveland was there to take initial photographs.
Sergeant Burns did not want to call out a C.S.I. team from the
Sheriff's Office until he was sure there was something worthwhile
in the shed.

After showing the search warrant to Mr. and Mrs. Tucker,
Jenkins removed the security lock and pulled up the overhead door
to the shed. The five detectives stood outside of the opened door
and peered inside. At first glance it appeared to be cluttered with
nothing more than miscellaneous household junk, but then
something in the right hand corner caught Jenkins' eye.

A red hand truck was leaning against the wall of the shed
partially concealed behind some boxes. A yellow windbreaker with

the words "Sunshine State Messenger Service" written on it in black lettering was draped across the handle of the hand truck. On top of a pile of boxes next to the hand truck was an unopened box with the words "Yamaha Model DSP-A2770 Stereo Amplifier" stenciled on it. Before Jenkins could celebrate the discovery of the evidence from the Good Guys crime, his attention was drawn to something else.

Lying on its back on the left side of the storage shed was a single-door upright refrigerator about five feet tall. A fifty-five gallon cardboard drum and several boxes were stacked on top of the refrigerator's single door. Irreparable damage would be done to a refrigerator from storing it lying down like this one was, so there was a good chance it was not being stored for future use. Jenkins then saw a small hole drilled through the side of the refrigerator and a horrific feeling came over him.

He shared his suspicions with the other detectives and they carefully began removing the items stacked on top of the refrigerator door. Detective Cleveland videotaped the process, and when the door was cleared Jenkins jerked it opened. The five men stared into of the filthy interior of the empty refrigerator, and it was Jenkins who first realized what they were looking at.

The inside of the refrigerator had been gutted of its food trays. All that remained was the freezer compartment covered by a blue plastic door, separated from the main part of the refrigerator by a metal shelf. It was the metal shelf of the freezer compartment that held Jenkins' attention and caused the hairs on the back of his neck to stand up.

The metal had been cut and peeled back in a semi-circular pattern to allow an opening between the freezer and the main refrigerator compartment. The opening was the right size for a human neck, and the blue cloth fibers covering the jagged metal around the opening were exactly the same as the ones Jenkins had seen around Kathy Powell's neck at her autopsy. He now knew where David Middleton had kept Kathy Powell during the last days of her life. Even more disturbing was he also now knew what caused the look of horror to be frozen on her face for eternity.

A large blue foam rubber ball with obvious teeth marks in it was lying on the floor next to the refrigerator. As Eddie Dixon so astutely put it, "That was used as a gag, and there ain't no reason to gag a dead lady. If she was here—she was alive for a while."

Sergeant Burns called for a C.S.I. team and the detectives backed out of the shed while they waited for them. Thirty minutes later Deputy Chuck Lowe and his boss Lieutenant Don Means from the county forensics team arrived and the detectives went back inside of the shed to continue their search.

The refrigerator was the initial focal point of the search. After first photographing it in place, the forensics investigators began to process the inside. Trace evidence of the blue fibers as well as small particles of skin were collected from the edges of the metal freezer tray cutout. There was not much visible to the naked eye, but the refrigerator was carefully loaded into the evidence truck so it could be moved to the crime lab and checked more thoroughly.

When the detectives stood the refrigerator up-right they saw that in addition to the small hole drilled on the right side, a cutout with another small hole had been drilled on the left side. They surmised these to be air holes, lending more credence to the theory Kathy Powell had been alive if she had in fact been held inside of the refrigerator. Once the refrigerator was moved out of the shed they began to make one morbid discovery after another.

Middleton had run a series of ropes and pulleys throughout the shed. The rope started at a hand-winch mounted to a heavy wooden speaker box. The speaker box measured four feet by four feet and was the type that might be seen on the stage of a Broadway play. Although the interior of the speaker box was hollowed out, they estimated it still weighed about three hundred pounds. It was definitely heavy enough to anchor the winch that operated the pulley system in the shed.

From the winch the rope ran through a series of industrial strength pulleys mounted to the ceiling beam inside of the shed. There was a clasp hook attached to the free-end of the rope, and human restraint devices were strewn around the floor near the hook. The forensic technicians found traces of hair and what appeared to be human skin on the restraint devices. With the way the restraint devices were rigged, it appeared the pulley system had been used to suspend a human body. As dark as cops' senses of humor can be there was no joking as the detectives silently went about their search of the shed.

Underneath the blue plastic tarp the detectives located an opened bag of Warp's Brothers Banana Bags with one bag missing. A bag of Ace Hardware brand black plastic bags matching the one that had been used to cover Kathy Powell's head was lying next to the banana bags. Receipts for the Commercial Hardware purchase of the bags and the original receipt for the Good Guys purchase were also located. White rope matching the one used to bind Kathy Powell, as well as a roll of duct tape were also found under the tarp.

Kathy Powell's answering machine, cordless phone, computer printer and portable computer were found toward the front of the shed. There were some compact discs and cassette tapes that had obviously belonged to Kathy Powell in a box on top of her computer printer. Jenkins reached into the box with a gloved hand and removed the top compact disc. It was titled "Trust Theory, 1992." Middleton had stolen her trust—figuratively *and* literally.

The detectives then began discovering things they really didn't want to find. A crate filled with sadomasochistic and bondage-type pornography, a box filled with assorted and well-used dildos and sex toys, and a machete with an animal skull and horns for the handle. God only knew what *that* was used for.

The last discovery of the day was two handguns in a box. One was a Smith and Wesson Model 15 .38 caliber revolver and the other was a Smith and Wesson Model 659 .9mm stainless steel pistol with a fifteen-round magazine. Also in the box was a rubber Halloween mask in the shape of the cartoon character Jughead's face. The cops called that a 2-11 kit after the California penal code for armed robbery.

They were now treading into a grey area as far as the search warrant was concerned. They were legally searching the storage shed, but were coming up with evidence that had nothing to do with either crime they came to investigate. After a brief discussion the detectives decided to seal the storage shed and go back in front of the judge in the morning in order to expand the scope of the search warrant. They bought a new lock from Mr. Tucker and locked the shed with the remainder of the contents still inside.

They were not yet a quarter of the way through their search of the shed, but they'd all seen enough for one day. Eddie Dixon summed it up the best when he said, "I sure picked a bad week to quit drinking."

Before leaving for his weekend training mission Douglas told Jenkins he'd keep his cell phone with him in case anything happened on the case. He would be returning from his trip later that night, but Jenkins knew he'd want to be filled in about the storage shed as soon as possible. It was a bittersweet phone call because the discovery was far too gruesome to warrant a celebration.

The detectives who were on scene at the storage shed on that cold and cloudy Sunday afternoon were hardcore veterans who had faced more than their share of death. Some of them had even faced their own mortality on more than one occasion, but none of them were prepared for the picture they now had of Kathy Powell's death. Bound with rope, gagged with a rubber ball, sealed inside an airtight makeshift coffin, gasping for her last breaths of fetid air filtering through two small holes in the refrigerator, alone and surely afraid. A death like that was worse than any of them could imagine.

When Dave Jenkins recounted the grizzly finding of David Middleton's storage shed to this author over a decade later, an eerie calm came over the veteran detective. He stared off into space and said, "My feelings were mixed. Part of me was elated because as soon as I saw what was in that shed I knew we had him. Another part of me was horrified thinking about what had been done to the victim in there."

They say if a person looks into the eyes of evil for too long, some of the evil is bound to seep inside of him. And so it was with David Middleton's chamber of horrors. Each man who entered it took away a little bit of the horror from within, and they will carry it with them forever.

Chapter 26

TWISTS

The detectives went back into the storage shed with their revised search warrant at 9:00 the next morning. The first thing they did was open the sealed fifty-five gallon drum that had been sitting on top of the refrigerator door when they originally entered the shed. They were surprised to find the drum half-filled with a variety of women's panties and lingerie.

At first they thought the clothing might belong to Evonne Haley, but as Douglas pointed out most people don't keep their underwear in a storage shed. Then Eddie Dixon held up a pair of tiny red lace thong panties and made another one of his astute observations. He said the only way these belonged to Evonne Haley was if she was using them as a nose warmer, because there was no way she was getting them over her butt.

The moment of humor ended when Douglas exclaimed, "Shit! He's taking souvenirs."

They all knew what that meant. Murderers were grouped into different categories based on traits they exhibited, and it was the serial killer who took souvenirs from his victims. By the time they got through searching the drum they collected thirty-seven pairs of panties, thirteen bras and six negligees. The garments varied in style, but most of them were designed for smaller women. Some were clean, but others had obviously been placed into the drum without being laundered since their last use. Each piece of clothing was logged and placed in a separate plastic bag for DNA testing. It would be a tedious procedure, but one that needed to be done.

The detectives theorized Middleton had been stealing women's underwear from their homes while he was working. When Middleton first moved to Reno he took a job working for Stanley Steamer Carpet Cleaners prior to being hired at the cable company. Both of those jobs would allow him unsupervised access to his customer's bedrooms where he would have had the opportunity to steal the undergarments. Even though this was a disturbing scenario, at least it would mean the women were live victims of perverse thefts instead of dead victims of a serial killer. What was buried underneath the clothing led them to believe they were dealing with more than just a thief with an underwear fetish.

At the bottom of the barrel were strands of long black hair, and not just a few of them. The hair was human and the strands were all at least twenty-four inches long. They pulled hair out of the barrel in clumps and laid it out on the folding table the forensics investigators were using to tag and bag the evidence. The split ends of the hairs told them it obviously did not come from a wig, and since the roots were still attached, the hair had been pulled out of a person's head.

The hair was too long and too dark to belong to either Kathy Powell or Middleton. The only other female they'd dealt with in the case was Haley, and the hair definitely was not her's.

The fact the hair was in the same drum as the women's underwear raised the possibility of another grim scenario for Middleton's souvenir collection. The detectives backed out of the storage shed and once again took the search warrant back to the judge for a revision. This time the scope of the warrant would include, "any evidence connected to murder victims presently referred to as Jane Does A through Z."

The search of the storage shed was completed on Tuesday, March 7, 1995 at 11:00 A.M. After everything had been removed from inside of the shed, the forensics team went over every inch of the interior with a black light looking for traces of blood or fingerprints. The place was clean—too clean for the inside of a storage shed.

A nearly empty industrial size jug of Clorox bleach was found inside of the shed. The detectives surmised Middleton would know from his police experience that bleach will obliterate DNA trace evidence, so had probably scrubbed the interior of the shed with it. This was another drawback of dealing with a suspect who was an ex-cop. They often knew how to get away with crime.

Kathy Powell's brother was allowed to view the property taken out of the shed to see if he recognized any of it. It addition to the items the detectives already knew of, he identified several distinctive pieces of jewelry, a camera and a hunting rifle that he said belonged to his sister. He said he had never seen the two handguns found in the shed, but he was certain they did not belong to Powell.

Both the revolver and the semi-automatic pistol looked like the types of guns cops carried as duty weapons. A brown leather shoulder holster for the revolver was also found in the shed. In addition to these items, they found Middleton's Boston P.D. cadet badge and police I.D. card in an official looking black leather badge wallet. The silver badge looked like a real police badge, and the word "Cadet" on the I.D. card was small enough to be easily overlooked if the credentials were flashed quickly. The photo on the I.D. card was of a much younger David Middleton, but it still looked like him.

There was a possibility Middleton either had in the past or was planning in the future to pose as a cop in order to commit crimes. They knew he'd used his badge to gain his victims' trust and lure them to him in Florida, so there was no reason he wouldn't try the ploy again. Someone who looked like a cop and flashed police credentials would certainly gain compliance if he approached the right person. They added sending a west coast law enforcement teletype checking sex crimes and unsolved murders where the suspect posed as a cop to their to-do list.

The talk of Middleton's guns looking like cop guns gave Jenkins an idea. It was nearly 5:00 P.M. on the east coast, but he took a chance and called the homicide division of the Miami Metro-Dade Police Department. He was put in contact with a detective, and after explaining the case they were working on asked if he would check the serial numbers on the guns found in Middleton's shed against their records. The detective said he would research the guns with the department range master and call back.

Fifteen minutes later Jenkins got a callback from the slightly embarrassed Miami detective confirming that both of the handguns had been issued to Middleton while he was with their department. Both weapons were listed as the property of the Miami Metro-Dade Police Department and still showed to be in service. The detective said their records also showed Middleton was issued a Remington Model 870 .12 gauge pump shotgun and asked if they had come across that weapon as well.

After flipping through his notes and comparing serial numbers, Jenkins confirmed the shotgun taken out of Middleton's apartment was the same one that had been issued by the Miami Metro-Dade Police Department. The detective assured Jenkins he would look into how Middleton had been allowed to keep his guns, and was relieved to hear they had not actually been involved in the crimes he was suspected of committing.

The phone call was followed by jokes about how great it must be to work for a department that let you keep your guns after going to prison so you could have something to fall back on when you got out, and how they should list the Miami P.D. as an accomplice to the ex-felon in possession of a firearm case. The jokes stopped when the detectives realized they didn't know if Middleton really *had* used the guns in the commission of a crime. They had no idea what Middleton was involved in before they found him. And even though Kathy Powell hadn't been shot, the possibility existed that Middleton used one of the guns to coerce her into submission. As Douglas put it, the case was getting twisted faster than a rattlesnake on speed.

Chapter 27

THE ACE OF SPADES

Even with the gruesome discoveries in the storage shed there still wasn't enough information or evidence to charge Middleton with the murder of Kathy Powell. All the detectives had at this point were their own theories and conjecture about what had happened in the homemade torture chamber, and that wouldn't be enough to convince a judge to sign a warrant for a murder arrest. They needed more concrete evidence and made it their mission over the next weeks to get it.

On Wednesday, March 8, 1995 Jenkins and Douglas started the process of taking evidence from Middleton himself. Douglas obtained a seizure order to take blood and hair samples from Middleton for DNA analysis. The order also gave them permission to take a dental impression from him for comparison to the bite mark on Kathy Powell's breast. The blood and hair samples were done at the County Jail and they took Middleton to a local dentist to have the dental impression done.

Middleton had invoked his rights so they could not discuss the case with him without his lawyer being present. The discovery of the storage shed had been a leading story in the local news, so the detectives were certain Middleton knew about it. But since he did not bring the subject up there was no discussion about it. Middleton made mostly small talk with the detectives. On their return trip from the dentist Middleton complained about the small portions of food at the jail, so Jenkins did a drive through at a Burger King. Douglas told Middleton it was the least they could do, since he used to be *one of them.*

The other detectives were also busy trying to tie up loose ends. Dixon was assigned to go to the storage facility and establish a timeline for Middleton's visits to his shed during the days Kathy Powell was missing. Each tenant had their own key code used to enter or exit the facility, so tracking him was just a matter of looking for his code and putting a time to his visits. There were also video surveillance cameras at the facility, but going through the tapes and matching them to the times would be time-consuming. The right man was on the job though.

Hunt and Depsynski interviewed Evonne Haley about the storage shed. She denied any knowledge of it, and said she had never heard of a company called Hal-Data. This was unfortunate since no identifiable fingerprints were found on the box of stereo equipment from Good Guys. They had nothing to charge her with unless she admitted knowledge of the crime.

The detectives also spoke to Haley's twelve-year-old daughter Natasha, who like her mother denied knowing about the storage shed. The young girl's hair did not match the hair found in the shed, but the possibility that the hair belonged to her or her mother would have to be eliminated since hair color and length can be changed. Without telling Haley the reason, Hunt told her they would eventually be getting a seizure order to take hair and DNA evidentiary samples from both her and Natasha.

Haley became upset and accused the detectives of ruining her life. She told them she'd already sent her ten-year-old son back to Colorado to stay with her parents, but her daughter wanted to stay in Reno with her. She told them due to the publicity the case was causing she couldn't stand having the neighbors staring her and her daughter down thinking they had been involved in murders, so now they were being forced to move. The detectives left without telling her most of the publicity was being caused by Middleton himself.

The local papers had once again hit the story with a feeding frenzy after the discovery of the storage shed was made public. Making the case even more of a media nightmare was the fact the Colorado newspapers had also picked up on Middleton's arrest and were running stories on his connection to the unsolved disappearance of Buffy Rice.

Walt and Bonnie Rice had been following the Reno case very closely and were fueling the media fire in Colorado. When the storage shed torture chamber was discovered in Reno they were quite vocal with their opinion that if the Montrose Police Department would have done its job with Buffy's case, these horrible things never would have happened in Reno. It had been sixteen months since Buffy disappeared and she still hadn't been found.

The case was picking up enough press interest that articles began filtering out across the country through the Associated Press. Middleton was making noise about being framed because he was black, and it wasn't being confined inside the white brick walls of the Washoe County Jail. The nation was still reeling from the Rodney King incident, so police-related racial issues were big news. Since Middleton wasn't talking to the press, there was little doubt that his defense team was helping get the word of possible racial overtones of the case out to the media.

Even though Middleton had not yet been charged with killing Kathy Powell, it was plain to see that that was the direction the investigation was heading. So far Middleton refused to do any jailhouse interviews with the local media, but he jumped at the chance to tell his story to television's *Inside Addition* reporter Tony Cox. The interview wouldn't actually air until September 29, 1995, but Middleton made it a point to throw in the "Mississippi of the west" comment. As an added bonus he told the reporter the police said they were going to "hang his black ass for the murders." Even though the police categorically denied both statements, the public still got to hear them.

The detectives tried their best to continue through their investigation and build a case against Middleton in spite of the negative publicity they were getting. It was statements made by Middleton's attorney Mike Specchio two weeks later that caused them to pull out what Douglas called their "Ace of Spades."

In an interview with *The Reno Gazette Journal*, Specchio was quoted as saying, "To me it stinks. They have nothing but circumstantial evidence on my guy. He admitted to dumping her body, and that was a terrible thing. If they want to charge him with that or with being in possession of some of her property that's one thing, but they want to go farther than that. This guy didn't kill anybody and he's not going to admit to killing anybody. We have to play by the rules, and the question is do the rules apply equally to whites and blacks?"

He ended the interview by saying, "Just because he's a black guy and a convicted felon doesn't mean he killed anybody. If this guy was a white college professor the case would be thrown out before it ever got to court."

At 3:00 in the afternoon on Wednesday, March 23, 1995, Detectives Jenkins and Douglas leisurely strolled into the office of the Public Defender and asked to speak to Mike Specchio. After waiting about fifteen minutes outside of his office his secretary told them he was available to see them. The attorney had never bothered to ask who the lead investigators were on the case, but he was about to find out.

Douglas walked into the office ahead of Jenkins and stopped in front of the desk Specchio was seated behind. With one of his best Eddie Murphy smiles, he said, "Let me introduce myself. I'm Detective John Douglas—the man who's gonna eventually be arresting your client David Middleton for the murder of Kathy Powell. Now we both know this ain't about race, so let's stop the foolishness. Its just gonna be me and Middleton in the newspaper photograph when we arrest him, and I'm even *blacker* than he is! Now how's that gonna look for you if you keep up this 'my client is a poor black man being framed' bullshit. We're doing our job clean, so how about you try that too?"

When telling this story later, Douglas said, "It was like the blood drained from the guy's face, and we just walked out and left him sitting there at his desk. It was the only time in my career I ever saw a lawyer speechless. Race was never an issue after that because he knew his smokescreen wasn't gonna work. I almost felt sorry for him. *Almost...*"

Chapter 28
LINES IN TIME

On Friday, March 31, 1995 the detectives assigned to the case held their last briefing of the week at 2:00 P.M. in the Detective Division conference room. Sergeants Burns and Tolliver were seated at the front of the room and four of the detectives were seated at the oval table looking over their notes. Eddie Dixon was standing at one of the white dry-erase boards mounted on the wall in front of the room putting the finishing touches on the storage shed timeline he'd developed. When he finished writing he began explaining what was known about Middleton's activities at the storage unit during the days Kathy Powell was missing.

According to the storage facility records, Middleton rented a five foot by ten foot storage unit under the name Hal-Data Research on June 30, 1994. On August 8, 1994 he requested a larger storage shed and moved into unit #16-28, which measured ten feet by ten feet. The entry records dating back to August were not available due to a change in security systems, but Dixon was able to accurately research back to February 3, 1995—the last day Powell was seen alive. The storage facility security system did not track exit times, but Middleton's entry times into the facility were outlined as follows:

- Friday, February 3, 1995: entered at 8:06 P.M.

- Saturday, February 4, 1995: entered at 12:37 A.M., 5:47 A.M., 6:49 A.M., 8:45 A.M., 11:53 A.M. and 5:38 P.M.

- Sunday, February 5, 1995: entered at 6:19 A.M., 11:09 A.M. and 3:30 P.M.

- Monday, February 6, 1995: entered at 9:26 A.M. and 3:15 P.M.

- Tuesday, February 7, 1995: NO ENTRIES

- Wednesday, February 8, 1995: entered at 6:49 P.M.

- Thursday, February 9, 1995: NO ENTRIES

- Friday, February 10, 1995: entered at 7:45 P.M.

- Saturday, February 11, 1995 (date Powell's body was discovered): entered at 7:26 P.M., VIDEO IS AVAILABLE OF THIS VISIT

- Sunday, February 12, 1995: entered at 12:53 A.M., VIDEO AVAILABLE OF THIS VISIT. SECOND PERSON IS WITH SUSPECT AT THIS TIME.

- NO FURTHER VISITS WERE MADE BY SUSPECT TO HIS STORAGE SHED BETWEEN 12 FEB 1995 AND DATE OF ARREST ON 23 FEB 1995.

Dixon went on to explain that the security system at the facility does not allow one car to follow another through the gate without entering a gate code. If a car tries to tailgate another one through the gate an alarm sounds. That would mean only the times listed for Middleton's code number were the times he was actually at the storage facility.

Additionally, the video surveillance system is activated 24 hours a day, but it scans the entire facility and does not fix on any one area. Middleton's truck was seen at the shed during most of the listed entries. During his visit to the shed on Monday, February 6th at 9:26 A.M. he was seen driving his T.C.I. Cable Company truck. Mr. and Mrs. Tucker both remembered seeing the T.C.I. truck there on other occasions. Two other notable pieces of evidence were found on the video tapes.

During Middleton's visit to the shed on Saturday, February 11th he can be seen loading a large cumbersome package into the rear of his International Harvester pickup truck. The quality of the tape and the lighting conditions were poor, but the package is clearly identifiable as the sleeping bag containing Kathy Powell's body. Middleton uses the ropes tied around the outside of the sleeping bag for handles as he carries the bundled body out of the storage shed and loads it into the back of his pickup truck. The time on the tape when he is seen loading the body is 7:40 P.M.—approximately two hours before it was discovered inside the dumpster.

The video also captured Middleton when he made his next trip to the shed five hours later on Sunday, February 12, 1995. His truck can be seen pulling through the front gate at 12:53 A.M. He is then seen walking out of his storage shed and getting into his truck to leave at 2:05 A.M. The interesting thing about that video clip was that Middleton was not alone during this visit.

A female was seen leaving the shed with him and getting into the passenger seat of his truck. Once again, the lighting and quality of the video was too poor to make out who the female was. It would never hold up in court, but judging from the height and weight, Dixon was reasonably certain the female was Evonne Haley. The tape had been sent to the F.B.I. for assistance with enhancement, but since the camera angle was bad they weren't hopeful that they could help.

After some discussion the timeline was updated with the other information they had. Since Kathy Powell had made phone calls to her fiancé in Philadelphia at 7:38 P.M. and to another friend at 8:00 P.M. the night she was last seen, they were certain she was still alive when Middleton stopped at his storage unit at 8:06 P.M. that night.

During the marathon interview, Middleton told Jenkins he had arrived at Kathy Powell's house for his date with her at 9:00 P.M. on Friday, February 3, 1995. Since Powell was never heard from after her 8:00 P.M. phone call that estimate was probably accurate. That meant Middleton stopped at his storage unit on his way to Kathy Powell's house, which is something a man doesn't normally do when he is on his way out for a date.

The probable reason for that stop was to retrieve the rope Middleton used to bind Powell and some type of weapon used to coerce her into submission. In addition to the other weapons discovered in the shed, they'd also located an electric stun gun. No marks from the prongs on the stun gun had been found on Kathy Powell's body, but the weapon was fully charged when it was recovered from the shed. The intimidation factor alone from a weapon such as that could cause a person to acquiesce to unreasonable demands, so not finding marks didn't rule out the possibility the stun gun had been used in the crime. The reason for Middleton's stop at the shed might never be known, but their logical conclusions were good enough for now.

Based on what they knew so far the detectives pieced together what they thought was a reasonable scenario for Kathy Powell's abduction and murder. Middleton had Powell with him when he returned to the shed at 12:37 A.M. on Saturday, February 4, 1995. Whether she had accompanied him there willingly or not will never be known because the video camera at the storage facility did not capture his arrival. What was known for certain was that Kathy Powell never left that storage shed alive again.

Middleton bound and restrained Kathy Powell during this initial visit to his storage shed and then left her there while he returned to her apartment to steal her belongings. With Powell out of the way Middleton would be able to take his time going through her apartment without fear of interruption. This would account for Powell's missing garage door opener, as he would have taken that with him in order to enter the condo surreptitiously through the garage. It would also explain why Powell's neighbors returning from their late night out at 4:00 A.M. saw Middleton's truck parked in front of her condo loaded with what they described as household goods.

Since there were nine entries into the storage unit over the next two days, Kathy Powell was most likely alive and held captive during that timeframe. Middleton would have used his frequent visits to perform whatever depravities the poor woman had been subjected to before her death. Exactly what he'd done might never be known, but the image of the homemade pulley system, human restraints and the rubber ball gag gave them a good enough idea to paint a morbid mental picture of the probabilities.

And then there was that horrendous refrigerator. Their original theory that Middleton bound Kathy Powell and kept her naked and gagged inside of the refrigerator when he was not at the storage unit was confirmed by the forensics evidence report. The blue fibers found on Kathy Powell's neck matched the fibers around the cutout in the freezer tray inside the refrigerator. The origin of these fibers was a shredded blue towel found on the floor next to the refrigerator.

It appeared Middleton had placed the towel around the cutout so Kathy Powell would not cut her neck on the jagged aluminum. It was an insanely humane gesture for a madman who was torturing his victim, and it apparently did not work. The skin fragments found on the cutout belonged to Kathy Powell too, so sometime during her struggle for freedom the towel placed there for her comfort became dislodged.

The forensics investigators also identified traces of skin and blood belonging to Kathy Powell on the interior of the refrigerator door. After taking measurements, they found these skin and blood traces matched the ante-mortem bruising discovered on Kathy Powell's body during the autopsy. DNA evidence and teeth marks taken from the blue ball gag also matched Kathy Powell. All of this meant she had been alive and struggling to get out of the refrigerator while held captive—a thought more horrific to the detectives than any other aspect of the case thus far.

Moving back to the timeline they saw there was a noticeable decrease in activity starting Monday, February 6, 1995. Their assumption was that Kathy Powell had died sometime between Middleton's last visit at 3:30 P.M. Sunday and his next visit at 3:15 P.M. on Monday. This timeframe would also coincide with the time of death placed by the coroner. Even though Powell had been murdered, a strange sense of relief came over the detectives when they realized her suffering would have ended by that time.

Middleton's next visit to the storage unit was the same day he purchased the plastic bags from Commercial Hardware—Wednesday, February 8th. It would have taken him a good deal of time to wrap Kathy Powell's body up in the manner it was found, so the detectives theorized he used his visits on February 8th and February 10th to do this. His visit to the shed when he removed the body on February 11th only lasted twelve minutes, so he must have had the package ready for travel before he got there.

Dixon had driven the most direct route he could think of from the storage facility to the location where Kathy Powell's body was found, making sure to take the drive at 7:40 P.M. on a Saturday so traffic would be comparable to what Middleton faced. It was 14.3 miles and doing the speed limit the drive took him twenty-one minutes. That meant Middleton dumped the body at roughly 8:00 P.M., so he had plenty of time to formulate his plan before going back to the storage facility.

Middleton's last visit to the shed at 12:53 A.M. Sunday, February 12th could have only been for one purpose—evidence eradication. Somewhere along the way he picked up the female who was seen leaving the shed with him. Dixon passed around some grainy black and white photos he made from the video tape of the woman seen leaving the storage unit with Middleton. The detectives were all convinced it was Evonne Haley, but they knew a jury might see it differently since the person in the photo was almost unrecognizable.

The one nagging question was why Middleton did such a good job cleaning up his shed, but left things like the blue ball gag, the restraints and trace evidence inside the refrigerator. After much discussion they came up with the only answer that made sense. If it *was* Evonne Haley who came back to the shed with Middleton, then maybe he just told her part of what happened. Admitting to having sex with Kathy Powell and her subsequent death inside of the shed might have been easy for him to explain away as an accident—just like he explained it to the police. But if he told Haley of the sadistic torture Kathy Powell endured before her death he might have risked shocking her into going to the police herself.

The detectives thought they had more than enough circumstantial evidence to justify charging Middleton with Kathy Powell's murder—even without a cause of death determination. All they needed to do was show criminal agency had been involved in her death to prove murder in the first degree. The fact they could show she had been kept alive inside of that horrid refrigerator for a period of days and then died while she was being held captive seemed more than enough to prove her death resulted from a criminal act.

Unfortunately, District Attorney Gammick disagreed. There were too many loopholes in the law when it came to prosecuting a murder case with an undetermined cause of death and he didn't want to lose this case through one of them. Middleton had already admitted to having sex with Kathy Powell, finding her dead and dumping her body. A good attorney could make it look like that was exactly what happened, and Middleton's attorney was good.

Gammick wanted more evidence before he approved charging Middleton with murder. If their case wasn't strong enough, there was a chance they would lose it and let Middleton go free to kill again. Double jeopardy was a concern, so if they lost him once they'd lose him forever.

The same went for charging either Middleton or Haley with the crimes related to the Good Guys' incident. There was enough evidence now to arrest them on that, but it was much smarter to wait until the murder charge was brought against Middleton so everything could be joined together in one all-encompassing case. The use of the credit card was just one step in the progression of criminal elements involved in the case. If they charged him with that crime prematurely the case would have to be tried separately and they might not be able to use evidence from it at Middleton's subsequent murder trial. Waiting was the right thing to do, but it wasn't easy.

Middleton was a captive audience, so the detectives weren't overly concerned with the District Attorney's decision. He was scheduled to go to court on his ex-felon in possession of firearms case on May 17th, and it looked like he would be pleading guilty in exchange for a one year sentence. The detectives still had time to come up with more evidence to support the murder charge, but they needed another lucky break. As they left for the weekend, they had no idea that break would come from a Golden Retriever named Nugget.

Chapter 29

STICKS AND BONES

Verdi, Nevada is a quaint little town nestled in the foothills of the Sierra Nevada Mountains twenty miles west of Reno on the California-Nevada border. The icy waters of the Truckee River fed by the mountain snowmelt flow swiftly through the Verdi Valley, making it lush with green vegetation. The hills are covered with Pinion Pine trees and Bitterbrush sage bushes, so the air always has a clean, crisp smell to it.

Bridge Street is the main thoroughfare running through Verdi. The two-lane road was aptly named for the wooden bridge spanning the Truckee River that connects Verdi to the main part of the valley. From Bridge Street a dirt road runs north into Dog Valley—a fifty square mile recreation area that is home to hikers, campers, horseback riders and off-road enthusiasts. On April 9, 1995 at 10:00 A.M. seventy-two-year-old Verdi resident James Warner* was walking his dog on the dirt road leading into Dog Valley. Unbeknownst to both man and dog, they were about to help turn the tide of the David Middleton investigation.

Warner was a retired cardiologist, so he knew the value of daily exercise. His routine was to take his eight-year-old Golden Retriever, Nugget for a three-mile walk every morning at 9:00 sharp. During the winter they kept to the lower lying trails along the river, but on this sunny Saturday morning he decided to hike into Dog Valley. Spring was in the air, the wildflowers were beginning to bloom on the hillsides and the snow had already melted off of the ground at the lower elevations in the valley.

Warner and his dog were on their return trip about a mile from town playing a game they both enjoyed immensely. Warner would throw a stick as far as he could into the sagebrush and Nugget would rummage around until he found it. The dog would faithfully return the stick to his master, who would then throw it again to start another round of fetch. The wind was with Warner when he threw the stick for the last time and it landed in a grouping of Pinion Pines about thirty yards off the trail. He watched Nugget bound through the sagebrush toward where the stick landed, only this time the dog didn't return right away.

After foraging around in the high sagebrush for a full minute, Nugget returned to his master holding his prize in his mouth—only it wasn't the stick he had originally gone after. Instead, clamped in the dog's teeth was what Warner instantly recognized as a human femur bone. Warner gently removed the bone from the dog's mouth and placed it on the ground beside the trail. He stuck a large stick into the semi-frozen ground as a marker, and then snapped a leash onto his dog's collar before following him to where he had found the bone.

When Warner was thirty feet from the copse of trees where he had thrown the stick he began to smell the distinctive odor of decay associated with death. The odor grew stronger as he got closer to the trees and was almost unbearable by the time he got to them. As Warner stepped into the clearing in the sagebrush directly underneath the pine trees he saw where Nugget had found the femur bone, and where the stench of death was emanating from.

Human skeletal remains had been partially unearthed from a shallow grave. Bones and bits of material were scattered around the site, which had apparently been dug up by scavenging coyotes. The skin that had once covered the bones had long since decomposed, but the clumps of long black hair still attached to the skull made the skeleton appear to have been from a female. Warner remembered from medical school that skin and organ tissue decomposed rather quickly, but hair sometimes remained for years after death.

The part of the skeleton still covered with dirt appeared to be enclosed in what looked like a sleeping bag. At first Warner thought this might have been a transient who had died while sleeping in a makeshift encampment and was then covered in dirt by a windstorm. But before backing out of the burial site to call the authorities Warner noticed something to change his mind. White rope was looped around the hands and neck of the skeleton, and Warner's morning walk turned into a jog as he rushed to call the police.

The site where the skeletal remains were discovered was in the jurisdiction of the Washoe County Sheriff's Office, so they responded when the jogger Warner flagged down for help called them. Warner remained on scene and led the first responding deputies to the site, then left after vowing to himself to keep to the river trails for his morning walks from now on.

By the time Lieutenant Don Means from the Forensic Investigation Unit arrived, a good-sized portion of Dog Valley Road had been cordoned off with yellow crime scene tape. Bodies dumped in the desert are not that strange of an occurrence—especially near gambling towns. But as soon as Lieutenant Means looked down at the partially exposed skeleton he knew this one was different.

Means noted a lot of animal activity at the site. In addition to the part of the skeleton still remaining in the shallow grave, there were bones and bone fragments scattered for several hundred yards. Intermingled with the bones were pieces of black plastic and shreds of fabric that appeared to have come from a sleeping bag.

Means helped investigate the discovery of Kathy Powell's body, so he was familiar with that case. He immediately saw the white nylon rope running through the matted hairpiece and around the hands of the skeleton was the same diameter and texture as the rope used to bind Kathy Powell. The knots in the rope were also strikingly similar in both cases.

As Means later put it, "Body dumps aren't that uncommon. But finding two of them where rope, trash bags and sleeping bags were used in this short of a time span *is* uncommon—even in Reno."

Detective Larry Canfield was the lead investigator on scene for the Sheriff's Office. After conferring with Means they agreed there were many similarities between the two cases, so they notified Reno P.D. and asked for the detectives working the Kathy Powell investigation to respond.

Jenkins and Douglas were called in from home and met at the police station so they could drive out to Verdi together. They brought along a binder containing every report of a missing female that had been filed with local police agencies since Middleton moved to Reno. Of the nineteen total reports, six were teenage runaways already returned home, three were elderly Alzheimer patients and two were disgruntled housewives who had fled their husbands and were now accounted for. After eliminating these they were left with eight missing females, but only four of them fit into the category of Middleton's past victims. These were the four cases they were in the process of following up on when they broke for the weekend.

The skeleton had not yet been exhumed from its shallow, earthen grave when Jenkins and Douglas arrived. They stood in the interior of the crime scene with Detective Canfield and Lieutenant Means, oblivious to the smell of death around them. After they were briefed they were allowed to take a closer look at the skeletal remains. It was then that they saw the long black hairs attached to the skeleton's skull cap, and they both instantly knew they'd seen that hair before.

The coroner was on scene and said the body would have had to have been buried there before the onset of the cold winter weather in order for that degree of decomposition to occur. The grave was only about six inches deep, so decomposition would have occurred quickly in the hot summer months. His best guess was the body had been buried for at least seven months, but it could have been longer. Using that timeframe, Jenkins eliminated all but one of the missing person reports in the binder.

They studied the Sparks Police Department missing person report of forty-two-year-old Thelma Davilla. An officer named Rocky Triplett took the initial report, and was experienced enough to have collected hair from Ms. Davilla's hairbrush to be used for later comparison. The case had then been assigned to Sparks Detective Dave Adams, who according to the report had dental records for Ms. Davilla on file. In addition to the hair still remaining on the skeleton, the jawbone and teeth were still intact. Because of the excellent preliminary investigation done in the missing person case it would be easy to quickly confirm whether the remains actually were Ms. Davilla.

The date Ms. Davilla was last seen showed to be August 8, 1994. Douglas looked up from the report and asked, "Why does that date sound so familiar?"

"Because we've seen it before," replied Jenkins. "Eddie Dixon had August 8, 1994 listed on his timeline as the day Middleton moved into his new and larger storage unit. Now we know the reason he needed more room."

"Shit! We should have seen that earlier."

"Well we didn't," replied Jenkins. "But we see it now and that's what matters. From the looks of our decedent it wouldn't have mattered if we would have noticed it when we got this report last week anyway."

Canfield said, "Well it's gonna save us a lot of leg work if you've got both the victim *and* the suspect identified in this case."

"I believe we do," said Jenkins. "But we need to be sure before you focus entirely on Middleton. If you will be so kind as to call Detective Adams from Sparks and have him bring the hair samples and dental records from his case, John and I will go to our department and retrieve the hair samples we took from Middleton's storage shed. We'll meet you at the crime lab in about an hour and see if things match up the way I think they will."

As the two Reno detectives were heading back to their car, Canfield called to them. "Hey D.J., how many more do you think there are?"

Jenkins looked at the binder in his hand and answered, "Only God and the devil can answer that question."

Douglas added, "And the devil ain't talkin without his lawyer."

Chapter 30

THELMA

The search of the Verdi gravesite and recovery of the skeletal remains were halted at 4:30 P.M. due to darkness. Forensic investigators spent the entire next day performing a painstakingly thorough grid search of the entire area where the remains had been located. By Monday morning April 11, 1995 the exhumed skeleton and all of the scattered bones collected at the site were in the custody of the Washoe County Coroner's Office. All of the forensic evidence was taken to the Sheriff's Crime Lab.

Washoe County Coroner Vernon McCarty positively identified the skeletal remains as Thelma Davilla through comparison of dental records. Additional identification came from Dr. Berch Henry, a criminalist for the Washoe County Sheriff's Crime Lab. Dr. Henry compared DNA taken from the skull cap of the skeleton to the hairs taken from Thelma Davilla's hairbrush and got a positive match. The hairs found at the bottom of the drum in Middleton's shed also matched Ms. Davilla's DNA. The detectives had anticipated this, but the DNA comparison yielded one surprising discovery.

Hair and small amounts of blood and skin had been located inside of the hollowed-out portion of the large speaker box inside of Middleton's storage shed. This trace evidence also matched Davilla's DNA. The only logical explanation for this was that

Thelma Davilla had at some point been placed inside the speaker box. The space was easily large enough to hold her small-framed body, and since she had been bound she more than likely was alive when placed inside the box. The detectives envisioned Middleton using the speaker box to hold Davilla captive the same way he used the refrigerator to hold Powell.

Investigator Richard Berger from the Sheriff's Forensic Science Division examined the rope found on and near Davilla's remains. Mr. Berger had also done the evidentiary analysis in Kathy Powell's case and said the rope used on both victims was consistent and similar in all manners. The rope was also consistent with the rope recovered from Middleton's storage shed.

An autopsy on Davilla's remains was not possible due to a lack of tissue, but a medical examination was performed by Dr. Frederick Laubscher from the Coroner's Office. Since the skull and other bones were intact, Dr. Laubscher ruled out gunshot, knife wound, crushing injury or any type of trauma as cause of death. However, he could not rule out suffocation or most other possible causes of death. After thorough examination his summation of cause and manner of death consisted of one word—*undetermined.*

The Davilla case now involved all three of Northern Nevada's biggest law enforcement agencies. She had been reported missing to the Sparks Police Department, her remains had been found in an unincorporated area under the jurisdiction of the Washoe County Sheriff's Office and her death was directly related to a Reno P.D. case. Since they were once again dealing with an undetermined cause of death the detectives would have to prove criminal agency was involved. They had their work cut out for them and decided it would be beneficial to both investigations to pool their resources.

A multi-jurisdictional task force would require the approval of the heads of all three agencies, and that would take time. As Douglas put it, if you put three police chiefs in the same room together they're not even going to agree about the time of day, never mind who's going to be lead agency on a task force. But there was nothing preventing the detectives from holding an impromptu meeting to discuss the cases between themselves, so that is what they did ay 9:00 A.M. on Tuesday, April 12, 1995.

They met at the Sparks Police Department since Detective Adams was the lead investigator on the Davilla case. Jenkins and Douglas had a vested interest in helping tie Middleton to the death of Thelma Davilla. If they could show Middleton had a predisposition for kidnap, torture and murder six months before he ever met Kathy Powell, it would make proving criminal agency in their case much easier.

In addition to Jenkins and Douglas, Sheriff's Detective Larry Canfield also attended the meeting. The three detectives listened intently as Detective Adams briefed them, each wanting to learn as much about the victim as they could.

Thelma Davilla was a Guatemalan immigrant who shared a one-bedroom apartment at 2244 Greenbrae Dr. in Sparks with her older sister Dora Valverde. At the time of her disappearance she was forty-two-years old-and unmarried. She had a sixth grade education, spoke very little English and worked bussing tables at the Hickory Pit Restaurant inside of the Circus-Circus Casino in downtown Reno.

She occupied the living room of her sister's apartment and slept on the couch. She enjoyed simple pleasures, like going to the mall or watching T.V. Since Davilla grew up in poverty in Guatemala she was never able to indulge in those types of activities. According to her sister one of the first things Davilla did after getting a job was buy a television and get cable installed in the apartment. Her cable T.V. provider was listed as T.C.I. Cable Company.

Davilla worked the 4:00 P.M. to midnight shift at the Hickory Pit Restaurant on Sunday, August 7, 1994 and was scheduled to be back at work at 4:00 P.M. the next day. When Ms. Valverde left for work at 8:00 A.M. on Monday, August 8, 1994 Davilla was asleep on the couch. The television was on and she was covered by a multi-colored Mexican-style blanket.

When Valverde returned home after work at 5:30 P.M. that same day she found the front door unlocked, which she said was unusual. The T.V. was still on, but Davilla and the blanket she had been using were gone. A plant near the couch had been knocked over, but that was the only thing appearing out of place. Davilla kept several hundred dollars in cash from tips in a coffee can near the couch and the money was still there.

Valverde was not overly concerned until she checked her telephone messages. There was a message from Davilla's dentist saying she had missed a morning appointment and another from the Hickory Pit Restaurant asking why she wasn't at work. Valverde knew her sister would not have willingly missed the dental appointment since she had been complaining of a toothache. She also knew Davilla had not missed a day of work during the six years she had been employed at the restaurant—a fact she was extremely proud of. Davilla was in good heath and would not have missed work without calling.

When Valverde still hadn't heard from Davilla by the next morning she notified the Sparks Police Department. Due to the uncharacteristic behavior of Davilla, the responding officers believed foul play might be involved. Detectives were called to the apartment and began their missing persons investigation.

Davilla's check book was on the living room table and the last check she wrote was dated August 8, 1994. The check was for seven dollars and it was written to the T.C.I. Cable Company. The detectives checked with T.C.I. and found Davilla had not been billed for a seven dollar charge. They also had no record of anyone from T.C.I. going to her apartment to collect any type of payment. Additionally, there was no specific service they provided where a seven dollar charge would have been billed. The information did not seem important at the time, so it was logged into the report with no further follow up.

Davilla had only three close friends she socialized with and did not have a steady boyfriend. One of her female friends said they often frequented a Latin nightclub called Cheers on West 4th Street in downtown Reno. She said Davilla liked to dance and occasionally dated men she met at the club. She added that Davilla had a preference for black men. Davilla and the friend had gone to Cheers on Saturday night August 6, 1994. The friend could not remember who Davilla had danced with, but they did leave the club together.

All three friends said Davilla never opened the door to her apartment without looking through the peep hole to see who was there, even when she was expecting someone. They said it was unlikely she would open the door for a stranger while she was home alone. The detectives noted in their report there was no sign of forced entry into the apartment.

Davilla did not own a car and used Citifare busses to commute. After canvassing the bus drivers the detectives found one driver who knew Davilla because she was a regular passenger on one of his routes. The driver remembered seeing Davilla at the Sparks bus station in the early evening on Friday, August 5, 1994. She was quite dressed up and told the driver she had plans to go out to dinner with friends. The driver recalled seeing a light colored pickup truck pull up to where Davilla was waiting. A black male was driving and a white female with curly reddish-blonde hair was in the passenger seat. The male got out and Davilla jumped in and slid into the middle of the front seat. The male then got back into the truck and drove off.

All investigative leads in Davilla's disappearance eventually turned into dead ends and the case was subsequently listed as open and inactive. Detective Adams said until Davilla's remains were discovered it was like she just vanished without a trace.

The words *vanished without a trace* echoed inside of Jenkins head, because he'd heard them before. News reporters in Colorado used those same words when telling the story of the disappearance of Buffy Rice-Donohue in Montrose, and again to describe the disappearance of fourteen-year-old Cindy Booth in Delta. But before he could dwell on that thought the phrase was chased from his brain by two words even more horrific. *Serial Killer!*

Chapter 31

BODY COUNT

Sergeant Burns called Jenkins as he and Douglas were leaving the Sparks Police Department to tell him that Lieutenant Tom Chinn of the Montrose Police Department and two other Colorado detectives were flying into Reno that afternoon. They hoped to look over the evidence taken from Middleton's storage shed and discuss similarities in the cases they were working.

The Colorado detectives arrived at the Reno Police Station at three in the afternoon and a meeting was set up in the Detective Division conference room to discuss their respective cases. Detectives Canfield and Adams representing the Sheriff's Office and the Sparks Police Department joined Jenkins, Douglas and Sergeant Burns for the meeting.

After being filled in on the Middleton investigation in Reno, Lieutenant Chinn brought the detectives up to date on the Buffy Rice-Donohue investigation. There was still no trace of Buffy and no new leads on the case. Chinn hoped something in Middleton's storage unit might link him to Buffy's disappearance and shed new light on his investigation. Their case was still listed as open and active, but they held little hope of finding Buffy alive after seventeen months.

Lieutenant Chinn eluded to the fact that Walt and Bonnie Rice had provided them with bad information that delayed their initial investigation in an attempt to steer the police away from any

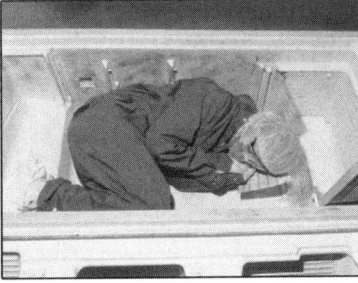

C.S.I. technician reenacting Kathy Powell's body placement while she was stored inside of the refrigerator in Middleton's storage shed.

Eddie Dixon and Steve Pitts standing in front of Middleton's "Torture Chamber" storage shed before it was searched. The refrigerator is in the left corner with the drum of souvenirs on top of it.

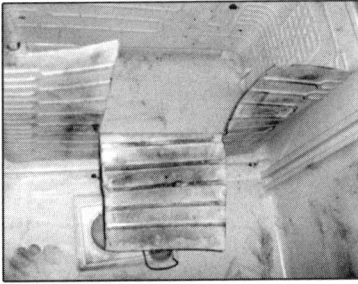

Cut out in the refrigerator that allowed Middleton to place Kathy Powell's head in the freezer portion.

Ropes and pulleys rigged inside of Middleton's storage shed.

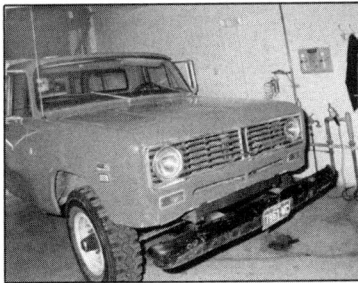

Middleton's 1972 International truck that first drew attention to him as a suspect in Kathy Powell's murder.

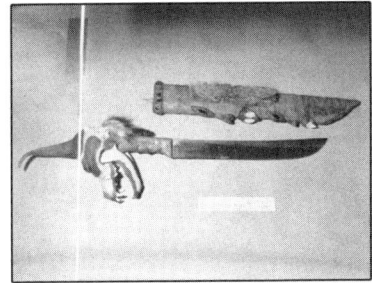

Voodoo machete used by Middleton in the Santeria ritualistic rape in Florida.

Middleton's Miami P.D. .357 Magnum
service revolver located inside
of his storage unit.

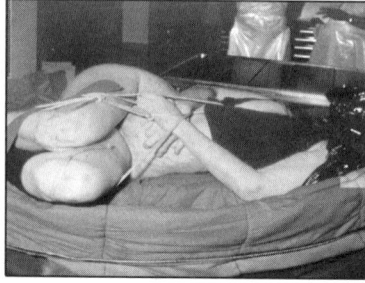

Kathy Powell's bound body after
it was removed from the sleeping bag.

Portion of the skeletal remains of
Thelma Davilla located in a
shallow grave North of Reno.

Middleton's Boston P.D. badge
and I.D. card located inside of
his storage shed.

Middleton's T.C.I. Cable Company
truck still held in storage
as evidence.

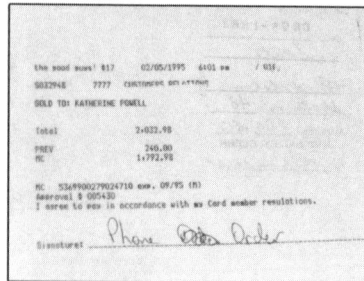

Credit card receipt from the
Good Guys purchase that
broke the case open.

possible drug connection to Buffy's disappearance. Middleton and Haley had been questioned during the investigation and they both took polygraph tests prior to leaving Colorado. The results for both of the polygraph tests were inconclusive. Since that time additional witness interviews had been done and Middleton and Haley were now considered the only viable suspects in the case.

The two questions the Nevada detectives had on their minds sat heavily in the room like invisible elephants. Why had Middleton been allowed to leave Colorado when he was the main suspect in Buffy's disappearance, and why hadn't he been arrested on the weapons charge when they had their chance to hold him? Those questions would remain unasked, because it just didn't matter now.

Detective Sergeant John Musick from Delta, Colorado next discussed the disappearance of fourteen-year-old Cindy Booth from his city. The teenager had last been seen riding her bicycle to the home of a family friend after school on the afternoon of August 4, 1993. Neither the girl nor her bicycle was ever seen again.

The family friend whose house Booth went to was forty-year-old Eugene Marvin Smith. The man was questioned after Booth's disappearance and was still the primary suspect in the case. Since a body had never been discovered and there was no physical evidence linking Smith to Booth's disappearance, he had not yet been charged with any crime related to the case.

Delta is twenty miles west of Montrose and the police department was interested in Middleton because Booth's disappearance occurred during the time he lived there. Eugene Smith and Middleton knew each other through construction work, so they wanted to explore the possibility that Middleton might have been involved in the disappearance. Smith refused to talk to the police, and had since been convicted on unrelated charges of molesting his three-year-old niece in 1992. He was due to be sentenced to fifteen years in prison, so, like Middleton, he was off the street while they investigated the disappearance of Cindy Booth.

Montrose P.D. Detective Kevin Walters then discussed a case he was working on in conjunction with the San Miguel County, Colorado Sheriff's Office. On November 13, 1994 the skeletal remains of a female in her early forties was found buried in a shallow grave in a rural area of Colorado about fifty miles east of Montrose. Her estimated time of death was in the early fall of 1993. This would have been just after the disappearance of Cindy Booth and during the time Middleton and Haley were living in Montrose.

The woman still remained unidentified, but it was believed she may have been a transient prostitute who was never reported missing. Detective Walters explained prostitutes often came to the Montrose area from Denver during ski season to ply their trade with vacationing tourists. He was working the case with the Sheriff's Department since the crime may have originated in Montrose.

The San Miguel County Coroner was able to establish blunt force trauma as the cause of death for the unknown female, so the case was classified as a homicide. The fact that Middleton preyed on street prostitutes in Miami had not gone unnoticed to the investigators, but it was the discovery of Kathy Powell and Thelma Davilla that really got them interested in him. Much like the Reno victims, the Jane Doe victim in the San Miguel County case had been bound with rope and placed inside a sleeping bag before being disposed of.

The Colorado detectives brought DNA and hair samples from all three victims with them. Thus far two hair samples and DNA evidence from five pairs of women's panties found in Middleton's shed were not matched with their owners, so arrangements were made for comparisons of all samples to be done at the Washoe County Crime Lab the next morning. There were no plans to charge Middleton with any of the Colorado crimes yet since he was already in custody in Nevada, but that could change if additional evidence was discovered. The Colorado detectives were also interested in interviewing Haley and Middleton while they were in town.

During the ensuing discussion Jenkins asked about the polygraph tests Middleton and Haley took. He had never before heard of a case where the polygraph results from two suspects involved in the same crime showed inconclusive, and he asked Chinn if he had a theory for the anomaly.

Chinn let out a sigh and said that question had come up before, but he didn't have an answer for it. He did say a lot of people were conned by Middleton, and most people in Montrose thought he was an honest ex-cop who had to get out of Miami after going undercover in prison. Jenkins had spent enough time talking to Middleton to be reasonably certain the Colorado lieutenant was probably a member of the group he had conned.

Several things were discussed by the Nevada detectives after their counterparts from Colorado left for their hotel. First and foremost, they all agreed a task force needed to be formed to investigate Middleton's crimes in Nevada. Part of the responsibilities would be to do an independent inquiry into Middleton's criminal activity in Colorado and Florida. They were not out to burn anyone—they just had to establish a pattern of criminal activity to support their case.

They needed to do this without stepping on the toes of the Colorado cops. None of them thought the Montrose Police Department had intentionally bungled their case against Middleton. Mistakes are sometimes made when small town cops get involved in big time investigations, but the mistakes had to be rectified.

The follow up in Florida was another matter, but it was just as essential. Somewhere along the line Middleton went from respected cop to serial killer and they all believed Florida was where they would find the answers. A road trip to Florida would definitely need to be made and the detectives would carry more clout if they represented a multi-jurisdictional task force. Sergeant

Burns agreed and said he would start the procedure first thing in the morning.

The conversation then turned to Evonne Haley. They all agreed she was currently more valuable to them as a free person then she would be if they arrested her on the theft charges from the Good Guys case. They had enough to proceed with the charges now, but her rights to an attorney would kick in if they questioned her about any of the murders while she was in custody. They decided to let her enjoy her freedom for now, but they all knew her days were numbered.

As they broke for the evening Douglas joked that if Middleton's body count got much higher he was going to make Norman Bates look like a boy scout. The detectives laughed, but inside they knew Middleton had already passed the magic number to be considered a serial killer. None of the men in the room had ever worked a confirmed serial killer before, but it was every homicide detective's dream to go up against one. Middleton was good, but now it was time to prove they were better.

Chapter 32

HEADS OR TAILS

The Colorado detectives flew home on Thursday, April 14, 1995. They had located nothing of evidentiary value to their cases during the search through the contents of Middleton's storage unit, and no DNA matches were found.

Speaking through his attorney, Middleton refused to talk to the detectives. When they called Haley for an interview her message to them was also quite clear. She told them to either arrest her or leave her the hell alone. The only things the detectives took with them were hair and DNA samples from Middleton. These might be useful for evidence comparison if the bodies of the two missing women should be discovered.

On Friday, April 15, 1995 Jenkins was flipping through the investigative report on the Buffy Rice case Lieutenant Chinn had left him. His instincts told him something was missing, so he got the phone number for the Rice family from the report and decided to call to see if they could shed some light on the case. He didn't know it at the time, but it would be the first of many conversations he'd have with the family throughout the course of the investigation.

Bonnie Rice was home when Jenkins called and was more than happy to talk to him about the case of her missing daughter. For the next hour Jenkins listened to the story of Buffy Rice-

Donohue's disappearance while taking notes on a yellow legal pad. Some of what Bonnie Rice told him he'd already read in the papers, but most of it was new and useful information.

The first bit of interesting information Jenkins learned was that Haley's father was an ex-cop with the Mesa County Sheriff's Office in Grand Junction, Colorado. According to Mrs. Rice, Haley's father had been fired for his involvement in some type of cover up during a murder investigation of a wealthy businessman in Telluride, Colorado. The adage about women being attracted to men like their fathers popped into Jenkins mind when he listened to the story.

Buffy knew that Haley's father was involved in law enforcement in Colorado and that Middleton had been a cop in Miami. She didn't know at the time Haley's father had been fired, and she believed Middleton had been an undercover operative while in prison in Miami. Buffy told her parents she trusted Middleton and Haley due to their involvement with law enforcement. Once again, the word *trust* was used by one of Middleton's victims.

Bonnie Rice described Buffy as a good student and an all-around good kid through her high school years. Buffy got engaged to her boyfriend Mason Donohue shortly after she graduated from high school. Bonnie said she and her husband would have rather seen her wait until she was older, but they liked Mason and were supportive of their daughter's decision. Buffy planned to become an x-ray technician, so she took the job at the Sizzler to raise money for school. Mason worked construction and the young couple moved into a rented mobile home in Montrose after they were married.

Buffy became involved with drugs three months before her disappearance. Mrs. Rice blames Middleton and Haley for this, as it became well-known that the two of them were involved in selling methamphetamine. Two weeks before Buffy disappeared she told her parents she had found out Middleton had raped a girl in Florida. She said she was terrified of Middleton and asked if she and Mason could move in with her parents. The young couple abandoned their mobile home and moved in with Bonnie and Walt Rice.

Bonnie had her own theory about Buffy's disappearance on the afternoon of Sunday, November 21, 1993. Evonne Haley had come to the Rice residence earlier that day to talk to Buffy, possibly about money Buffy owed her. Haley was parked in front of the Rice house talking to Buffy when Walt Rice yelled to Buffy that he wanted her to get the family car washed later that afternoon. Bonnie Rice felt Haley heard that exchange.

The apartment Haley and Middleton shared overlooked the parking lot of the car wash, which was located in the same shopping complex as the Wal-Mart Buffy's car was later found parked in front of. Bonnie believed Haley waited for Buffy to pull into the car wash and then confronted her there. Witnesses saw Haley drive into the car wash parking lot in her red RX-7 and then follow Buffy to the Wal-Mart. The same witnesses saw Buffy get into the passenger seat of Haley's car, but said it looked as though she was at first trying to walk away from Haley.

When Buffy did not return home by 4:00 that afternoon her parents knew something was wrong and suspected Middleton and Haley were involved. They called the Montrose Police Department and an officer responded to their house. Although the officer did not take an official report at that time, he did write down the address Mrs. Rice gave them for Middleton and Haley as a place they thought Buffy might be.

Mrs. Rice said she went to Middleton's apartment three times that night looking for Buffy, but no one answered the door. She went on to say that several of Buffy's friends gave statements to the police, including the store clerk Jenkins had read about who saw Middleton carrying bags out of the apartment that night. Not only did the police fail to follow up with some of these witnesses, a year later they contacted one of them and asked her to fill out another statement because they lost her original one.

On one of the visits Mrs. Rice made to Middleton's apartment that first night she noticed a window screen had been partially pushed out and she saw what looked like a bloodstain on the inside of the windowsill. She reported this to the police, but they did not go to the apartment until two days later. According to Bonnie, Lieutenant Chinn and two officers went to Middleton's apartment on Tuesday, November 23, 1993 to check her report. Lieutenant Chinn said the alleged bloodstain looked like paint, so no photos were taken and no evidentiary sample was collected.

Lieutenant Chinn told Mrs. Rice it was during this visit to the apartment that he asked Middleton about the report of him loading bags into his car the night Buffy disappeared. Middleton said the bags contained laundry and showed Lieutenant Chinn several empty laundry bags inside of the apartment. Lieutenant Chinn believed this story, even though Middleton offered no explanation for why he was loading heavy bags of laundry into Haley's car at midnight in a town that didn't have a twenty-four hour laundromat.

Jenkins asked Bonnie Rice about the article concerning the nude photos of Buffy. She confirmed the story to be true and went on to explain how the police came into possession of the photos. Due to the Rice's frustration with the way the police were handling the case, they hired a private investigator named Nelson Jennett on December 1, 1993 to help find Buffy. Unbeknownst to them, Jennett had close ties to the Montrose Police Department and was reporting back to them without the Rice's consent. The Rice's got word of this and fired Jennett on December 20, 1995.

Bonnie said Jennett notified Lieutenant Chinn that he was no longer working for the Rice's, but he asked if he could continue working with the police to assist on the case. Jennett received a phone call from a man named Ken Newman on January 2, 1994. Newman was the manager of the mobile home park where Buffy and Mason Donohue had been living prior to moving in with the Rice's. He told Jennett he had found an undeveloped roll of film while cleaning out Buffy and Mason's trailer and wanted to know what to do with it.

Jennett went to the mobile home park and picked up the roll of film. While he was there, Newman told him there was a second roll of film still inside the trailer. Newman let Jennett into the trailer and he retrieved the second roll of film. He then got the film developed and turned the photos over to Lieutenant Chinn. The photos were from Buffy and Mason's honeymoon and did, in fact, contain nude photos of Buffy. Not only did the photos have no possible evidentiary value to the missing person case, the family actually did confirm the police had shown them around in public on more than one occasion.

The film was the property of Mason Donohue and it was taken out of a trailer the rent was paid up on. Mason made repeated requests for the police to give the photos to him, but thus far they had refused. Bonnie said the situation was particularly frustrating because even if the photos did have some evidentiary value, it was her understanding that they could not be used in a court of law. The private investigator was acting as an agent of the police, so a search warrant should have been obtained before the film was taken out of the trailer. This last statement led Jenkins to believe perhaps Bonnie Rice had a better understanding of the law than did the people investigating her daughter's disappearance.

Bonnie went on to say it was shortly after the first confrontation they had with the police over their display of the photos that charges were filed against her husband for the

Waterdog Mountain incident and against her for trespassing at Middleton's apartment. She said Haley admitted in a recorded phone conversation with her that the police who responded to the apartment the night Middleton pulled the shotgun on her told Haley to press charges against her. Bonnie was told by her attorney this tape was inadmissible in any court proceedings because it was recorded without Haley's knowledge. It was still enough to convince the Rice's that the police were siding with Middleton and Haley.

Jenkins then asked Bonnie to tell him more about the shotgun incident. She described the shotgun in great detail and her description exactly matched the weapon taken out of Middleton's apartment. She said when Middleton pointed the shotgun at her it was so close to her face that she could see clearly all the way down the barrel. She said she honestly believed Middleton was going to kill her, but at that point and time she didn't care. Deep inside she knew her daughter had been killed, so a part of her was already dead.

As an afterthought, Jenkins asked Mrs. Rice what her opinion was regarding Middleton and Haley both passing their polygraph tests. She surprised him when she immediately answered they hadn't passed the tests, the results were inconclusive, which was a big difference. She had obviously done her homework, because she knew polygraph test results depended largely on how the operator posed the questions.

In the case of Middleton and Haley, the polygraph operator was the father of the owner of the construction company Middleton worked at. Both men were friends and members of the group of people Middleton had conned into believing he was an undercover cop when he was in prison. Bonnie had no doubts the polygraph test results were inconclusive because the operator *wanted* them to be so.

Bonnie then gave Jenkins one more piece of surprise information. She had been in Reno following Middleton and Haley the week Kathy Powell's body was discovered. Bonnie Rice, her mother-in-law and a family friend drove to Reno for the purpose of following Middleton and Haley in hopes they would do something to lead to the discovery of Buffy.

The three women sat in their car at the end of Middleton's street and followed either him or Haley until they would lose them. They arrived in Reno two days after Kathy Powell was abducted, but they never saw Middleton go to his storage shed and they were not following him when he dumped the body in the dumpster. They actually spent more time following Haley because they were convinced she was dealing drugs out of a downtown Reno car repair shop.

Before hanging up Bonnie said she wished Jenkins luck in bringing Middleton to justice for the murders he committed in Reno. She said not knowing who was responsible for her daughter's disappearance was a living hell, but seeing Middleton go to prison would make it a little easier. She said she would pray for the detectives, and Jenkins believed her.

By the time Jenkins hung up the phone he'd accumulated more information than the entire case file Lieutenant Chinn left for him contained. It was not uncommon for animosity to develop between a victim's family and the police when a case went unsolved for an extended period of time. But in this case the story told by the police was completely different than the one told to him by Bonnie Rice. A story was much like a coin—each having two sides that sometimes bore no resemblance to each other. Now that he'd heard both sides of this story it was time to figure out which one was heads and which one was tails.

Chapter 33

TASK FORCE

It is a proven fact in law enforcement that the best way to screw up an investigation is to keep getting more police agencies involved in it. The old adage of "too many chiefs and not enough Indians" comes into play every time. By the end of April this is exactly what happened with the Middleton investigation. Every police administrator wanted their department to be the one that broke the case, and they *all* were putting pressure on the District Attorney's Office to file murder charges against Middleton.

On Friday, April 21, 1995 at 8:00 A.M. a meeting was held at the Washoe County Sheriff's Office. In attendance were representatives from the Reno and Sparks Police Departments, the Washoe County Sheriff's Office, The Washoe County District Attorney's Office and the State of Nevada Division of Investigation. The cops who were actually working on the case were finally going to get what they had asked for. A task force was being formed to more efficiently investigate the murders of Kathy Powell and Thelma Davilla.

Members of the task force would be Detective Dave Adams from the Sparks Police Department, Detective Larry Canfield from the Sheriff's Office, Investigator Mary Haugen from the Nevada Division of Investigation and Detective Dave Jenkins from the Reno Police Department. Other detectives from those agencies would be utilized as needed, but they would take their assignments from these lead investigators.

District Attorney Dick Gammick and his assistant Dave Stanton would be following the case closely, but Deputy District Attorney Tom Viloria was assigned exclusively to the Middleton case. Even though Viloria was handling the case, Gammick made it perfectly clear that any decision to file murder charges against Middleton would need *his* personal approval. This would take some of the heat off Viloria, but it would also insure the case was prepared the way Gammick wanted it before his office prosecuted it.

From the onset it was decided the job of the task force would be to investigate *only* the Powell and Davilla murders. Their investigative efforts in Colorado, Florida or anywhere else the case led them would be confined to fact-finding inquiries to establish information that would aid them in the prosecution of Middleton for these two murders.

Any crimes Middleton committed in other jurisdictions either had been or were in the process of being investigated by the proper agencies. The task force would liaise with these agencies and render any assistance they were asked for, but that was it. The fear was that if the detectives uncovered possible malfeasance that allowed Middleton to remain a free man his defense attorney would use that at trial. It was a very realistic possibility that a good attorney could turn everything around and point the blame at the police for not doing their jobs and allowing Middleton to continue killing people. It only took one juror with a grudge against the police to believe that type of ploy and poison the entire jury.

The task force was given one week to gather all the information known about Middleton, Haley and both murder cases. Another meeting would then be held the following Friday to discuss the status of the investigation. The District Attorney would review the case at that time and make a determination about what else was needed to support murder charges against Middleton.

The next task force meeting was held at the Washoe County Sheriff's Office crime lab on Friday, April 28, 1995 at 10:00 A.M. The detectives had worked hard at putting their cases together during the week and felt they were close to having enough on Middleton to file murder charges against him. The refrigerator and several other items of evidence taken from Middleton's shed were displayed at the meeting. In addition to the task force detectives, representatives from the administrations of each agency and the District Attorney's office were in attendance.

Jenkins started the discussion by giving background information on what was known about Middleton's past criminal history in Florida and Colorado. He included Haley's involvement with Middleton and what they had learned from the Colorado detectives about the three open murders in the Montrose area while the couple was living there. He also told the group what he had learned during his conversation with Bonnie Rice.

Everyone at the meeting was familiar with the evidence gathered thus far linking Middleton to the two Nevada murders, but some important evidentiary findings had come in since the last meeting. Middleton's dental impression and the bite mark on Kathy Powell's left breast were examined by Dr. Raymond Rawson, a professor of dentistry. This comparison was important because no saliva had been found on the bite mark, possibly because Middleton had cleaned it with bleach. Dr. Rawson confirmed the bite mark had been inflicted by Middleton. He further concluded that this was a very hard and painful bite since it caused bleeding below the skin. Because of this bleeding he determined the bite was inflicted while Powell was still alive.

Dr. Rawson also compared the teeth marks in the foam ball to Kathy Powell's dental impression. He confirmed the teeth marks in the ball were Powell's and that she had bitten into it extremely hard to cause those marks. From the positioning of the teeth marks he concluded the ball had been shoved into Powell's mouth in its entirety. Since the saliva on the ball also matched Powell's the ball would have been placed into her mouth while she was still alive. The body does not produce saliva post mortem, and additionally there would be no reason to gag a dead person.

The forensic report on the rope used on Powell and Davilla had also returned. White nylon twelve-strand rope with a one-quarter inch diameter had been used to bind both victims. This was the same type as the rope found in Middleton's storage shed, but the rope was a common type sold commercially. The knots in the rope were listed as "SS granny knots" which are a very common knot.

Further analysis had also been done on the hairs found in Middleton's shed. In addition to the hair discovered in the barrel, hairs found on a blanket, in a rolled up ball of duct tape and on one of the human bondage restraints had also been identified as coming from Davilla. This was positive proof that Davilla had been held inside of the storage shed at some time prior to her death.

Detective Adams went on to further discuss the Davilla investigation. Davilla and her sister had T.C.I. Cable service installed in their apartment in June of 1993. Middleton was not the installer listed in the company records. The cable service at their apartment was serviced on July 23, 1994, approximately two weeks before Davilla disappeared. Middleton was not the listed technician on this service either. The technician who did the service recalls Middleton helping him on several occasions, but could not accurately recall if the July service call was one of them. It was possible that Middleton was on this service call and met Davilla at that time.

Another possibility was that Middleton met Davilla at the Cheers nightclub in Reno. The manager of Cheers picked Middleton out of a photo lineup and recalled him being in the club on more than one occasion. He also recognized the photo of Davilla, but could not recall if he ever saw the two of them together.

A third possibility was the Sierra Stix bar in Sparks. This was directly across the street from Davilla's apartment and she sometimes went there with friends. Jenkins recalled from his interview with the bartender Suzanne Atkinson that she first met Middleton at the Sierra Stix Bar in the summer of 1994. When they re-contacted her she said she believed this was either in late July or early August of 1994.

Where Middleton met Davilla was irrelevant, because they could now show that he *had* known her on August 8, 1994. During a canvass of Davilla's apartment complex the week prior, one of her neighbors identified Middleton from another photo lineup. The neighbor said he recalled seeing Middleton at 6:45 A.M. the morning of August 8, 1994 at Davilla's apartment. He said he watched Middleton walk partway up the stairs leading to the apartment. He then saw Middleton stop and stand on the stairs as if he was listening to something, then turn and walk back down the stairs and away from the apartment.

In a follow up interview with Ms. Valverde she told detectives 6:45 is the time she normally eats breakfast before going to work, and the kitchen is just inside the front door of the apartment. Detectives theorized that Middleton planned to make contact with Davilla during the 6:45 A.M. visit, but left the apartment when he heard Valverde making noise in the kitchen. It was possible that he remained in the area and returned to the apartment when he saw Valverde leave for work. Records at T.C.I. showed Middleton was scheduled to work at 8:00 A.M. on Monday, August 8, 1994, but he called in sick.

The detectives also had a theory about how Middleton had taken Davilla from the apartment. Since the plant was knocked over near the couch where Davilla was sleeping, there was probably some type of struggle. Middleton could have used his stun gun on her or he could have simply overpowered her. They were reasonably certain Middleton had carried Davilla out of her apartment wrapped inside a blanket. Ms. Valverde identified a large hand woven Mexican blanket found inside of Middleton's storage shed as the one her sister was covered with when she last saw her sleeping on the couch on August 8, 1994. In addition to the blanket, Ms. Valverde also identified a black lacy top and a red hair scrunchy found inside the shed as belonging to Davilla.

Since hair and DNA evidence from Davilla was found inside of the large speaker box in Middleton's shed, that is where he most likely held her captive when he first took her to his old storage unit. Once there Middleton must have realized his storage shed was too small for whatever he had planned for Davilla, so he rented the larger one. Since Davilla's hair was found in the balled-up duct tape it was probably used as a gag. That meant she was kept alive in the storage shed for at least some period of time, and was more than likely bound and gagged inside the speaker box while Middleton moved his belongings into his new storage unit.

What was done to Davilla and how long she was held captive inside of Middleton's chamber of horrors might never be known. One thing that was certain is she never left that storage shed alive.

The discussion then moved to when murder charges would be filed against Middleton. A rather heated debate began between

Sergeant Tolliver and District Attorney Gammick. Tolliver thought there was enough to move ahead with the murder charges and accused the D.A. of wanting the entire case gift wrapped for him. The undetermined cause of death ruling was still a stumbling block and Gammick would not budge on the issue.

Sergeant Burns intervened and suggested they meet again after Middleton's May 17th sentencing on the weapons charge. Middleton might slip up and give them something they could use against him during the court proceedings. The frustrated task force detectives agreed, but each of them felt there was a far better chance of Middleton slipping *away* than slipping *up*.

Chapter 34

DEATH OF A CHEERLEADER

David Middleton pled guilty to one count of conspiracy to being an ex-felon in possession of a firearm on May 17, 1995. In exchange for his guilty plea he was sentenced to one year in jail. He would be given credit for time already in custody and would be allowed to serve the rest of his term in the Washoe County Jail instead of the Nevada State Prison. The sentence was light, but prosecutor Tom Viloria knew other charges would be brought against him before he was ever freed from jail.

If Middleton behaved while incarcerated he would be given credit for "good time" and be out in six months. The detectives could always charge him with the Good Guys crime to keep him in jail longer, but they wanted more. They knew Middleton had tortured and killed Kathy Powell and Thelma Davilla, and they wouldn't rest until he was made to answer for the unspeakable crimes he'd committed against them.

The next notable event in the Middleton investigation was as much of a fluke as Nugget's discovery of Thelma Davilla in Verdi. On May 24, 1995 a forty-three-year-old woman was hiking in the rugged hills near Norwood, Colorado. Norwood is a small town about forty miles west of Montrose and the outlying areas are a good place to find Indian artifacts and animal bones. The woman was looking for deer antlers and stopped underneath a tree where the brush had been disturbed. She used a small shovel to dig through six inches of loose dirt, but instead of finding antlers she unearthed the remains of Buffy Rice-Donohue.

Jenkins first learned of the chance discovery that same day through a phone call from Bonnie Rice. The coroner had not made an official identification of the body yet, but investigators were certain it was Buffy. The living hell of the unknown was over for the grieving mother, but the investigation into Buffy's death would prove to be a different kind of nightmare.

Buffy's body was discovered in the jurisdiction of the San Miguel County Sheriff's Office, but the Montrose Police Department retained the lead in the investigation since she was last seen in their city. The task force detectives in Reno followed the Colorado investigation closely because they were certain Buffy's killer was already in their custody. Any evidence the Colorado detectives could come up with linking Middleton to Buffy's murder would strengthen the Reno cases.

The cold Colorado temperatures and the fact Buffy's body had remained buried slowed the decomposition process considerably. Unlike the Thelma Davilla case, the San Miguel County Coroner was able to perform an autopsy on the remains of Buffy Rice-Donohue. By Friday, May 26, 1995 the preliminary report from that autopsy had been completed and a copy was faxed to Dave Jenkins.

The task force detectives sat in the Detective Division conference room at the Reno Police Department reading copies of the autopsy report with great interest. The coroner was able to determine a cause of death after examining Buffy. The death was caused by blunt force trauma and was officially listed as a homicide. That ruling alone would make the case much easier for the Colorado detectives to work.

In addition to the cause and manner of death, the coroner's exam also found Buffy had been raped prior to her death. Like the Kathy Powell case, the suspect left behind no DNA evidence. This meant he probably wore a condom as he did with Kathy Powell. Unlike DNA evidence, trace evidence left behind from a condom will dissipate over time. The detectives knew from the interview with Tina Bronson that Middleton carried his own Trojan Brand condoms with him, so this information fit his *modus operandi.*

Buffy had been bound with white nylon rope and her body was covered with black plastic garbage bags. Duct tape had been wrapped around her head and mouth to gag her. Several deep teeth marks and tearing found on the gag showed that Buffy was alive for quite some time after being bound. Keeping his victim bound and gagged while engaging in sexual torture was another similarity between this and the Kathy Powell murder case.

Some hairs and carpet fibers were found inside of the plastic bags covering Buffy's body. The preliminary report showed the hair matched the samples from David Middleton and the carpet fibers were the same color as the interior carpet in Evonne Haley's RX-7. Since the hair samples used for comparison were given to the Colorado detectives by the Reno detectives, there was some question about their admissibility as evidence. To alleviate this problem the Colorado detectives would be returning to Reno in the near future to take hair and carpet samples under a court order. Until such time they could not officially say the hairs found on the body belonged to Middleton.

The murder of Buffy Rice-Donohue was a tragedy, but the task force detectives believed her death would not be in vain. Unlike the Reno murder cases, the Colorado case was strong. They had a confirmed cause of death, a coroner's ruling of homicide, a motive of sex and money for the murder, and forensic evidence on the victim's body. Added to this were the facts the victim was last seen with Haley and a witness had seen Middleton loading a large bag similar to the one Buffy was buried in into the back of Haley's RX-7 the night of her disappearance. The detectives knew there was no such thing as a slam-dunk case, but this was about as close to one as they could get.

The proper way to proceed with the investigation was obvious. Once the Colorado detectives officially matched Middleton's hair and the carpet samples from Haley's car to the evidence they found on Buffy's body, they would have enough to charge one or both of them with her murder. Middleton was still in custody for his firearms charge, but no other charges had yet been filed against him. The process of extraditing him to Colorado and trying him for Buffy's murder would be fairly easy since there were no pending court actions in Nevada.

The best case scenario would be that Middleton would be found guilty in Colorado. The detectives could then file murder charges on him resulting from the Powell and Davilla cases and extradite him back to Nevada for trial. Since he would have already been found guilty of a murder that bore so many similarities to the Nevada cases they would be able to use the Colorado case during Middleton's trial. Even if they were precluded from using it during their case in chief, they would surely be able to bring his conviction in during the penalty phase to show prior criminal acts.

The worst case scenario was that Middleton would be found innocent in Colorado. That seemed unlikely, but stranger things than that had happened. The murder trial of O.J. Simpson was beginning its fifth month and adding a new twist to the adage of "anything can happen in a jury trial." The prosecutor in the Simpson case had called it a slam-dunk, but she was losing ground on a daily basis.

Even if Middleton *did* beat the Colorado charges it would still help the Reno cases. There is no statute of limitations for murder and the more time they had to gather evidence the better. They could defer charging him until after the Colorado case was adjudicated so they would not have to worry about violating the time element dealing with Middleton's sixth amendment right to a speedy trial. The clock started ticking when they officially charged him, so time was on their side.

It was a win-win situation for the Nevada detectives and they left for their weekend feeling good about the latest developments in Colorado. Their revelry was short-lived when they received updated information from Colorado on Monday, May 29, 1995. Montrose District Attorney Wyatt Angelo ruled that regardless of what evidence was gathered connecting Middleton to the murder of Buffy Rice-Donohue, no charges would be filed against him at this time.

Angelo's decision was based on the cost of extraditing and trying Middleton when he would surely be charged with the Reno murders soon. He estimated the cost of a murder trial to be $100,000 and said there was no reason for the taxpayers of Montrose to bear that type of expense if there was a chance Middleton would be found guilty of two murders in Nevada.

The detectives investigating the Powell and Davilla cases were amazed by the Colorado prosecutor's decision. Publicly they had to be very careful not to express their opinions, so all press inquiries were directed to the Montrose Police Department for comment. Their private opinions were another matter. One of the detectives couldn't come close to mustering his Eddie Murphy smile when he called the prosecutor's decision *bullshit!* Another one summed it up even better by calling the prosecutor a *fucking clam.*

Jenkins had been out of the room taking a call from Bonnie Rice and after returning he told the other detectives about his phone conversation. Bonnie had just finished an interview with the

Rocky Mountain News about the district Attorney's decision, and after hearing it the detectives all wished murders were prosecuted by mothers instead of lawyers. Her quote was, "This should never be a money matter at all. A murder took place in our county, and the murderer should be prosecuted."

Buffy Rice-Donohue's life was taken away from her at the age of eighteen. The perky former cheerleader for the Montrose High School Indians had aspirations of someday being a marine biologist. Those who knew her had no doubt she would someday achieve her goal. At her wedding five months to the day before Buffy disappeared, she told guests her one wish was for happiness and a long life. Every cop sitting in the conference room knew who had taken that wish away.

Other detectives had crowded into the conference room to hear what was going on. Jenkins told them the Rice's were in the process of having a tombstone made for Buffy's grave. The inscription on the back of the heart shaped stone read, "We promise you Buffy, Mom and Dad will never stop fighting for you."

There was one detective in the group who was harder than the slab of marble that parental promise was chiseled into, but even the former Army Ranger had trouble keeping his emotions in check when he heard that. He said, "Nobody's gonna put this fuckin clam away for us, so let's get to work."

Chapter 35

GIRLFRIEND-EN-STEIN

The detectives were still unable to talk to Middleton without him first contacting them, so they decided to work the case from a different angle. At 9:00 A.M. on Tuesday, May 30, 1995 Jenkins called Evonne Haley and asked if she would agree to a follow up interview. Haley said she would talk to him, but she did not want the police to come to her apartment. Jenkins made arrangements with Haley for him and Depsynski to meet her at a coffee shop two blocks from her Carlin Street apartment in forty minutes.

The detectives worked out their interview strategy on the way. They would mention nothing to Haley about the discovery of Buffy Rice-Donohue's body, but if she brought the subject up they would listen and play dumb. They didn't want to tip Haley off to the fact the Colorado detectives would be in Reno the following week to take their evidentiary samples from her car and from Middleton.

The main reason for the meeting with Haley was to discuss the storage shed, her involvement in the Good Guys case and to ask her if she knew Thelma Davilla. In addition to the bus driver originally interviewed in the Davilla case, some of her coworkers also gave a description matching Haley as a person Davilla had been seen with just prior to her disappearance. Haley and Davilla worked in downtown Reno casinos that were only two blocks apart. Additionally, Haley's place of employment was only a block from the nightclub Davilla frequented. Bonnie Rice was convinced that Haley singled out female victims and brought them to Middleton, so this possible connection needed to be explored.

Another possible theory on how Middleton met Davilla recently surfaced and the detectives wanted to ask Haley about it. The Cheers Nightclub on West 4th Street in Reno was in the middle of an area known for prostitution activity. The parking lot of the food and liquor store right next to Cheers was a popular congregating place for prostitutes. Since Middleton had been known to troll for streetwalkers in Florida, the detectives thought there might be a connection there.

When Detective Adams took a photo lineup to the store, one of the clerks recognized Middleton's photo as a man he knew as "Big Dave." He said Middleton often bought burritos at the store in the afternoon and parked his T.C.I. Cable Company truck in the parking lot while he ate his lunch. He also remembered Middleton coming into the store on occasion during the night to buy liquor. The store had a large plate glass window in the front, so the clerk had a good view of the parking lot. He said he had seen women he knew were prostitutes leave the lot with Middleton on more than one occasion in both his T.C.I. Cable Company truck and his International Harvester pickup.

There was no indication that Davilla had ever been involved in prostitution activity, but this was definitely a place where Middleton might have first seen her. The route from the closest bus stop to Cheers crossed directly in front of the convenience store parking lot. Davilla was known to dress nicely when she went out dancing and often wore short skirts that accentuated her legs. The possibility that she attracted Middleton's attention and he followed her inside of the nightclub was worth exploring.

During the interview Haley denied knowing Thelma Davilla. She said she read about the case in the newspaper and did not recognize Davilla from the news photo. She also read the news stories saying the police were looking into Middleton's involvement in the Davilla case and accused them of trying to frame him for the Davilla murder in order to make it look like he killed Kathy Powell. She was convinced Middleton never met Davilla and had nothing to do with her death.

Haley told the detectives she had no knowledge of the Good Guys' thefts and denied knowing anything about the existence of Middleton's storage unit. The conversation then moved to Haley's sexual relationship with Middleton. She said they had never practiced or discussed any type of bondage, sadomasochism or any other type of unusual sexual activities.

Jenkins told Haley that information had been uncovered during the investigation that conflicted with her claims of ignorance regarding some of the issues they were discussing. Haley suggested that she might be better off if she took a polygraph test to resolve those conflicts. Jenkins hid his excitement about Haley making the offer and excused himself from the table so he could call the station to set a time for the test.

The polygraph test was set for the following Thursday morning at 9:00 A.M. Since the police still had Haley's car in custody at the evidence yard Jenkins said he would pick her up and drive her to the station for the exam. She agreed, but said she would be living at her new trailer in Sun Valley by then since she had to be out of her Carlin Street apartment by the first of the month. Haley gave Jenkins her new address of 5722 Flynn Drive in Sun Valley and left the coffee shop.

The detectives knew through a jailhouse informant that Middleton made nightly phone calls to Haley from jail. They were hopeful she would tell Middleton about her interview and that he might make contact with them to see what was going on. They were also reasonably certain Middleton would tell Haley not to submit to the polygraph test. With an unbiased polygraph operator and Middleton not there to offer Haley guidance, they were certain she would not be able to defeat the test.

Their suspicions about the polygraph test were confirmed when Jenkins went to pick up Haley at her Sun Valley residence at 8:30 A.M. on Thursday, June 1, 1995. Haley was not home and the trailer was locked. Sun Valley is only fifteen miles north of Reno, but it is sometimes referred to as the biggest trailer park in the world. Haley's trailer was located in the type of neighborhood where people get selective memories when dealing with the police. None of her neighbors admitted seeing Haley or anyone else around the trailer that morning, so Jenkins drove to Haley's Carlin Street apartment to look for her. She was not there, but he found her daughter Natasha sitting on the front steps of the apartment.

Jenkins asked the girl why she was not in school, or at least inside the apartment. She told him she had spent the night at a friend's house and when she returned to the apartment she found she was locked out. Natasha told him she had not eaten since the day before and she was very hungry. Jenkins agreed to take her to a local fast food restaurant to get something to eat before driving her to school and notifying Child Protective Services of the situation.

During the drive Jenkins asked Natasha if she had ever been to Middleton's storage unit in Sparks. She said she had not, and wasn't even aware Middleton had a storage unit. She then asked him why the police thought Middleton had killed women. She said she was ready to hear about the investigation, so Jenkins gave her an abbreviated version of what the police knew so far. He then dropped her off with the principal of her school and made another unsuccessful attempt to contact Haley.

On Tuesday, June 6, 1995 the detectives decided to make another attempt at getting Haley to take a polygraph test. They did not have a new phone number for her so Jenkins, Canfield and Adams drove to her Sun Valley trailer. She was home when they got there and told them she would re-schedule the polygraph test. When asked if she would take it that afternoon, she said she couldn't because she was trying to find a ride to take her to pick up her daughter from school.

Adams suggested they schedule the test at the Sparks Police Department and they could pick up Haley's daughter along the way. Haley consented to this, but once at the Sparks Police Department she said she had changed her mind. She said she was not mentally prepared to take a polygraph test and could not understand why the detectives could not take her at her word regarding the storage shed, the Good Guys case and her not knowing Davilla.

Since the detectives' last meeting with Haley, two of Davilla's coworkers had picked her out of a photo line up, saying they had seen her with Davilla on two separate occasions shortly before she disappeared. One other coworker said he saw Haley with Davilla at a doctor's office in Sparks in early August of 1994. Haley said they must have her confused with someone else and again denied ever meeting Thelma Davilla. She then started making a scene in the lobby of the police station and asked for her and her daughter to be driven home.

All three detectives got the same vibes from Haley. If the theory was true about sociopaths attracting other sociopaths, she and Middleton were a match made in hell. Except if Haley actually *was* bringing Middleton his victims, then who was the bigger monster? It went back to the Frankenstein theory. Was the *real* monster the creator or the created?

Even though the detectives knew Haley was lying they could not force her to take the polygraph test. During the drive back to Sun Valley Haley asked Jenkins why he hadn't spoken to Middleton recently. She said she talked to Middleton on the phone the previous night and he told her he wanted to talk to Jenkins again, but felt the detective didn't want to talk to him.

Jenkins smiled and was grateful Canfield was in the car with him to hear the exchange. He told Haley that if Middleton wanted to talk, he would be more than happy to oblige his request for contact. His plan to have Haley feed Middleton information was working, and he was about to get another crack at the devil.

Chapter 36
TRUE LIES

On Wednesday, June 7, 1995 Detectives Jenkins, Douglas, Canfield and Adams drove to the Washoe County Jail to attempt an interview with Middleton. The secondhand request through Haley for Jenkins to talk to Middleton was questionable, but they decided to make contact with him and see how it went.

Middleton agreed to an interview, but said he would only talk to Jenkins. The detectives knew Middleton was trying to play them, so they decided to use this to their advantage. Jenkins would take the lead on the interview and let Middleton believe there was some type of cop-like bond between the two of them. The other three detectives would video record the interview from an adjacent room, and act as a safety net for Jenkins. If they saw Middleton starting to get the upper hand in the interview they could call Jenkins out and re-direct their strategy.

The detectives left Middleton alone in the interview room while they formulated their strategy. His hands were cuffed to a belly chain and his right leg to a steel eye-bolt mounted in the floor. The idea was to make him as uncomfortable as possible while he was alone and then improve his level of comfort when Jenkins came into the room. Having him associate comfort with talking to the detectives might give them a psychological edge.

The interview room was devoid of furnishings with the exception of a square metal table and three chairs in the center of the room. The hard metal chair for the interviewee was slightly lower and smaller than the two padded chairs on the opposite side of the table designed for the interviewers to sit in. Taking the high ground was another mental game used to put the prisoner at a disadvantage during the interview.

Jenkins walked into the interview room and set two Styrofoam cups of steaming black coffee on the table. After removing the restraints from Middleton's hands and ankles he suggested the prisoner stand and stretch before starting. Middleton went to sit back down on the prisoner chair, but Jenkins pushed one of the more comfortable interviewer chairs around to the other side of the table for him to use. He told Middleton he wasn't going to insult his intelligence by playing cop games with him. While this small gesture put Middleton at ease, it also showed him Jenkins was in control of even the simplest things in his life right now.

Unlike the interview rooms seen on T.V. cop shows, there was no one-way glass built into the walls or video camera hanging from the ceiling in this one. The camera and microphone for the state of the art video and audio equipment being monitored by the detectives in the next room were concealed in the smoke detector hanging from the ceiling. Even though the interviewee had to be advised they were being recorded, people sometimes talked more freely when the camera wasn't staring directly at them.

They sat sipping their coffee and making idle conversation for a few minutes, more about the NBA playoff games than about Middleton's time in jail. When the light on the smoke detector went from flashing red to solid green, Jenkins knew the recording equipment was on and it was time for him to start talking about the real reason he was sitting in the room with a murderer.

Jenkins began the interview by asking, "So what's going on here, David?"

Middleton shrugged his shoulders, and in a soft voice said, "I guess Evonne told you I wanted you to come up here and talk to me. I'm glad you did, because I'm going crazy in here."

"I'm flattered," Jenkins said. "But that's not what I was asking about. I want to ask you some questions, and they're not related to Kathy Powell. Have you been reading the newspapers lately?"

Middleton replied, "I haven't read the papers or watched the news in the last three weeks. I plead guilty to the gun thing, so I'm gonna be in here for a while. If I read about things going on out there while I'm stuck in here I just get more depressed."

Most people's eyes look up and to the left when they lie, but Middleton wasn't most people. He stared right into Jenkins' eyes when he gave his answer. Jenkins knew from the jailhouse informant that Middleton had watched the T.V. news story about his link to the deaths of Kathy Powell and Thelma Davilla. The informant described Middleton as becoming catatonic after seeing the news show. Jenkins didn't put much faith in informants, but the deputy assigned to Middleton's cell block had confirmed the story.

"Does the name Thelma Davilla mean anything to you?" Jenkins asked.

Middleton again stared Jenkins straight in the eyes. He said, "I never met the lady. Her name was in some of my plea agreement paperwork and my lawyers said you might be asking me about her. My lawyers also told me you make your living lying to people and that you were gonna lie to me. They told me not to talk to you."

Middleton was deflecting his guilt back to Jenkins, but the detective wasn't falling for the trick. He said, "If your lawyers say not to talk to me, then don't talk to me. I'll get us another cup of coffee and we can bullshit about basketball some more before they take you back to your cell. If that's what you want, then it's fine with me."

Middleton smiled and said, "You're good, Jenkins. I'll talk to you, but I wouldn't mind another cup of coffee too."

Douglas was waiting in the hallway when Jenkins stepped out of the room to get the coffee. The other detectives were satisfied the Miranda requirements had been met after Middleton's last statement agreeing to talk to Jenkins, so they decided it was time to push him. They also agreed that the way Middleton could look him in the eye and lie was nothing short of eerie.

Jenkins returned to the room with the coffee and got right back into the questioning. He asked, "Have you ever been to the Cheers nightclub, David?"

Middleton sipped his coffee while staring across the table at Jenkins. He answered, "I know where it is, but I've never been inside the place. I used to get my lunch at the store right next to the club sometimes while I was working. I'm not much of a bar person though, so I never got the urge to go in the club."

"Would you be referring to the Al Collins Food and Liquor Store when you say you got your lunch near Cheers?"

"That's the one," Middleton replied. "They make a mean burrito there, and the price is right. When I was working that area of town I liked to sit outside the store in my truck and people-watch while I ate my lunch. There're a lot of interesting characters hanging on 4th Street."

Jenkins took a sip of his coffee then asked, "What if I told you the manager from Cheers picked your photo out of a lineup and said he remembers you being inside the club?"

Without hesitation Middleton replied, "I'd say all of us brothers look alike to you white people, so the manager's statement wouldn't hold up in court."

Jenkins smiled and said, "I never mentioned that the manager was white. You're slipping, David."

For a fleeting second Jenkins saw a panicked look on Middleton's face, but it was gone as quickly as it had appeared. Middleton stared at Jenkins with his cold dark eyes and said, "Like

I said before, Jenkins, you're good. That's why I like you. But for the record, I was just guessing the bar manager was white because most of them are. I've never been inside of Cheers so I have no idea what the manager looks like."

"Fair enough," Jenkins said. "Let's move on. Have you ever been inside of the Sierra Stix Bar in Sparks?"

Middleton's gaze didn't move when he said, "Nope. I've never been inside of that one either."

It then became crystal clear to Jenkins how Middleton could lie so convincingly. He was a true pathological liar and in his demented brain he wasn't lying at all, because he'd convinced himself he was telling the truth. Jenkins had studied this phenomenon and had even crossed paths with pathological liars on occasion, but none as deviant as this one.

Middleton had the ability to move the real truth across a bridge inside of his brain and store it in a place where there was no return route in the informational journey. He was well aware of his evil deeds, but his lies seemed truthful because he was able to answer questions with the part of his brain that was guilt-free. This is why he was such a good con man, and why he was able to defeat the polygraph test. It was also why Jenkins now knew he could beat the devil.

Jenkins decided to try an experiment. He made a face like he just smelled something sour and asked, "Did you brush your teeth today, David?"

Middleton looked confused and replied, "Of course I did. I brush my teeth every day. Why?"

Jenkins shrugged and said, "No reason, really. It's just that your breath is so rotten I can smell it clear over here. I think you're lying about brushing your teeth, but that's your prerogative."

Middleton jumped up and yelled, "What the hell are you talking about? Why would I lie about brushing my teeth?"

Jenkins remained seated. He knew the line of questioning would confuse the other detectives who were watching him, but they wouldn't intervene unless they thought he needed help. He calmly said, "Sit down, David. Perhaps I'm mistaken."

Middleton's anger calmed as he sat back in his chair. He said, "Damned right you're mistaken. It's probably just this rank cop-shop coffee that's making my breath bad. Now I've got a question for you. Did you tell Evonne I was having a homosexual relationship in jail?"

Jenkins had made mention of this to Haley the day before, mainly to see is she would leak it back to Middleton during her nightly conversation with him. He answered, "I received information from a jailhouse informant that you were having a homosexual relationship with someone in jail. I don't normally believe much of what I hear from informants, so I asked Evonne if you may have had any proclivity to homosexual involvement in the past. Not that it matters to me—I just wanted to confirm the credibility of the informant."

"Well I ain't no punk," Middleton said. "You can tell your informant to go fuck himself, and tell Evonne that whole thing is bullshit."

Jenkins said, "I'll do that. Have you spoken to Evonne lately?"

"Not in a few days. Sometimes the lines are long at the jail phones."

Jenkins knew this was also a lie since Middleton must have spoken to Haley sometime since he leaked the information to her. There was no reason for him to lie about this, but another trait of a pathological liar was they lied even when they didn't have to. Middleton was passing every test Jenkins threw his way.

Changing the subject, Jenkins said, "Tell me about your storage shed, David."

Middleton looked straight at him and said, "I store shit in there. Sometimes I do a little work in there too."

"Were you working on that old Tappan refrigerator you had in the shed?"

A smile slowly spread across Middleton's face and he responded, "I got a good deal on that thing. I thought I could fix it up, but now I think it's beyond repair. You can throw it out if you get back over there. I can always get another one when I get out."

Jenkins nodded his head slowly and said, "Let me think about that. How about all the clothes in the shed? Where did they come from?"

"That stuff all belongs to Evonne and Natasha," Middleton replied.

This was another lie. Hair and DNA samples had already been taken from Haley and her daughter. Nothing from the shed matched either of them, and they both denied having anything stored anywhere other than their apartment. Jenkins let the lie go and continued, "What if I told you Thelma Davilla's sister identified a blanket and some clothing found in your shed as belonging to her sister?"

Middleton said, "I'd tell you that I got that blanket in Nogales, Mexico when me and my old Metro partner Harvey Honig were down there for an extradition about seven years ago. Anybody that says different must be mistaken. A lot of those Mexican blankets look alike."

Jenkins continued smiling but said nothing. There were several different kinds of blankets inside the storage shed, and he'd never mentioned the one he was talking about was a Mexican blanket. Moving along, he asked, "Did you ever bring Evonne, Natasha or any other woman to your storage shed?"

Middleton held the detective's gaze, "No."

Jenkins looked at his notes and said, "I have a statement from the storage facility manager that says he saw you bring a woman to your shed."

"What did he say she looked like?"

Jenkins leaned back in his chair. "Why would that matter? If you said you never took a female to your storage shed, then the manager must be mistaken, right? Just like the informant was wrong about your homosexual relationship in jail, Ms. Davilla's sister was erroneous about the blanket and I was incorrect about your forgetting to brush your teeth. Everybody makes mistakes in your life except you, right, David?"

Middleton looked away from Jenkins and once again became visibly upset. He exclaimed, "Hey! All this stress I've been under has been giving me terrible headaches! I forget shit sometimes. I did take a girl to the storage shed, but only one time and one girl. She was a black girl I met when I was eating lunch outside of that store one day."

Jenkins raised his eyebrows and asked, "The store next to cheers?"

"That's right. I was in my company truck eating lunch and the girl came up to the window and started talking to me. All I remember is her name was Jennifer or something like that. I gave her a ride to Sparks, but we stopped off at my storage shed first."

"And why would you take a girl you just met to your storage shed, David? I've been there, and I can honestly say there is not much to do that would appeal to a girl you just met."

Middleton calmed down again and slipped back into his macho role. He said, "That depends on what you're planning on doing. Sometimes when girls get around me they can't control themselves. This girl said she wanted to have sex with me. I couldn't take her to my place because Evonne was home and the girl said she lived with her parents or something. The storage shed was close to where she was going, so I figured it was as good a place as any."

Jenkins hid his excitement at the fact Middleton had just admitted to taking a girl to his shed for sex. Now was the time to play up to his ego to keep him talking. He continued, "There are a lot of prostitutes that hang out around that store, David. The romantic tryst you've just described to me sounds surprisingly similar to a prostitution deal. Was this girl Jennifer a 4th Street prostitute?"

Middleton gave Jenkins a smile evil enough to make the real Satan take a step backwards. "I didn't ask, but do I look like a man who needs to pay for it? I never paid for pussy in my life."

Jenkins smiled back and said, "That may be true, but when you get things on credit, the payment comes due sooner or later. I think your bill has just been sent to a collection agency."

"We'll see," Middleton said. "I'm getting another headache, so I want to go back to my cell now."

Once the prisoner requests to end a voluntary interview anything else said cannot be used as evidence. Jenkins stood up to get the jail deputy, but before he got to the door Middleton said, "Hey Jenkins. I heard they found Buffy. Is that right?"

"That's right," Jenkins answered. "A couple of your old friends from Montrose are coming to visit you on Friday, so I'll let them tell you about it. And speaking of old friends, it seems I'll be in Miami on Monday. Is there anyone you'd like me to say hello to for you while I'm there? Maybe an old partner, ex-wife, former female co-worker or girl you met when she was sixteen? I'll be glad to give them your regards. Call me when you'd like to talk again, David."

Jenkins walked out of the interview room leaving his statement about going to Florida hanging in the air for Middleton to think about. Jenkins himself had plenty of new information to think about before his pending trip to Miami.

They now had to research any missing person cases or unidentified dead bodies that could possibly be the girl Middleton admitted to taking to the shed. They would also have to show Middleton's photograph to *every* street prostitute they could find to see which of them had contact with him. If he admitted to taking a black girl to his shed that meant she was probably a white or Hispanic girl. The legal prostitution ranches east of town would also need to be checked since some of those girls moonlighted as streetwalkers on their days off.

All this was running through his head when Douglas stepped out into the hallway and said, "I've got twenty bucks bet with these clowns that Middleton's bad breath has something to do with the murders. You better not let me down."

Jenkins looked at him and said, "Have I ever?"

"Not today," Douglas replied. "Let's talk."

Chapter 37

YOUR OWN WORST ENEMY

The four detectives went to the first floor cafeteria to discuss the interview. After ordering coffee and sandwiches they sat at a table in a far corner of the room away from the other patrons. The cafeteria was for employees only, but people talked about things they overheard, and privacy was important.

When they were seated, Canfield asked, "So what was that all about in there?"

"I was giving our boy a series of tests," Jenkins replied. "I now know we are dealing with a true pathological liar, and that fact will shape the way we handle him from now on."

Douglas swallowed a mouthful of turkey and cheese, and then said, "I could have told you Middleton was a liar, even *without* asking him about his teeth."

Jenkins said, "Not just a liar, John—a *pathological* liar. There's a big difference between a pathological liar and your run of the mill *slime ball* liar. I'll show you."

Looking at Adams, Jenkins said, "I'm going to ask you a very simple question, Dave. I want you to take your time answering it, but I want the answer you give me to be something you know to be an obvious lie."

"OK," Adams said. "Just don't ask me if I ever thought about screwing a chicken. That's the one question they always ask you on those police psych tests that there's really no way to answer without making it look like you thought about screwing a chicken sometime."

"You're reading too much into this little test," Jenkins said. "The question I'm going to ask you is much simpler than your thoughts on animal husbandry. What is your name?"

Adams paused in thought while he stared at an imaginary spot on the ceiling to his left. He then looked at Jenkins and answered, "John Douglas."

"That's original," Douglas said.

"It may not be original," Jenkins said, "but it proves my point. Did you see the way he looked up and to his left before he answered with a lie? That is because a *normal* person needs to go into the prefrontal cortex of their brain to retrieve information they know isn't true. In Dave's case this action was overt—probably because lying doesn't come easy to him."

"You wouldn't say that if you ever played golf with him," Canfield interjected.

"Well now you know what to look for the next time he tells you his score," Jenkins said. "The looking to the left action is sometimes much more subtle than we just witnessed. It's often nothing more than the eyeballs looking up and left for a fraction of a second, but it's always there in a normal person. A pathological liar has increased amounts of white matter and decreased amounts of gray matter in the prefrontal lobe of their brains. The study I read said this is the reason they can look you straight in the eye and lie like it was second nature."

Douglas said, "You know entirely too much shit that a cop just ain't supposed to know about."

Jenkins smiled and said, "I find if I learn a little about a lot of things and not too much about any one thing in particular than I can at least *sound* fairly intelligent in most settings. At any rate, the way Middleton handled the question about brushing his teeth was atypical behavior for a pathological liar. They can't always tell the truth from a lie, so when you call them on something small that they haven't had a chance to process yet, they will go into a rage. It didn't matter whether Middleton brushed his teeth or not. What mattered was that I called him on it and his brain wasn't prepared for a response to the unexpected question."

Canfield said, "So why can he lie so easily about murder and torture, but then can't deal with something as insignificant as brushing his teeth?"

"Because the pathological liar re-writes history in their brain, so to them it never really happened. Some normal people do this too, but pathological liars take it to the extreme. Lies are normally unplanned and impulsive. But pathological lying is a behavior, and a behavior needs to be repeated over a long period of time."

"Are you sure we should even be talking about shit like this?" Douglas asked. "We might be opening the door for an insanity defense if his lawyers get wind of this psychobabble."

"Middleton is just as sane as any of us sitting at this table," Jenkins assured. "Well, that might not be the best comparison to use, but he *is* sane. Just because someone fits this definition doesn't mean they are necessarily evil either. Some very famous and charismatic people throughout history were pathological liars—including a couple of our most popular presidents."

Douglas said, "You're not referring to our current president, are you? Who in the hell doesn't inhale when they smoke pot?"

"I'm not referring to anyone in particular. I'm just saying a pathological liar may not readily recognize truth from lies, but he certainly knows right from wrong. The McNaughton rule says the prosecution only needs to prove the defendant knew his criminal acts were wrong in order to meet the burden of proof. If Middleton didn't think what he did was wrong he wouldn't have lied in the first place, so that just strengthens our case."

"So now that we know Middleton is a pathological liar, how do we use it against him?" Adams asked.

"Several ways," Jenkins responded. "I am by no means an expert on this, but there *are* some out there who would be willing to testify to this phenomenon. The class I took was put on by a professor from USC and I'm sure he would offer expert testimony if needed. After that, the defense would never be able to bring up the fact Middleton passed a polygraph test, and they *certainly* would never risk putting him on the witness stand.

"In addition to that, there are traits exhibited by pathological liars we can use to our advantage. They need a crowd to perform in front of and to always be the center of attention. The more times they tell their story—the more improved their lies get. They are manipulative, egotistical and legends in their own minds. Where is Middleton currently housed in the jail?"

"He's in G.P.," replied Canfield. This was the jail terminology for the general population housing units.

"Can that be changed?"

Canfield thought for a moment and then answered, "I could get him moved to the SHU," again using a jail acronym to refer to the Special Housing Unit. "He'd be in a solitary cell there and would only be let out one hour a day for exercise. He wouldn't be allowed to go to the recreation yard either. I'll need a reason to keep him there though. If I just get him moved without cause his lawyer will file a writ for cruel and unusual punishment."

Jenkins said, "How about threats of suicide and the potential for violence as the reason for the move? You heard him talking about depression, and we all know he's going to snap when we finally charge him with the murders."

"I'll give it a try. The worst the jail commander can do is say no, but I think I can call in some favors and make it happen. Why do you want him out of G.P.?"

"We need to take away his audience," Jenkins answered. "Middleton will go crazy if he can't be on stage. Did you see the look on his face when I told him we were heading to Miami? He has no idea what we've dug up on him and that is going to eat away at him twenty-four hours a day if he doesn't have a diversion. If I remember right he won't be able to make nightly phone calls to Haley while he's locked up in the S.H.U., so his information pipeline will be cut off too. I want David Middleton alone and worried for the rest of this investigation. He can share a cell with his own worst enemy from now on, and that enemy is the devil's incarnate himself."

Chapter 38

WELCOME TO MIAMI

When Jenkins, Canfield and Adams stepped outside through the front doors of the Miami International Airport at 5:15 P.M. on Monday, June 12, 1995, they instantly learned the meaning behind the phrase, "it's not the heat, it's the humidity." The ninety-three degree air temperature was only slightly warmer than what they left behind at home, but Reno's humidity level normally hovered in the area of five percent. The informational T.V. monitor in the baggage area said Miami's current humidity was ninety-eight percent—a mere two percent from the air turning into water.

By the time they found a taxi and made it to the Miami Airport Holiday Inn they were hot and clammy, and their clothes were sticking to their skin. They decided to stop at the lobby bar and enjoy some cool conditioned air and even cooler beers before checking in. Since it is impossible to stop for *a* beer when two or more cops get together, they were still in the bar enjoying steak dinners and libations at eight o'clock that night.

Their investigative plans for Miami were based on information obtained during a series of phone calls made the prior week. Middleton had been well liked for the most part during his police career and they wanted to keep their interviews as neutral as possible. On the list of officers they would talk to were five of

Middleton's former partners, his supervisor at the time of arrest and the detective who investigated his rape case.

There were also three civilians they would interview who might be able to shed light on Middleton's past. This list included the civilian records clerk who he videotaped himself having sex with, his ex-wife and the victim of the rape that brought Middleton's criminal activities to light.

Jenkins also made phone contact with Metro-Dade County District Attorney Kathleen Hoague prior to leaving Reno. There were no plans to interview her while they were in Miami, but she would be providing them with some valuable assistance. They would need to review the case files for Middleton's rape arrest, his personnel file and his Internal Affairs file. They would need an administrative search warrant to get some of this information and the D.A.'s office would help with that.

The combination of their late night planning session, jetlag and the intense morning humidity made the detectives feel like they were moving in slow motion when they met in the hotel restaurant at 7:00 the next morning. Nevertheless, by 8:30 they were pulling out of the Airport Hertz lot in their rented white Crown Victoria headed for Downtown Miami.

None of them had ever been to Miami before and they took in the sights as they drove along Highway 836, better known as the Dolphin Expressway. The morning commuter traffic was heavy even though it was the off-season, but the cold air blasting out of the dashboard vents felt good while they crept along the highway at a steady twenty-five miles per hour. When they neared the end of their nine-mile drive to the courthouse, the ocean came into view on the other side of the Miami skyline.

The sun was shining through the hazy morning sky over the ocean, which seamed out of place to the three west-coasters. The detectives were used to the Pacific Coast where the sun was over the ocean in the afternoon. They felt sorry for the people living near the east coast beaches since they didn't get to see the spectacular sight of a bright orange sun setting into the ocean. It was almost a ritual in coastal areas on the Pacific to toast the ocean sunsets with some type of adult libation. Tossing back a couple of cold ones while watching the early morning sun pop up over the Atlantic Ocean could also be considered a ritual of sorts—albeit one that might require substance abuse therapy.

The twenty-eight story Dade County Courthouse was built in 1928, making it the oldest building in downtown Miami. For many years it was the tallest building south of Baltimore, but those times were long gone. The early twentieth century architecture of the beautifully constructed white building made it stand out like an ancient stalagmite in the midst of the modern glass-walled skyscrapers. Since it was the only building of its kind in the city, it was easy for the three tourist detectives to locate. They parked in a downtown parking structure and endured the heat and humidity one more time during their half-block walk to the courthouse.

Jenkins met with the assistant district attorney who was assigned to help with the required paperwork while the other two detectives researched Middleton's court case in the first-floor records section. The attorney's office was on the twenty-sixth floor and had a view of downtown Miami. The six-lane MacArthur Causeway with Miami Beach and the Pacific Ocean beyond it could be seen in the distance. Jenkins considered checking out the famous Miami Beach nightlife while they were in town, but then thought better of it. The Holiday Inn bar was better suited to their tastes than a nightclub would be. He'd heard the South Beach nightlife didn't start until midnight, and unless he was being called out for a murder, he was normally asleep long before then.

With signed warrants in hand, Jenkins met the other two detectives in the courthouse lobby at 11:30. They decided to have lunch at a restaurant next door and discuss what they learned before heading to the police station. The restaurant had a sidewalk dining area where patrons sat underneath misters to stay cool, but the three desert-dwelling detectives opted to sit inside and take advantage of the air conditioning.

Adams and Canfield had copied several of the reports in Middleton's court files, but they didn't learn anything new. They'd already obtained most of the information through news articles and phone conversations with the prosecutor.

Judging from the court transcripts it looked like the jury did their best with what they had to work with when reaching the verdict in Middleton's trial. Pre-trial defense motions kept some of the most damaging evidence from ever making it to the jury. It appeared the jury had come to the only verdict they could because they were never allowed to hear about the evidence of the rape. There was some question about the judge's decisions and jury instruction, but since he had been removed and prosecuted himself, those questions would never be answered.

The next step for the detectives was to get into Middleton's personnel and I.A. files which were kept in the main police station located twelve miles inland in the city of Doral. Afternoon traffic was light so they made the drive in fifteen minutes. The four-story glass and marble building was easy to find, and they parked in the visitor's lot adjacent to the building. The Metro-Dade Sheriff's Department had changed its name to the Miami-Dade Police Department in early 1994, but shading from the old lettering could still be seen over the door as they walked through the main entrance.

They were escorted to the Investigative Services Division, and the first thing they noticed was they were highly overdressed. All the Miami detectives wore summer-weight short sleeve shirts and slacks. None of them bothered wearing suit coats to cover their guns and badges like the Reno detectives did, and they decided an evening clothes shopping trip might be in order.

The Reno detectives sat shooting the breeze with some Miami detectives while they waited for their warrant to be reviewed by the dayshift lieutenant. They were treated cordially and the Miami cops were very curious about the case, since none of them actually knew Middleton. After twenty minutes the detectives were led to a conference room where they were allowed to review Middleton's personnel and I.A. files in private.

According to the documents in Middleton's personnel file, he had been an outstanding police officer during his early years with the Metro-Dade Police Department. During his first year he earned a series of commendations and above average performance evaluations which resulted in a promotion to detective in the Warrants Bureau. After that it looked like he was on the fast track for upward movement in the department.

The records showed he continued to excel in his career during the next six years, but in early 1988 he began having trouble with tardiness and unexplained absences from work. The first major incident they found was documented in March of 1988. Middleton was removed from his detective job and assigned to station duty while being investigated by Internal Affairs. This stirred their interests, so they switched over to Middleton's I.A. file to learn more.

The I.A. investigation began when a detective from the County Prosecutor's Office in Somerset, New Jersey contacted the Warrants division at the Metro-Dade Police Department on February 17, 1988. The detective had received a letter from the Miami-Dade Warrants section in support of a suspect named Jaabir Muhammand who was incarcerated in New Jersey on narcotics trafficking charges. Muhammand was being held without bail due to the serious nature of his crimes. The letter in question was a request to have Muhammand granted a low bail amount since he had proven to be an asset to the Metro-Dade Police Department in the past.

The New Jersey detective found the request strange and called to verify the authenticity of the letter. It was written on official letterhead from the Metro-Dade Warrants division and signed by Detective David Millington, badge number 3261. The Metro-Dade Warrants division sergeant who had taken the call told the New Jersey detective they didn't have anyone named Millington working there, but they did have a David *Middleton*, and, coincidently enough, his badge number was *3361*. He also said any request for bail assistance from within the department would be highly unusual and would at the very least have to be approved by the division commander.

The New Jersey detective then asked if the sergeant had ever heard of a Ms. G.A. Thomas, or a company named Total Concept Cleaning Inc. The detective also received a letter in support of Jaabir Muhammand from Ms. Thomas the same day he received the letter from Detective Millington. Ms. Thomas said in her letter that Muhammand was a business associate of hers and that she would vouch for his credibility should he be granted bail. Although she listed her address as a post office box in Delaware, the letter was postmarked in Miami. The detective said Muhammand was a hardcore criminal, and it was odd to get even *one* letter in support of him, never mind two in the same day bearing the same postmark

Neither G.A. Thomas nor the company name sounded familiar to the Metro-Dade sergeant. He also didn't think Detective Middleton would write a letter such as the one described, but he told the New Jersey detective he would ask a few questions and get back to him.

Those few questions turned into a full-blown one-year Internal Affairs investigation. The investigative report read like a dime store crime novel, and if the three detectives didn't know what they did about Middleton they would have thought they actually were reading a work of fiction instead of a police document.

It turned out that Ms. G.A. Thomas was actually an alias for a Gerrilyn Smith, an ex-felon for fraud and narcotics related offenses. Smith had served a year in the Tennessee State Prison after being picked up on felony warrants in Miami in early 1984. The arresting officer when she was picked up in Miami was Detective David Middleton from the Metro-Dade Police Department Warrants division.

When the I.A. investigators checked with the prison officials in Tennessee they discovered Middleton had later written a letter in support of Smith vouching for her and guaranteeing her employment if she should be released on early parole. The letter was written on Metro-Dade Police Department letterhead, and the employment Middleton guaranteed was at a company he owned called Total Concepts Cleaning Inc. in Miami. As a result of this letter Ms. Smith was paroled and allowed to move back to Miami.

The investigators then researched Total Concepts Cleaning Inc. and found it was a Delaware-based company with an office address in Miami. Since Delaware has the most liberal state tax laws in the country, it is not uncommon for companies to register there and then base offices in different states. What *was* uncommon was Total Concepts Cleaning Inc. listed David Middleton as the president and his brother-in-law Albert Heredia as vice president. Gerrilyn Smith and New Jersey prisoner Jaabir Muhammand were listed as board members. It was later determined Smith and Muhammand were sister and brother.

The I.A. file contained transcripts from several interviews with Middleton where he denied writing the support letters for Smith and Muhammand, knowing either one of them and involvement in Total Concepts Cleaning Inc. He said the company was formed by his brother-in-law as a tax shelter, and he had no idea his name was on the corporate paperwork. A polygraph test given to him during the investigation surprisingly enough proved inconclusive.

At the end of the investigation it was determined that Middleton did write both of the support letters and had been lying about them from the start. He changed his name to Millington on the New Jersey letter to avoid getting caught. It was also determined that Middleton had been having a long-term affair with Smith that began when he arrested her in 1984.

Research was done on Total Concepts Cleaning Inc. and it showed to be an active company—at least on the surface. Money was moving through the company, but they did not actually have any customers. There were allegations that profits from Muhammand's drug trade might have been laundered through the company, but the detectives could not find any supporting documentation in the files showing follow up investigation was done in this area.

The Internal Affairs investigation determined Middleton was guilty of associating with known criminals, assisting known criminals, misrepresentation and falsification of police documents, lying during a police investigation, and not reporting outside employment. He was given a suspension of ten days without pay, but was allowed to give up vacation days in lieu of some of them. Middleton had been assigned to desk duty throughout the investigation, but he was returned to his position in the Warrants section on February 15, 1989. This was nineteen months *before* he kidnapped and raped the sixteen-year old girl in Miami.

A criminal investigation was not initiated on Middleton even though several crimes almost jumped off the pages of the report at the detectives. Even if the only crimes investigated were tax evasion and money laundering, Middleton still would have been at least fired, if not put in prison. In most departments just a sustained allegation of lying during an investigation warrants termination because the officer's credibility during court testimony is diminished.

The Reno detectives knew if this original investigation had been handled differently they would not be sitting in Miami right now, and several women might still be alive. Before leaving the room they gathered up their notes and reminded each other they were here to investigate their own case, not critique the handling of the Miami case seven years earlier. They would keep their opinions to themselves, but they also decided to cancel their shopping trip to buy clothes better suited for the Miami weather. Not fitting in with the Miami cops didn't sound like a bad idea at the moment.

Chapter 39

SEVEN-AND-O

The detectives were given use of the conference room in the Robbery-Homicide division at the main station in Doral for their interviews. Their plan was to interview all seven Miami cops that day, and the first one met them at 9:00 A.M. on Wednesday, June 14, 1995.

Sergeant Harvey Honig was currently working in the Auto Theft Bureau, but he had been Middleton's partner in the Warrants division from 1983 to 1987. The first thing he told the detectives was that he was shocked by the possibility Middleton was involved in a serious crime. But he then added he was equally shocked when Middleton had been arrested in Miami for rape.

Sergeant Honig described Middleton as being very personable, intelligent and a hard working police officer. He said he had not worked or socialized with Middleton for over a year before his Miami arrest, and realized that people do change. He said he'd never known Middleton to do anything that would be considered illegal, although he did have some questionable ethics when it came to his sexual behavior.

Jenkins asked Sergeant Honig if he recalled the extradition trip to Mexico where Middleton said he bought the Mexican blanket found in his shed. Sergeant Honig said he distinctly remembered the trip, because out of country extraditions were unusual. He and Middleton had flown to Nogales, Mexico to pick up a wanted drug trafficker who had turned himself in at the U.S. Consulate there. While in Mexico, Sergeant Honig said he bought several Mexican style blankets, but was reasonably certain that Middleton did not buy any or any other souvenirs. Middleton's transference of the blanket purchase from his partner to himself also fit the profile of the pathological liar.

The next scheduled interview was with Middleton's former supervisor in the Warrants division. Sergeant Wesley Dallas currently worked in the Miami-Dade Narcotics Bureau. Due to the nature of his assignment, the task force detectives drove to his Miami office instead of asking him to come to the main police station.

Sergeant Dallas also used the words intelligent and personable to describe Middleton, but added he wasn't an easy employee to supervise. He said Middleton was constantly late or absent from work and he had to discipline him twice for this. Aside from these problems he said Middleton was a good cop and he never suspected any drug, alcohol or ethical problems.

When Middleton was identified as a suspect in the Miami rape case, Sergeant Dallas was assigned to bring him in for questioning. It was Sergeant Dallas who tracked Middleton down and located him in Mississippi after he'd skipped town. He was also one of the two Miami cops who flew to Mississippi after Middleton was arrested to extradite him back to Florida.

While in Mississippi the local police detectives gave Sergeant Dallas two video tapes that had been in Middleton's possession when they arrested him. The sergeant said he was by no means a prude, but these tapes could only be described as sexually deviant in nature. One tape showed Middleton having sex with several women who appeared to be prostitutes. The tape was obviously recorded in Miami, and most of the sex was rough bondage type.

The other tape showed Middleton having sex with a civilian Metro-Dade Police records clerk inside the department's main station. Sergeant Dallas recognized the woman and said in addition to her being an employee she was also married to a Metro-Dade police officer. The tapes were not pertinent to Middleton's rape case, so they were returned to him. These were the same tapes found in his storage unit during the Reno investigation.

At the end of the interview Sergeant Dallas added one more interesting piece of information. Middleton's brother-in-law and corporate vice president, Albert Heridia was currently in prison for drug trafficking charges. The charges stemmed from money laundering allegations associated with Total Concepts Cleaning Inc. Middleton was out of state by the time Heridia was arrested, but it still raised questions about his involvement in the drug trade while he was in Miami.

Officer Art Wellons was waiting for the detectives when they returned to the conference room at the Doral station. Officer Wellons was currently assigned to an elementary school as a school resource officer, but he had worked in the Warrants division with Middleton shortly before his arrest on the Miami rape charges.

When asked to describe Middleton, Officer Wellons replied, "He's weird." He then went on to say Middleton seemed obsessed with sex and often bragged about video tapes depicting him having sex with various women. Officer Wellons said he never personally saw any of these tapes, but other detectives in the unit told him they had seen them. Aside from his sexual peculiarities, Officer Wellons described Middleton as a personable and likeable officer.

Detective Greg Benjamin was waiting outside the conference room for his interview when Officer Wellons left. Detective Benjamin was currently working in an auto theft task force, but he had been Middleton's partner in the Warrants division at the time of his arrest on the rape charges.

Detective Benjamin said he had limited contact with Middleton away from the job, but he was familiar with his relationship with Evonne Haley. Detective Benjamin coached the junior league football team Haley's son was on, so he knew Middleton was having an affair with her. He knew Middleton was married, but also was aware he was involved in several extra-marital affairs. He said Middleton had a post office box he used to keep things from his wife, but never knew him to have any type of storage unit while they were working together. Without putting it into words, the detectives could tell Detective Benjamin did not think too highly of his former partner.

Detective Paul Kuiper still worked in the Warrants division and had been partnered with Middleton at times during 1985 and 1986. He said he became fairly close to Middleton at work, but did not socialize with him away from the job. He said Middleton was married at the time, but was very sexually active and always hitting on someone. At one time Middleton confided in him that he was having an affair with his wife's sister and often had sexual trysts with her and other women in his house when his wife was not home.

Detective Kuiper described Middleton as a schemer and as always talking about ways he could make a lot of money. He also said he knew Middleton drank heavily and had become very sloppy in his appearance during the months just prior to his arrest. This detective also did not sound like a big fan of Middleton's.

The next interviewee was *definitely* not a member of the David Middleton fan club. Detective Ellen Christopher was the lead investigator in Middleton's rape case. She had nothing good to say about Middleton, or the way his investigation was handled at the levels above her. She said the victim in that case was credible and she had no doubt Middleton was guilty of the rape.

Detective Christopher seemed agitated and said she could not go into the details of the case or the subsequent prosecution. The task force detectives didn't push her on this because they got the impression she wanted to talk to them, but had possibly been told not to. Before leaving the brief interview she did tell them she was certain Middleton had been involved in previous cases similar to the one that resulted in his arrest. She said it was her opinion these cases either went unreported—or uninvestigated.

Their last interview of the day proved to be the most informative. Detective Linnard Broom was also still assigned to the Warrants division, and had known Middleton from his first day in the division until the day he was arrested. He had never been permanent partners with Middleton, but they had been friends and went on several extradition trips together. Detective Broom described Middleton as personable and likeable, but wasn't surprised at all that he was in trouble with the law.

Detective Broom said it was his opinion that Middleton had no morality when it came to his sexual activities, and described him as having a very large sexual appetite. Middleton often bragged about his extra-marital sexual encounters to Detective Broom, and showed him several videos he'd taped of himself having sex with other women. One of these was the tape of him having sex with the civilian police employee and Middleton joked about her husband being a Miami police officer. Detective Broom was also aware of Middleton's affair with his wife's sister.

According to Detective Broom Middleton was well liked and highly respected in the division prior to his arrest. But he added, "I always knew his joint would end up getting him in trouble."

The rape allegations shocked Detective Broom, so he asked Middleton about them while visiting him shortly after his arrest. Middleton admitted having sex with the juvenile, but denied raping her. He said the girl willingly had sex with him and then made up the rape allegations later. Middleton was so convincing when telling the story that Detective Broom went back to the station and told his coworkers the whole thing was no big deal and Middleton would probably be back to work soon. It was after that he learned Middleton had been wearing his uniform at the time of the alleged rape incident.

He told the task force detectives, "That was the one thing above everything else that made me doubtful of Mr. Middleton's innocence. Officers in the Warrants division wear plain clothes, so there was no reason he should have been on the street in uniform. I went back and asked him about it, but he had no explanation. He actually went into a rage, so I just wished him the best and never saw him again."

The three tired detectives sat in the Airport Holiday Inn restaurant that evening discussing the day's interviews over dinner and drinks. Although some opinions varied about Middleton's personality, one thing was certain. All seven cops said Middleton had sexually deviant tendencies long before he ever reached Reno. They were 7 and 0 establishing the groundwork for Middleton's premeditated behavior, and any team would be proud of a win-loss ratio like that.

Chapter 40

OEDIPUS

Thursday, June 15, 1995 would be the detectives last full day in Florida. They had three more interviews to conduct, and were looking forward to escaping the Florida weather. Their first interview of the day was with Middleton's ex-wife Julia "Tina" Heridia.

Ms. Heridia agreed to talk to the detectives at her home located twenty miles south of Miami in an area called Cutler Ridge. The detectives arrived at the modest two-story home Ms. Heridia had once shared with Middleton at 10:30 in the morning. Ms. Heridia answered the door wearing a white cotton sundress and white sandals. The thirty-five year old single mother of two was pretty in wholesome sort of way. Her long dark hair, dark complexion and slight stature matched the characteristics of all the victims attributed to Middleton thus far.

A pitcher of iced tea with lemons floating in it was in the middle of the kitchen table Ms. Heridia led the detectives to. Once they were seated she poured them each a glass before sitting down herself. Her demeanor was quite cordial and her conversation was candid. She told the detectives she and Middleton had been high school sweethearts while growing up in Boston and had gotten married right after graduation. They moved from Boston to Miami after Middleton took the job with the Metro-Dade Police Department.

Shortly after they moved to Miami Ms. Heridia said she became aware Middleton had been involved in several extra-marital affairs. She described Middleton as a chronic liar and said he would often tell her unbelievable stories to cover his relationships with other women. She also said he would lie about everything.

She then told the detectives she believed her ex-husband's life began to change for the worse after his mother's death in 1987. She noticed he began drinking excessively and his affairs became more blatant. When asked to describe Middleton's mother, the detectives noted Ms. Heredia could very well have been describing an older version of herself—or any of Middleton's other victims.

It was also around this time that Middleton's sexual appetite and aggressiveness began to gradually increase. Ms. Heridia said on several occasions Middleton requested that she hurt him, scratch him or bite him. He also wanted to handcuff her and even bit her on a couple of occasions. She said she had been unwilling to participate in these types of activities and refused to have sex with him when he became insistent that she try these things. She also said Middleton told her that her unwillingness to participate in unusual sex practices resulted in him leaving home to find more willing partners.

When Middleton was arrested in Miami, Ms. Heridia said she questioned him about the allegations made by the police. Even though Middleton steadfastly denied the charges and said the young female victim was lying, she always knew in her heart her husband was guilty. The couple had a son and a daughter, but both were very young when their marriage began to fail.

Ms. Heridia filed for divorce while Middleton was in prison. Her uncontested request was granted in January of 1999 and she legally changed back to her maiden name. Middleton stayed at her house for two weeks when he got out of prison, but then left to join Evonne Haley in Colorado.

Since that time he had not been in contact with either her or their children. There were no child support payments and Middleton did not request visitation with his children. Since he gave up his parental rights, the children's last names were also legally changed to Heridia. When asked if she would be willing to testify in court to the things she had just told them, Ms. Heridia answered yes without hesitation.

Their next interview was forty miles north in the city of North Miami with Alyssa Cervantes*, the sixteen-year-old runaway Middleton had raped in 1990. She was now twenty-one-years-old and lived with her husband and two-year-old daughter in a small house in North Miami.

The detectives made the drive up the Florida Turnpike in a little under an hour and were pleasantly surprised when they got out of the car in front of Ms. Cervantes house. A cool breeze blowing in from the Biscayne Bay had caused the air temperature to drop to eight-eight degrees and the humidity to plunge to eighty-five percent. This was considered a cooling phase for the Miami area, but the Renoites still felt like they were walking through a steam room as they made their way to the front door.

Ms. Cervantes was visibly nervous when she opened the door for the detectives and asked that her older sister be allowed to remain with her during the interview. They sat at a table in a small but very neat dining room, and Jenkins began the interview by asking generic background questions to put Ms. Cervantes at ease. She said she was employed as a fulltime customer service representative at a local firm and was also attending night school for physical therapy. On the outside it looked like Ms Cervantes had moved on with her life, but something in her eyes told the detectives this was just a façade.

As Ms. Cervantes began telling the story of what happened to her when Middleton picked her up on September 29, 1990 there was no doubt she was still haunted by the nightmare. She did her best to maintain her composure as she recounted the events, but as she described being brutally raped by Middleton while she was handcuffed and helpless in the back seat of his police car, she lost control and began sobbing heavily.

The detectives offered to cease the interview, but Ms. Cervantes said she wanted to continue. After calming herself she went on to say the only reason she was out that night in the first place was that she had had a fight with her boyfriend and decided to walk home from a party they were attending. She had always been taught to respect the police, so when Middleton pulled up and told her to get into his police car she did as she was told.

She said, "I wasn't aware that I had to be cautious with this man. He had a uniform on. I was supposed to respect him, so that's what I did."

The young girl had the same long dark hair, the same dark Latina skin and the same small build shared by Middleton's mother, his ex-wife and all of his other victims. She said when Middleton climbed into the back seat of his police car and started undressing her she resisted, but he easily overpowered her. She said she pleaded with him, but he just kept telling her to shut up.

After Middleton raped her he opened the car door and told her she could run if she wanted. He made no offer to take off the handcuffs or let her get dressed, and she had no idea where they were. She asked him if he could drop her off closer to her home and remained in the back seat while they drove to the area where he picked her up. Ms. Cervantes said Middleton was like a different person during the drive. He made no mention of the attack and talked about his daughter and family. She said it was like he was two different people.

Ms. Cervantes did not initially report the rape out of fear no one would believe her. Two days later she broke down and confided in her sister who was a corrections officer at a nearby state prison. Her sister persuaded her to go to the police and took her to the Miami-Dade Police Department to make the report.

After Middleton's conviction, Ms. Cervantes' sister found out he was being allowed to serve his time in a county facility as part of a protective custody program for former law enforcement officers convicted of non-violent crimes. Her sister was outraged and went to the administration of the prison where she worked to complain. Middleton was soon transferred to the very same prison where Ms. Cervantes' sister worked to serve the remainder of his time. Judging from the smile on the correctional officer's face as she told the story, the detectives were reasonably certain his time spent in her prison was not easy.

As the detectives were leaving the house Ms. Cervantes told them she had pangs of guilt about testifying against Middleton now that she knew he had killed some of his victims. She said, "Because I came forward he lost his job and went to jail. He learned from that, so he wasn't about to take the chance of letting his victims go again. The only difference between what he did to them and what he did to me is he made sure they couldn't testify against him."

They assured Ms. Cervantes she had done what was right by coming forward and testifying against Middleton, but each of them knew she was right about one thing. Middleton was a man who learned from his mistakes, and in his mind letting his victim live was the only error he ever made.

When they were back in the car, Adams said, "Freud would have a field day with Middleton's mommy issues. First he married a girl who looked like his mother and then after she died he started raping and killing girls who looked like her. What do they call that?"

"A friggin psycho," Canfield replied.

Jenkins said, "Actually, Dave, it's funny you should mention what Freud would think. He called what Middleton has the Oedipus Complex. He named it after the Shakespearian character Oedipus Rex who allowed his sexual feelings for his mother to control everything else in his life."

"Douglas is right," Canfield said, "you do know too much shit a cop ain't supposed to know about."

Adams asked, "So, do you think all that Freudian crap will help Middleton's defense out?"

"Nope," Jenkins answered. "People lose their loved ones every day, but they don't go out killing people who look like them. From here on out we will never mention Freud again. We're cops, not shrinks. We'll be much better off going with the Larry Canfield theory that Middleton is just a friggin psycho. Is anyone besides me hungry?"

Chapter 41

FATHER DAVE

After a seafood lunch at a bayside restaurant, the detectives called the work phone number for their last interviewee. Ms. Barbara Fortunato* was the former civilian employee for the Miami-Dade Police Department who had had sex with Middleton in the station's D.U.I. room. She did not want the detectives coming to her place of employment, but she agreed to meet them at a North Miami McDonald's a block from her office.

The three detectives were sitting inside the McDonald's sipping Mc-milkshakes when Ms. Fortunato walked into the restaurant. They knew it was her because her looks were interchangeable with the other two women they had talked to that day. She was very pretty and had long dark hair, dark skin and a petite build. She also recognized the detectives upon sight because they were probably the only three people in Miami wearing suit coats and ties during the current heat wave. Ms. Fortunato sat down at the table and introductions were made all around. She began telling the detectives the strangest story they had yet heard during the weirdest investigation any of them had ever been involved in.

Ms. Fortunato was a thirty-one-year-old Cuban immigrant when she met Middleton while working at the main Miami-Dade Police station in 1989. Ms. Fortunato was a practicing member of a local Santerian religious sect—a fact she often discussed with Middleton. Santeria is a West African based religion imported to south Florida by Cubans who were used as sugar plantation slaves in the early 1800's. Some of their voodoo-type rituals include animal sacrifices, putting people into trances and worship of gods.

One day Ms. Fortunato confided to Middleton that she was having marital problems with her husband who worked in the Patrol division in one of the Miami-Dade substations. It was then that Middleton informed Ms. Fortunato that he was a practicing Santerian priest and could help her solve her problems. Ms. Fortunato told the detectives a Santerian priest is called an Ifa, pronounced *ee-fah*. She said an Ifa is the most powerful person in the religion, and receives knowledge and wisdom directly from the gods. She said she was honored to be in the presence of an Ifa and told Middleton she would do whatever he told her.

The detectives let Ms. Fortunato continue without interruption. They knew Middleton was conning her, but did not want to make her feel foolish. Middleton was no closer to being a priest than Satan himself, but there was no sense pointing out what was surely obvious to her by now.

Ms. Fortunato said one afternoon shortly after Middleton revealed his religious secrets to her he phoned her in the Records section and told her to meet him in the department D.U.I. room. Middleton was alone when she got there. He locked the door and handed her a chicken egg. He then told her to insert the egg into her vagina as the first part of the ritual. He said that if the egg remained inside her for ten minutes without breaking it would show she was pure enough to continue with the remainder of the cleansing rituals. Ms. Fortunato explained that chickens and chicken blood are common in Santerian rituals, so the request did not seem odd to her.

Ms. Fortunato did as she was instructed. After ten minutes she removed the unbroken egg from inside of her and gave it back to Middleton. The detectives didn't have the heart to tell the woman she had most likely not been handed a raw chicken egg. Father Middleton, or whatever his official title was at the time, had probably bought a hardboiled egg at a local deli while preparing for the ritual and then ate it for lunch after he was through cleansing her.

The next thing Middleton told the woman was that his semen contained wisdom and power bestowed upon him by the Santerian gods. He said she needed to accept his semen into her body in order to be helped with her marital problems. Once again she did as instructed and accepted his magical bodily fluids both orally and vaginally. What she didn't know was the religious acts were being captured on video courtesy of Father Dave.

The following week Ms. Fortunato told Middleton her marital problems were continuing, so he suggested she come to his house where he could perform a more detailed cleansing ritual. Ms. Fortunato was reluctant to go to his house until Middleton assured her his wife and children would be there. He said his entire family practiced Santeria, so she would be among friends.

Ms. Fortunato went to Middleton's house the following Sunday and was surprised to see he was the only one home. He assured her his wife would be home shortly, but suggested they begin the Santerian cleansing rituals without her. Middleton excused himself from the room and when he returned he was wearing a black hooded priest's robe and some type of white rubber mask, and had a machete with an animal head for a handle attached to his belt. Ms. Fortunato said the skull handle had a sharp horn about eight inches long attached to it. Based on the description, the detectives knew this was the same machete they had found in Middleton's shed.

The room they were in had animal heads mounted on the walls and large plants in each corner. The tile floor had been covered with a large plastic tarp, and Middleton told Ms. Fortunato it was for the ritual. She became nervous and asked him about the priest's robe, the mask and the large machete. He told her it was all part of the ritual and would need to draw blood from her before they continued.

Middleton had Ms. Fortunato strip naked and stand in the middle of the plastic tarp. He then took out the animal skull machete and cut her finger to draw blood. She was telling the story as calmly as if she were describing a day at the beach, and the detectives were on the edge of their cheap plastic seats waiting to hear what happened next. As she continued they certainly were not disappointed.

After a small puddle of blood had dripped out of the cut on Ms. Fortunato's finger, Middleton retrieved a burlap bag from the backyard and brought it into the house. He pulled a live chicken out of the bag and handed it to the naked, bleeding woman. He then instructed her to hold the chicken by the neck and swing it around until the neck broke. Ms. Fortunato did as she was told and then handed the deceased chicken back to Middleton. The masked priest then took out his machete, decapitated the dead chicken and covered Ms. Fortunato with chicken blood.

Ms. Fortunato said things began getting a little strange after that. Middleton made her put on a pink dress and told her he was going to handcuff her while he introduced more magical semen into her body. Since Ms. Fortunato was familiar with the use of animal slaughter and chicken blood as normal parts of Santerian religious rituals, she didn't give them much thought. But she had *never* heard of handcuffs being used in *any* religion, so she decided to make a hasty retreat out the front door.

Unfortunately for Ms. Fortunato, Middleton was much quicker than her. He caught her before she was able to get out of the house and struck her across the back of the head with the animal skull handle of his machete. She was knocked unconscious, but said she remembered Middleton sexually assaulting her vaginally and anally. He used the horn on his animal head machete handle for the anal penetration.

When Ms. Fortunato went to Internal Affairs to complain about the incident they did not believe her story. They told her it was their opinion she made up the bizarre tale to cover up the fact she had sex with Middleton in the D.U.I. room. Ms. Fortunato volunteered to take a polygraph test, but the department elected instead to fire her for having sex in the workplace. Perhaps if they would have looked a little harder and found the animal skull machete and Jughead Halloween mask currently sitting in the R.P.D. evidence room they might have put more credence in the story.

The detectives were eerily silent in the car as they drove back to their hotel after bidding farewell to Ms. Fortunato. Each one of them believed her story, but they'd had the advantage of meeting the David Middleton no one knew existed when she reported it to the Miami cops. They could all picture Middleton running around his house with his black hood partially covering his Jughead mask, swinging a machete in one hand and a headless chicken in the other. It was a sight they'd all rather forget.

Canfield said, "Middleton's one hell of a marriage counselor. I wonder if she ever straightened out her problems."

"I don't know," said Jenkins. "But I've gotta call Douglas as soon as we get back to the hotel."

"To tell him about that weird shit?" asked Adams.

"No, to say I told you so," replied Jenkins. "He was swinging that machete around the evidence room like he was some kind of Samurai warrior, and I told him he should have been wearing gloves. Maybe he'll listen next time."

Chapter 42

THE ARREST

The investigation in Reno progressed nicely while the three detectives were on their Florida fact-finding trip. The lab reports from Thelma Davilla's remains were now officially completed and several DNA matches had been located on items found in Middleton's storage shed. The most damning of these evidentiary matches was hair and blood from Davilla found on the Mexican blanket her sister had identified as coming from their apartment. The rope used to bind Davilla was also now positively matched to the type of rope found in Middleton's shed.

During a task force meeting on Monday, June 19, 1995 District Attorney Dick Gammick said he was finally convinced there was enough evidence to file murder charges against Middleton. He wasn't certain how much of what the detectives learned in Florida could be introduced at trial, but the story of the Santeria ritualistic rape was something he would like to get in front of a jury.

A meeting was set with Deputy District Attorney Tom Viloria for Thursday, June 22, 1995. The arrest warrants would be written on that day and presented to the judge for his signature. The decision was made to file all charges against Middleton in one single indictment instead of charging each murder separately. This way only one jury would hear everything connected to both cases.

That would eliminate taking the chance of two juries considering the evidence differently and arriving at conflicting verdicts. Since juries were unpredictable, it was better to keep exposure to them as limited as possible.

The legal term for bringing separate cases together was called a *joinder,* and there were pros and cons involved in using the process in this case. On one hand, the prosecution would not have to worry about evidence from one of the murders being excluded from the other case if it was ruled prejudicial to the jury. But on the other hand, they stood a chance of losing their strong case in the Powell murder due to the weaker case in the Davilla one. They still hadn't proven a solid link between Middleton and Davilla, and the only man who knew what that link was wasn't giving it up.

The final decision on the joinder of the cases was left up to Tom Viloria since he would be prosecuting them. To him this decision was another no-brainer. If there was ever a case worthy of the death penalty, this was it. In Nevada the same jury that hears the case-in-chief also sits for the penalty phase, so he would prosecute one case in front of one jury. The joinder wouldn't be easy, but he welcomed the challenge.

The law said two or more offenses could be charged in the same indictment with a separate count for each if the prosecution could prove certain things about the crimes. In this case, Viloria would have to prove the criminal acts were either connected together or were parts of a common scheme or plan. Since there was no obvious connection between the two murders, the latter would have to be proven in order for the cases to be joindered.

The common scheme or plan displayed by Middleton in the two murders was to meet women, abduct and hold them captive, abuse and kill them, and then dispose of their bodies. The similarities between Powell and Davilla were that both were unmarried women of about the same age and physical stature, alone at home when they disappeared and their homes had been serviced by T.C.I. Cable Company. Middleton had also met both of the victims before they disappeared. Even though Middleton hadn't admitted knowing Davilla, Viloria would be able to introduce witness testimony that would suggest he had met her at least once.

The storage shed was the key piece of evidence to prove a common scheme in the murders. He visited that shed on the day each victim disappeared, DNA evidence and property from both women was found inside of the shed, and rope similar to the one used to bind both victims was also stored there. Viloria was confident he could successfully joinder all of the charges together into one indictment, and Judge Fidel Salcedo agreed with him when he signed the arrest warrants at 11:30 A.M. on Thursday, June 22, 1995.

Detective Canfield met Jenkins and Douglas in an interview room at the Washoe County Jail. After Middleton was brought into the room they sat him down at a table and let him read through the arrest warrant and the affidavit in support of it. The detectives did their best to hide their jubilance while they watched Middleton deflate like a used Mylar balloon as he read through the papers detailing his crimes.

After Middleton was through reading the documents he was officially placed under arrest for two counts of murder in the first degree, two counts of kidnap and charges of credit card fraud related to the telephonic purchase at Good Guys. The arresting officer listed on the paperwork was Detective John Douglas, and it would be his face smiling his best Eddie Murphy grin that would appear on the front page of the local paper the next morning when the story of the murderous cable guy ran. Any racial overtones left lingering around the case would then be gone forever.

Middleton asked no questions until the jail deputies were leading him out of the room. His cockiness returned when he stopped at the door, looked over his shoulder at Jenkins and said, "This ain't over. Not by a long shot."

Jenkins and everyone else involved in the case knew that was an understatement. A major part of the investigation had just come to a close, but they were far from finished. A preliminary hearing was set for July 15, 1995 to determine if there was enough evidence to bind Middleton over to District Court for trial on the charges against him. This would be their first hurdle in what would surely be a long and complicated legal battle, and they still had work to do if they were going to make it over the top.

The task force detectives planned to meet for a victory dinner at the Harrah's Casino Steak House at 6:00 P.M. None of them would rest until Middleton was convicted in court, but arresting him for his criminal acts was the first reason the detectives had to celebrate since Kathy Powell's body was discovered nearly five months earlier. Before Jenkins and Douglas could join the others for the impromptu victory party, they had one more job to do.

The decision had been made earlier in the day not to charge Evonne Haley with any crimes related to the Good Guys case even though they would have no problem proving her involvement in them. Tom Viloria wanted her to testify against Middleton, but if they arrested her before the preliminary hearing they would run into trouble with co-conspirator testimony. For the time being she would remain free, but they would subpoena her as a witness for the State. There was no doubt she would perjure herself on the stand in order to save Middleton, but exposing her lies would be more damning to the defense than if she actually told the truth.

It was 4:00 in the afternoon when Jenkins and Douglas pulled their unmarked detective car into the rundown Sun Valley trailer park where Evonne Haley shared a rusted forty foot single-wide trailer with her daughter. Jenkins instinctively parked two spaces down from Haley's trailer so they would not be seen as they walked up to serve the witness subpoena on her.

When Haley opened the door she was once again highly agitated. The living room floor of the small trailer was covered with broken glass and a table in the center of the room was overturned. Haley said she had flown into a fit of rage when one of

Middleton's attorneys called to tell her of the murder arrest. She accused the detectives of framing the man she loved and ruining her life. As an almost insignificant afterthought, she then told Jenkins it was *his* fault her daughter just threatened to commit suicide.

Jenkins asked Haley what she meant by that statement, but she dismissed the question without answering and asked why the detectives were at her home. Douglas explained the witness subpoena to Haley while Jenkins wandered around the trailer looking for her daughter. He found the girl crouched in a corner of the small cluttered bathroom. She was crying and using a large pair of scissors to slice through the veins in her right wrist.

Blood was already dripping from a wound on her left wrist, and Jenkins knew better than to rush in and try to grab the scissors from the girl. He kept his voice as calm as he could as he talked the young girl into putting down the scissors and stepping away from them. The wounds were deep enough to need stitches, but fortunately she had not yet cut all the way through her veins. Jenkins wrapped towels around the girl's wrists and then called out to Douglas asking him to radio for backup and an ambulance. It looked like their victory dinner would have to wait for another day.

Chapter 43

PEOPLE vs. MIDDLETON

David Stephen Middleton was formally arraigned in Judge

Fidel Salcido's courtroom on Thursday, June 22, 1995. He was

dressed in an orange jail-issued jumpsuit and stood stoically next

to his attorney behind the defense table as the judge read the

charges against him. When Judge Salcido asked if Middleton

understood the charges, he nodded his head and quietly answered,

"Yes sir."

When the judge asked Middleton if he wished to enter a

plea, the question was answered by his attorney. Mike Speccio's

booming voice echoed of the wooden walls in the courtroom when

he said, "My client pleads not guilty to *all* of the State's charges."

Judge Salcido looked down at Middleton from his perch

behind the ornate judge's dais. He said, "Mr. Middleton, I hereby

order you to remain held in custody without bail at the Washoe

County Jail. You will return to this courtroom at 9:00 A.M. on July

14, 1995 for a preliminary hearing. At the conclusion of that

hearing I will make a determination on whether you should be

bound over to the District Court of Washoe County for trial. Do

you have any questions?"

Middleton answered no and was led out of the courtroom

by two jail deputies. A photo of Middleton with his head hanging

low, shoulders slumped and wrists shackled to a belly chain as he shuffled out of the courtroom was on the front page of the local newspaper the next day. Even though Middleton had held several different jobs in the six years since he ceased being a police officer, the headline in bold print above his photo read, "EX-COP CHARGED IN DOUBLE MURDER!" The task force detectives figured there just wasn't enough sensationalism in reporting the arrest of a cable guy, so an ex-cop was better for sales.

Pre-trial publicity was heavy during the three weeks prior to the preliminary hearing. In a last ditch effort, Middleton's attorneys filed a motion to get Judge Salcido removed from the case. They cited the judge's involvement from the onset of the investigation would prejudice him, but their appeal was overruled. Salcido remained the presiding judge, and the hallway outside of his courtroom was crowded with spectators and reporters on the morning of Friday, July 14, 1995.

The preliminary hearing was expected to last at least three days. Dave Jenkins was scheduled to be the first witness for the prosecution and his testimony was expected to take up most of the first day. Jenkins had been meeting with Tom Viloria on a daily basis preparing for the hearing, and when he arrived at the courthouse at 8:30 in the morning he wasn't surprised to see the crowd waiting to get inside the courtroom.

Evonne Haley had contacted Tom Viloria and said she would refuse to testify in the hearing. She cited her Fifth Amendment right against self-incrimination as the reason, since she would be asked to testify in a case she might later be charged in. Jenkins spotted Haley and her daughter seated on a wooden bench in the hallway outside of the courtroom and he knew they were there as spectators—not witnesses. Viloria had initially wanted to subpoena Haley's daughter, but thought better of it after Jenkins explained the girl was currently in therapy after her botched suicide attempt. She'd already been through enough, so they would spare her the added trauma of testifying against a man she once trusted.

Jenkins recognized several family members and friends of both Kathy Powell and Thelma Davilla in the crowded hallway. He'd met most of them during the investigation and exchanged somber greetings with them as he worked his way toward the courtroom. A man and woman standing quietly in the corner attracted his attention. He didn't recognize them, but the large buttons bearing the smiling face of a once-popular cheerleader they wore pinned to their shirts immediately told him why they were interested in the case.

Jenkins walked over and shook hands with Bonnie and Walt Rice. They had driven fourteen and a half hours through three states in order to hear testimony against a former Miami cop who they knew in their hearts had taken their daughter from them. Underneath the beaming photo of Buffy on the pin they wore over their hearts was written the words, "WE WON'T FORGET YOU BUFFY."

Bonnie Rice told Jenkins they would be staying in Reno for the duration of the court proceedings. She said, "I want to see

Middleton and I want him to see me. I want him to know that we know what happened to our daughter. He took the most precious thing in our lives away from us—our only daughter."

Walt Rice added, "It's gong to hurt to see him knowing what he did to our daughter, but knowing that he's locked up and can't hurt anyone else will give us some satisfaction."

After hearing that, the hardened homicide detective who was about to testify about dumpster diving and death whispers was so overcome with emotion he could barley talk. Jenkins fought to regain his calm veneer and assured Bonnie and Walt Rice he would do his best to make sure David Middleton never walked the earth as a free man again. He then introduced them to the Powell and Davilla families and left them alone to bond in a way that only survivors of common tragedies can understand.

The deputy guarding the courtroom door recognized Jenkins when he approached and stepped aside so he could enter before the doors were opened for the public. The room was designed to hold about a hundred people, but there were more than that waiting outside the doors. Jenkins found the court bailiff and arranged to have a row of seats close to the front of the courtroom reserved for the victim's family members through the proceedings. Since he was a witness he knew he would be unable to stay inside the room and listen to the testimony of other witnesses, but he wanted to make sure the family members heard what they had come for.

Judge Salcido had denied the defense motion to bar the press from the proceeding and at 8:45 A.M. members of the media were allowed to take their places in the section of the courtroom reserved for them. After that the general public was allowed to enter and by 9:00 the room was filled to capacity. Tom Viloria walked in and placed his briefcase on the prosecution table located to the right of the defense table in the front of the courtroom.

Jenkins walked through the swinging gate of the wood rail separating the attorney tables from the rows of wooden spectator benches and approached Viloria. After a hushed conversation, Viloria followed Jenkins to where the victims' family members were seated. He introduced himself to Bonnie and Walt Rice, Kathy Powell's mother and brother, and Thelma Davilla's sister and uncle. The emotional moment ended abruptly when the side door opened and David Middleton was escorted into the courtroom.

Middleton walked into the room with the confident stride of a man on a mission. During the trial phase of the court proceedings he would be allowed to dress in street clothes so the jury would not be predisposed to thinking he was a criminal due to his mode of dress. But since the judge presides over a preliminary hearing without a jury being present, Middleton was still dressed in his jail overalls. His curly black hair was pulled back into a short ponytail and the sleeves of his jumpsuit were rolled up tight over his muscular arms. Even though his hands were still cuffed to the belly chain around his waist, he presented an intimidating figure as he stared around the packed courtroom.

Mike Speccio was already seated at the defense table with the two attorneys from his office who would be assisting him. Before Middleton got to his designated seat next to his attorney, he spotted Bonnie and Walt Rice sitting in the second row on the prosecution's side of the room. He locked eyes with Walt Rice and then leaned down to whisper something to his defense team. The three attorney's representing Middleton turned and looked at the Rices and then engaged in a hushed conversation between themselves.

Jenkins and Viloria witnessed the exchange, but before they could discuss it the bailiff exclaimed, "All rise! The preliminary hearing related to the matter of the People of the State of Nevada versus David Stephen Middleton will now begin."

Chapter 44

THE BLACK CLOUD

Judge Salcido walked into the courtroom through the rear door leading to the judge's chamber and took his seat behind the ornate oak dais. He told the crowd to be seated and asked the defense and prosecution attorneys if they were ready to begin. Attorney Mike Speccio stood and asked to approach the bench for a sidebar conversation before the proceeding started. His request was granted, and he and Viloria walked to the front of the room to speak to the judge out of earshot of the spectators.

Jenkins was seated in the first row of spectator benches and watched nervously as the two attorneys stood to the left side of the judge's dais speaking in hushed tones. Criminal cases were more often won or lost by legal maneuvering than by testimony and evidence. Jenkins knew Speccio was good at what he did, and didn't like the fact he was raising legal questions before the proceedings even started.

The topic of the sidebar conversation was the buttons being worn by Bonnie and Walt Rice. Speccio argued this would be prejudicial to Middleton since it implied he was already guilty of murdering their daughter in Colorado. Since Middleton had never been charged in that case, Speccio claimed it was unfair to bring anything related to it into this proceeding. His first request to have the Rices removed from the courtroom was denied by Judge

Salcido since this was an open proceeding. His second request to order them to remove the buttons bearing the photo of their murdered daughter was also denied due to the possibility of First Amendment rights violations.

The judge's ruling was binding and Speccio was clearly frustrated. Before leaving the bench, he was overheard telling the judge, "This will gain media attention that is going to prejudice Mr. Middleton in both Nevada and Colorado. Maybe that's what we should do, have Mr. Middleton tried in the public opinion polls instead of court!"

The attorneys returned to their respective seats and Judge Salcido told Viloria to call the prosecution's first witness. When Viloria called Detective Dave Jenkins to the stand he walked purposefully to the witness chair attached to the right side of the judge's dais and stood erect as the bailiff swore him in. The courtroom spectators and media representatives watched intently as Jenkins took his seat in the witness chair, but it was Middleton who the detective locked eyes with as he adjusted the microphone in front of him.

Speccio stood and asked Judge Salcido to invoke the exclusionary rule before Viloria began questioning his witness. This rule was commonly used to keep witnesses from hearing each others testimony, so all persons testifying in the case would have to leave the room unless they were currently on the stand.

Since Viloria knew Jenkins would be testifying throughout most of the day he did not have any of his other witnesses scheduled to come in until the afternoon. The only other prosecution witness in the room was Thelma Davilla's sister Dora Valverde. It had to be explained to Ms. Valverde several times why she would not be able to remain in the room, and she was visibly upset by the fact she would not be able to hear testimony in the case. Viloria waited until she was escorted out of the courtroom and then began his questioning.

The prosecution's job in a preliminary hearing is to prove a crime has been committed and that there is enough probable cause of the defendant's guilt in that crime to bind him or her over for trial in District Court. Once the defendant is bound over, the burden of proof beyond a reasonable doubt kicks in before a jury can find him guilty of committing the crime. This is the reason the prosecution introduces as little testimony and evidence as possible during the preliminary hearing. If they show the defense too much too early, it can hurt their case in chief when it gets in front of a jury.

Viloria skipped having Jenkins introduce his resume into the record since he was already well known to the judge and defense attorneys. He would save that impressive show of credentials for the jury in order to lend credence to the detective's testimony. He asked only if Jenkins was employed as a homicide detective with the Reno Police Department on the night of Saturday, February 11, 1995. When Jenkins answered yes to the question, Viloria began leading him through the initial steps of the investigation.

During the next three hours Jenkins took the judge and courtroom spectators on a journey that began with the discovery of Kathy Powell's body and ended with the subsequent arrest of David Middleton. Viloria acted as the tour guide for the audience, using a series of questions and answers designed to extract the information that lead Jenkins and the other detectives down the winding path the investigation followed. Most questions were designed to be answered with a simple yes or no reply to avoid giving the defense too much information. Viloria had prepared his questioning well, but his timing was the most important aspect of his presentation.

The noon lunch break actually starts at 11:30 in most court proceedings, and it was precisely 11:00 when Viloria's questioning led Jenkins to the discovery of Middleton's storage shed. It was at this point in the detective's testimony that Viloria stopped leading him and let him describe in narrative what was found inside the shed. This style of testimony would give the horrific torture shed the most descriptive value, and Viloria wanted the impact to settle in on all who heard it during the ensuing lunch break.

Middleton's attorneys had sat quietly through Jenkins' testimony thus far, but they raised their first objection when Viloria asked him about the discovery of the storage shed. Court documents showed the detectives used Middleton's keys to determine this shed actually belonged to him. Since Middleton specifically told Jenkins he did not want the police to have his key ring, the defense argued they were illegally in possession of his keys. Therefore, any evidence discovered by using the keys should be dismissed.

This was a reasonable objection and Jenkins tried not to appear nervous as the attorneys for the defense and prosecution argued the point of law. He knew their case would be severely damaged if they were not able to introduce the contents of the storage shed into evidence, but Viloria handled the objection perfectly. Since Middleton had relinquished custody of the keys to Evonne Haley and she subsequently gave them to Jenkins, Judge Salcido ruled the police legally possessed the keys. Jenkins spotted Evonne Haley seated in the audience and noticed her face had turned a bright shade of red after realizing the error she had made in turning over the keys to him.

Jenkins was allowed to continue his testimony. He told of discovering the storage shed and outlined for the judge some of the items located inside. He described finding the Warps Brothers Banana Bags, bondage devices, gags, a stun gun and sexual paraphernalia. The last thing Jenkins described was the refrigerator they theorized Kathy Powell had been held captive inside of. This drew the second defense objection because they said it was only speculation on the part of the investigators that Powell had been alive when she was placed into the refrigerator.

This was another area of testimony carefully planned out by Viloria, as he had anticipated the defense objection. The judge granted Viloria's request to clarify the statement, so he asked Jenkins what led him to believe Kathy Powell had been placed inside of the refrigerator while still alive. Jenkins went on to describe the air holes drilled into the refrigerator, how the blue fibers found around the freezer cutout matched the fibers found around Powell's neck and how the blood and skin fragments found inside of the refrigerator were linked to her by DNA comparison.

He finished by saying, "That transfer of fiber, blood and skin could only have been caused by the decedent thrashing about inside of that refrigerator. It has been my experience through many years of homicide investigation that when a person stops living—they also stop moving. Therefore, the only logical conclusion to be reached is that at some point prior to Ms. Powell's death, she was held in a horrible captive state inside of that refrigerator."

The statement exploded in the room like a bomb, and loud sobs could be heard coming from the audience. Jenkins looked over and saw Kathy Powell's brother putting his arm around his mother to comfort her. This was the first official mention of how the refrigerator had been used, and Jenkins knew the grizzly picture of Kathy Powell being held inside of it would be forever ingrained in the minds of her family members.

What the prosecution planned to introduce into evidence next was even more horrific than Jenkins' description of the refrigerator. Before Viloria brought out blowup photos of the crime scene and the refrigerator itself, he told the court the photos would be highly disturbing in nature. He asked the judge to ban the press from photographing the evidentiary photos, and gave anyone who might be bothered by them a moment to leave the courtroom if they so desired. The judge granted the request, but everyone in attendance remained in their seats.

Several eight-by-ten photos mounted on heavy white poster boards were placed on easels in the front of the courtroom. Judge Slacido swiveled his chair to better view them, and Viloria asked Jenkins to describe what was depicted in the photos.

The first set of photos was of Kathy Powell as she was found inside the dumpster. In the second set she had been removed from the plastic bags and sleeping bag. Jenkins pointed out how the ropes had been tied around her in a manner that would choke her if she moved too much, leading him to believe she had been tied up by someone other than herself.

The last set of photos was of a demonstration staged using a crime scene technician who was about the same height and weight as Kathy Powell. The woman was dressed in protective clothing and had been placed inside of the refrigerator to show the position of Kathy Powell's body as determined by matching her injuries to the corresponding blood and skin samples taken from the refrigerator walls and door. The technician's body was twisted in a grotesque position and a murmur went through the crowd as they realized this was how Kathy Powell spent the last days of her life.

The photos had a devastating effect on everyone in the room with the exception of one man. As Jenkins got back into the witness chair he looked at Middleton and saw he was staring straight ahead as if the photos were not even in the room. Middleton had disassociated himself from the crime in the way only a true sociopath could.

At precisely 11:30 A.M. Viloria said he had no further questions for Jenkins, but would be recalling him for additional testimony at a later time. The defense deferred cross-examination until Jenkins' testimony was competed and Judge Salcido recessed the courtroom for lunch. Middleton was led from the room followed by his attorneys. Once he was gone, the press people rushed out to start their bi-lines. They'd been given a glimpse of life through the eyes of a madman, and the story would definitely lead off the evening news.

Jenkins and Viloria had a brief discussion about the day's events and they were both pleased with how the testimony went. They were by no means out of the woods yet because they still had to deal with the major hurdle in their case. There was no doubt that Middleton was evil and had murdered in the past, but that was not what they were here to prove. They had to show that Kathy Powell and Thelma Davilla died at his hands, and one single word hung over the case like a black cloud waiting to burst over their heads. *Undetermined.*

Chapter 45

ROCKY

Testimony resumed at 2:00 in the afternoon when the prosecution called Detective Larry Canfield to the stand. Canfield testified to the facts surrounding the discovery of Thelma Davilla's decomposed remains and how Middleton was linked to the crime. He introduced into evidence hair samples matched to Davilla through DNA, the blanket she had been wrapped in when her sister last saw her and some of the clothing she had been wearing. Canfield testified that all of these items had been in the possession of the Reno Police when Davilla was found and the items had come from Middleton's shed.

Canfield then detailed the formation of the task force and their investigative efforts that led to charging Middleton with the murder. No mention of the Florida trip or anything they learned there about Middleton's past was brought up. Viloria was still uncertain if he would be able to get any of that information into evidence, but if he could, he would save it for trial.

Speccio asked only two questions of Canfield during cross examination. The first question was if Canfield had ever investigated a homicide case where the cause of death was undetermined. The second question was whether Thelma Davilla's cause of death had ever been determined. The detective quietly answered no to both questions.

Sparks Police Detective Dave Adams was the next to take the stand. He testified to the facts surrounding Thelma Davilla's disappearance and how the police initially handled the case. He then said the case was put in the opened and unsolved file until the discovery of her body. After that he was brought back into the case since he was the lead detective when she initially disappeared.

Adams testified to the many man-hours the task force detectives put in interviewing known associates of Davilla. At least three of those people established possible links between Middleton and Davilla before her disappearance. Adams then testified to the service calls performed by T.C.I. Cable Company at Davilla's apartment and the possible link to Middleton.

He also testified that he and Canfield spent several hours doing interviews at the legal brothels east of Reno. Middleton was a frequent patron in two of the houses of prostitution, but they found a common theme throughout their interviews. Middleton never engaged in any sexual activity with the prostitutes when he visited the brothels. He would sit at the bar and drink with the girls, then try to get them to go out on dates with him. The word *stalker* surfaced several times during their investigative interviews.

Upon cross examination Speccio asked Adams the same two questions he asked Canfield. Had he ever investigated a homicide with no known cause of death and had a cause of death been established in the Thelma Davilla case? Like Canfield, Adams answered no to both questions.

The fourth and final witness of the day was by far the most compelling. Dora Valverde took the stand and broke down in tears twice during her testimony. She described her sister as a hard working and caring person who loved living in the United States, and never caused anyone any harm during her entire life. She recounted her story of leaving for work on August 8, 1994—the last day she saw her sister alive. She also identified the blanket found in Middleton's storage shed as the same one her sister had been sleeping in when she last saw her.

Speccio did not cross examine Ms. Valverde and Judge Salcido dismissed everyone for the weekend after she was through testifying. Court was due to reconvene Monday morning and that was when Viloria planned to address the issue of cause of death.

Much of the morning of Monday, June 17, 2008 was spent with the defense team reviewing documents. It was common practice for documentation to be admitted into evidence without testimony to support it if the defense and prosecution both stipulated to the fact it would happen anyway if the person who prepared them actually testified in court. This was a time saving practice at the preliminary hearing stages of a criminal case, but the actual experts would be called to testify if the case was bound over for trial.

Viloria decided not to call Dr. Roger Ritzlin or Dr. Frederick Laubscher to the stand at this point to testify regarding the autopsy of Kathy Powell or the examination of Thelma Davilla's remains. Speccio agreed to have the reports prepared by both doctors and the death certificates issued for both women entered into evidence without testimony. All documentation listed the causes of death as undetermined, so the defense had nothing to gain by having the doctors testify.

It was 1:00 P.M. by the time Viloria called his first witness of the day. Deputy Chuck Lowe testified to gathering evidence at both crime scenes, Middleton's storage shed and apartment, and finally at the homes of Kathy Powell and Thelma Davilla. He authenticated the photos on display in the courtroom as ones he had taken and testified to noticing similarities in how the victims in both cases were dumped.

Viloria next asked Lowe if during the hundreds of deaths he had responded to as a forensic technician, had he ever seen one where the death resulted from natural causes and the decedent was bound in the manner Kathy Powell was. Lowe answered no, and it was his opinion no one would willingly want to be bound in the manner Kathy Powell was.

Speccio objected to this last statement as conjecture, but Judge Salcido allowed the answer to remain on record since Lowe was testifying to his expert observations. Viloria felt he had just taken a very big step in proving criminal agency in the case.

The next witness was Richard Berger, the Sheriff's Department criminalist who examined the rope, fiber and hair evidence in the case. Berger testified that the rope found in Middleton's storage shed was similar and consistent with the rope taken from the bodies of Kathy Powell and Thelma Davilla. Mr.

Berger next said the blue fibers found on Kathy Powell's neck and body were virtually indistinguishable from the fibers found in the refrigerator in Middleton's storage shed.

During cross examination Speccio asked Mr. Berger if the rope used on either Powell or Davilla was a 100% match to the rope found in Middleton's shed. Berger said that it was impossible to get a 100% match with rope unless the two ends of a cut rope were present for comparison. Speccio asked no further questions, leaving the possibility that the ropes were unrelated hanging in the air for consideration.

Dr. Berch Henry, also a Sheriff's Department ciminalist took the stand next. Henry was a DNA specialist and had done the DNA testing in both cases. He testified that the hair recovered from the bondage clamps in Middleton's shed was Kathy Powell's. He also said the DNA samples taken from the foam rubber ball gag and from the inside of the refrigerator all matched Kathy Powell.

Dr. Henry said he tested the hair found inside the barrel and on the Mexican blanket found inside of Middleton's shed. He testified that those hair samples matched DNA evidence he had retrieved from inside of the skull cap of Thelma Davilla.

When it was Speccio's turn to question the witness he asked if the hair sample matches were determined to be 100% accurate. Dr. Henry answered the hair sample matched to Powell had an assigned population frequency of one in 24,000 for Caucasian donors. In Ms. Davilla's case the frequency was one in 17,000 for Hispanics.

Even though these numbers were well above what was considered a positive match, the fact that the comparisons were not an exact match might be enough to cast a shadow of a doubt on the evidence if it were presented to a jury. Viloria made a mental note to do a better job laying the groundwork for the expert testimony at trial because Speccio was obviously doing his homework.

The last prosecution witness of the afternoon was Gary Cable, the Good Guys salesperson who had taken the phone order from the person identifying themselves as Kathy Powell. This part of the case presentation was tricky, since Cable would also be called to testify against Evonne Haley when she was eventually charged with her part in the crime.

Viloria decided it was best to put only Cable on the stand during the preliminary hearing and save the testimony of his coworker Mike Serrateo for trial. Evonne Haley was once again in the courtroom, and if Serrateo saw her it might lessen his credibility when he identified her in later court proceedings. Since Haley refused to testify in the Middleton case there was no reason not to charge her for her part in the Good Guys case now.

Cable testified that he took the phone order for the stereo equipment and his first impression of the caller was it was a man disguising his voice as a woman. He identified the sales receipt found in Middleton's shed as the one he made for the phone sale and authenticated his hand writing on the bottom where the words "phone order" were written. He also identified the stereo equipment found in Middleton's shed as the same merchandise purchased during the phone order.

Speccio asked only one question of the witness during cross examination. He asked Cable if he had ever received any training on voice identification. Cable said no, but he usually talks to hundreds of people a week while performing his job and had become quite good at matching people to their voices. Viloria liked the answer and Speccio seemed angry that he had asked the question.

There still was no solid evidence to show cause of death or criminal agency, but Viloria was pleased with the groundwork he'd laid with circumstantial evidence throughout the day. He wished he had more, but he'd play with what was dealt him. Rocky Balboa always fought harder when he was against the ropes with the cards stacked against him, and so would he.

Chapter 46

GREAT EXPECTATIONS

There was only one prosecution witness left when court reconvened at 9:00 the next morning. Viloria called Detective Dave Jenkins to the stand to sum up the case. The courtroom was once again crowded with spectators and reporters, but Jenkins picked out Bonnie and Walt Rice sitting in their reserved seats as he made his way to the witness stand. They pledged to remain in town until the end of the proceedings and had kept their word. They also still wore their buttons with Buffy's photo on them pinned to their shirts.

Judge Salcido reminded Jenkins he was still under oath from his prior testimony, and Viloria began the questioning as soon as the detective was seated in the witness chair. This line of questioning was concerning statements Middleton made to Jenkins during some of his interviews.

Jenkins recounted the statement Middleton made to him during their first contact while they were walking to the Records section at the Reno Police Department. He said this was the first time he was inclined to believe Middleton had something to do with Kathy Powell's death because he said he had knowledge of it but then recanted the statement when Detective Douglas joined them.

He next went on to inform about the bizarre explanation Middleton gave him regarding the circumstances of Kathy Powell's death. Middleton originally denied knowing her, but then admitted to having consensual sex with her. Finally he said she was alive and well when he left to go to the store, but dead and tied up when he returned. Jenkins also told the judge about Middleton's "Pig in a Poke" offer to the District Attorney in order to gain clemency from prosecution.

Viloria asked Jenkins if in his professional opinion these were the actions of an innocent man. Speccio objected, but he was overruled by the judge since Jenkins was considered an expert in the areas of interview and interrogation. Jenkins did not go into the pathological liar theory, since that too would be saved for trial. He did say based on his training and experience there was no way an innocent person would answer questions in the manner Middleton had.

Viloria was feeling good about the testimony, until it was time for cross examination. Speccio hit Jenkins hard about the marathon interview and asked if he had ever come upon an instance where a suspect tells the police what they want to hear just to put an end to the questioning. Jenkins reluctantly agreed he had heard of such incidents, but it had never happened to him and assuredly was not the case with this interview.

Speccio stood up and said, "I just have a couple more questions for you, detective. Have you ever investigated a homicide where there was an undetermined cause of death?"

Jenkins took a deep breath and replied, "Yes I have. Three cases come immediately to mind, but there may have been more."

"OK," Speccio said. "Let's just talk about these three that you can remember. Were they all adult victims?"

Viloria stood up and objected to the line of questioning based on relevance to the current case. Speccio asked for the court's indulgence, saying he would show relevance with the next couple of questions. The objection was overruled and Judge Salcido instructed Jenkins to answer the question.

Jenkins said, "Of the three cases, two of the victims were infants in what initially appeared to be S.I.D.S. deaths, but were later proven to be intentional acts by the parents. Only one case of undetermined death where the victim was an adult immediately comes to mind."

Speccio remained standing and said, "And who was the victim in that one case you investigated, detective?"

Jenkins paused and then answered, "A thirty-eight-year-old woman who was found deceased in a downtown Reno motel room on August 4, 1993. The coroner was unable to establish cause or manner of death during her autopsy, but we subsequently arrested and convicted her boyfriend for her murder."

"And what is the current status of that case?" Speccio asked.

"It is currently in front of the Nevada State Supreme Court on appeal from your office," Jenkins replied.

Speccio stepped closer to the witness stand and inquired, "And do you know the basis for that appeal, Detective Jenkins?"

Jenkins smiled and answered, "I'm certain we both know the answer to that question, Mr. Speccio. The conviction is being appealed because your office feels the state did not accurately prove the corpus delecti for the crime of murder, since the coroner could not rule criminal agency was involved in the death."

"Thank you, detective," Speccio said. "No further questions."

Viloria chose not to ask Jenkins any questions on re-direct examination, and the judge told him he could step down from the witness stand. Since there were no other witnesses scheduled to testify, Jenkins was allowed to remain in the courtroom to listen to the closing arguments. He stood in the back of the room next to Douglas who had come to court to listen to the last of the testimony.

Speccio hadn't called any witnesses for the defense during the proceedings, and he certainly wasn't going to put Middleton on the stand to testify in his own defense. Viloria would have loved to get a chance at picking Middleton's story apart under oath, but unfortunately that would probably never happen. People like Middleton were the reason the Constitution guaranteed a person the right not to testify in their own trial. He wouldn't be able to keep himself from lying and those lies would never stand up against a skilled attorney like Viloria.

Middleton sat erect and stared straight ahead as Viloria began his closing arguments. Viloria remained standing behind the prosecution table as he spoke, and kept his summation brief. A link had been established between Middleton and both victims. DNA evidence from both women was found inside of Middleton's makeshift torture chamber, meaning they were both alive at some point when they entered the shed. Both women were found dead after their bodies were dumped, which meant their lives ended while Middleton held them in captivity. Kidnap, torture, rape and murder were the common theme in both cases. Viloria ended by saying the prosecution more than proved there was enough probable cause to bind Middleton over for the crimes he was charged with.

The closing arguments for the defense consisted of two statements. Speccio stood and said, "The prosecution has not shown a link between these two cases, nor have they proven criminal agency was involved in either death. At this time the defense moves that the charges against David Middleton be dropped."

Judge Salcido studied his notes for a moment and then announced that he found enough probable cause to bind Middleton over for District Court trial on all charges. A trial date would be set as soon as he could consult the court calendar.

There was a commotion in the room as the news reporters hurriedly left to start preparing their stories. A photo of a confused Middleton with the headline "EX-COP GOES TO TRIAL FOR

THE CABLE GUY MURDERS" would be printed on the front page of the morning paper. The task force detectives lamenting about poor press coverage were pleasantly surprised the news didn't dub the case the "Ex-Cop Murders."

After Middleton had been led from the courtroom, Jenkins and Douglas stood in the hallway waiting for Viloria. They watched Bonnie and Walt Rice hugging the families of the other victims in celebration inside of the emptying courtroom. These were people who hadn't known each other a few short days earlier, but would now forever be kindred family.

Viloria walked up to the two detectives and said, "Well, we made it past the first step."

"We did," Jenkins agreed. "But Speccio brought up the Frutiger case, and that concerns me."

Viloria said, "Frutiger was guilty and he got convicted of murder. We can't help what happens after that."

Douglas said, "The rumor I'm hearing is the State Supreme Court is about to reverse his conviction and set him free."

"That's a pretty credible rumor," Viloria said. "That means Speccio is already planning his appeal, and that's something an attorney does when he knows he has a guilty client who is going to be convicted."

"I still don't like it," Jenkins said. "I'd feel a lot better if we had a solid cause of death to base our case on. Like Charles Dickens said in *Great Expectations*, 'Take nothing on its looks, but take everything on evidence.' Our case is a little short on evidence for my liking."

Viloria rolled his eyes and said, "What they say about you is true. You really do know too much shit for a cop. We'll worry about the Frutiger case and causes of death later. Middleton is guilty and we're gonna send him back to hell where he belongs, so let's go celebrate with a nice lunch."

Chapter 47

FRUTIGER

On August 4, 1993 the manager of the Regency Hotel in a seedy part of downtown Reno sent a maintenance man to investigate a putrid smell possibly coming from a broken sewer line under one of the buildings. The custodian crawled under the hotel and found the sewer lines intact, but determined the foul odor was originating from room thirty-five.

The manager knocked on the door to room thirty-five which was answered by a man named Clinton Frutiger who rented the room with his girlfriend, Peggy Poulter. Frutiger told the manager he was just about to call her to report the odor, but was waiting for Peggy to get out of the shower. He asked the manager to return in about ten minutes and he would allow her to come inside to check for the source of the smell.

While the manager waited inside of her office she was surprised to see Frutiger hurry from the hotel room alone and speed out of the parking lot driving Peggy Poulter's beige 1985 Oldsmobile Cutlass. The manager went back to room thirty-five. She could hear the shower running, but there was no answer when she knocked on the door. She entered the room and found there was no one in the shower, but the room was swarming with flies and there were towels stuffed under the closet door.

The manager fought her way through the flies and pulled open the closet door. She found Peggy Poulter wrapped in plastic lying on the closet floor in a puddle of dried blood. She was the source of the foul odor, and judging from the amount of maggots crawling over her body, she had been dead for quite some time.

Reno Police Detective Dave Jenkins was assigned the case and he responded to the hotel with his partner, Detective John Douglas. After their initial investigation was completed, Poulter's body was removed from the closet. With the assistance of the coroner, they removed the plastic bag that was covering her head and some of the plastic wrapping from her body. There were no immediate signs of trauma, but there was a suspicious looking bulge in the plastic that remained wrapped around her body.

The detectives carefully unwrapped more plastic and then found what was causing the protuberance. The killer had wrapped Ms. Poulter's cat inside of the plastic so she could take her beloved pet with her into the afterlife. Unlike Poulter, the cat's cause of death was immediately distinguishable since its head was grotesquely twisted 180 degrees from its natural position. Killing the cat showed aggression associated with someone close to the victim, so Clinton Frutiger became the likely suspect in what certainly appeared to be a murder. An attempt to locate was broadcast for Poulter's Oldsmobile, but by then Frutiger had a four-hour head start and was not located.

An autopsy was performed on Ms. Poulter the next day by Dr. Roger Ritzlin—the same doctor who would perform the autopsy on Kathy Powell six months later. Dr. Ritzlin observed Poulter's body was severely decomposed and estimated she had been dead about a week. He said he could not determine a cause of death due to the decomposition, but found her liver was enlarged and her blood alcohol level at the time of her death was a .341.

Dr. Ritzlin determined Poulter could have died from heart disease, a cirrhotic liver, alcohol consumption at a lethal level or strangulation. He found bleeding in Poulter's neck area, but said it was a small amount and not consistent with trauma caused by strangulation. The plastic bag covering Poulter's head was described as being "draped over her head and not wrapped in a way that would cause suffocation," so that was also ruled out as a cause of death.

After completion of Peggy Poulter's autopsy, Dr. Ritzlin listed the cause and manner of her death as *undetermined.* The case was reclassified as a *suspicious death* with Clinton Frutiger listed as a person of interest. Since Frutiger had unrelated outstanding warrants, Jenkins and Douglas went in search of him to see what he knew about the death of Peggy Poulter *and* her cat.

The next day Poulter's car was located in the parking lot of a casino in Carson City, thirty miles south of Reno. The detectives staked out the car and took Frutiger into custody when he returned to it. In his wallet they found Peggy Poulter's ATM card and two of her credit cards. Subsequent investigation showed Frutiger had been withdrawing the maximum amount from Poulter's bank account since July 1, 1993 and had made several charges on her credit cards after the time of her death. Inside of the car they also found a briefcase loaded with personal papers belonging to Ms. Poulter.

Based on the circumstances, the case was upgraded to a homicide and Clinton Frutiger was arrested for the murder of Peggy Poulter. Throughout his trial, his defense stuck to the story that Ms. Poulter had died of natural causes and Frutiger hid her body because he was afraid to call the police. They explained the cat had been hit by a car and Frutiger thought it was humane to burry the cat with its owner. He was subsequently convicted of murder and sentenced to life in prison.

An appeal was immediately filed by the Public Defender's office. The basis for the appeal was the State did not adequately prove criminal agency was involved in the death of Peggy Poulter when they presented their case to the grand jury. Since a cause and manner of death was never determined and there was a possibility Poulter died of natural causes, the defense argued the case never should have reached trial in District Court. Criminal agency was the *corpus delicti* in the charge of murder, so it was now up to the State Supreme Court to determine if the prosecution had met its burden of proof.

The Nevada Supreme Court was in the process of reviewing the Frutiger case at the time David Middleton was bound over for trail. Three murder cases being tried in different parts of Nevada could possibly be effected by the Nevada Supreme

Court ruling in the Frutiger case. One of them had been officially dubbed "The Cable Guy Murders."

Chapter 48

HABEAS CORPUS

Middleton's murder trial was scheduled to be heard in the Washoe County Courtroom of District Court Judge Peter Breen on November 13, 1995. As soon as Middleton's defense attorneys were notified of the date, they made a request for a continuance of at least ninety days in order to prepare their appeal of Judge Salcido's decision in the preliminary hearing.

Since Middleton was being held in custody and it was his own decision to forfeit his right to a speedy trial, the request for continuance was granted. A new trail date was set for Monday, February 12, 1996. The State Supreme Court would certainly rule on the Frutiger case before they recessed for the Christmas holidays, so the prosecution knew the defense had an ulterior motive for their continuance request.

Middleton's attorneys went to work on their appeal almost immediately after he was bound over for trial at his preliminary hearing. On August 30, 1995 Public Defender Mike Speccio and his Chief Appellate Deputy Attorney John Reese Petty filed a nineteen-page Writ of Habeas Corpus with Judge Breen seeking a reversal of Judge Salcido's decision.

Habeas corpus is a Latin term which translates to *you should have the body.* A Writ of Habeas Corpus is a legal document filed by a detainee seeking relief from unlawful imprisonment due to insufficient evidence against him. In Nevada these writs are heard *ex parte*—another Latin term that means *from or for one party*. It would be up to Judge Breen alone to decide on the Writ of Habeas Corpus without any involvement of the prosecution. This would be the first test of the strength of the prosecution's case against Middleton.

The main argument in the writ was that there was insufficient evidence presented to the Justice Of The Peace at the time of the preliminary hearing to establish the corpus delicti of murder. The writ read in part:

"Notwithstanding the substantial amount of time spent in the preliminary hearing held below it is significant, for purposes of this petition, that the State failed to produce any evidence as to the cause of death for either Ms. Davilla or Ms. Powell. Indeed, according to the death certificates admitted into evidence, Ms. Davilla's cause of death could not be determined and as to Ms. Powell, the cause of death could not be determined "after autopsy."

In this case in order to establish the requisite probable cause to support a belief that crimes of murder had been committed and that Mr. Middleton had committed the crimes, the prosecution was obliged to prove the corpus delicti of the alleged crimes. To establish the corpus delicti of murder, two elements must be proven: (1) the fact of death; and (2) the criminal agency of another responsible for the death, (Hooker v. Sheriff, NV. 506-1262 1973).

Here there was no evidence, direct or circumstantial, showing criminal agency as the cause of either Ms. Davilla's or Ms. Powell's deaths; nor was there evidence, direct or circumstantial, that Mr. Middleton was involved in the cause of either death.

Simply put this is a case where the Justice Of The Peace was presented with no evidence to support the corpus delicti of murder—yet without so much as an explanation—bound Mr. Middleton over to the district court on both counts of murder. The Justice Of The Peace simply said, 'In this case the State has brought a lot of evidence before the court, and I'm not going to try to even near elaborate over all of it. I'm not going to even try to do that...' and then bound Mr. Middleton over for trial. But the fact of the matter was that there was no evidence showing criminal agency as the cause of either death.

We are a nation who prides ourselves on following the rules of law. Thus, the rule of law applies equally to both citizens and governments in our constitutional scheme. Under the rule of law Mr. Middleton should not have been bound over on the two counts of murder because the State failed to offer any evidence supporting the criminal agency prong of the corpus delicti of the crime.

For the reasons and authorities set forth above it is respectfully submitted that the State failed to establish the corpus delicti of murder in the case of either Ms. Davilla or

Ms. Powell. Accordingly, Mr. Middleton respectfully requests that this court grant the Writ of Habeas Corpus and discharge the two counts of murder."

Judge Breen took the writ under advisement and eventually gave both the defense and prosecution a chance to argue their cases. On Wednesday, October 18, 1995 Judge Breen called the attorneys into his chambers and issued his ruling. He rejected the Writ of Habeas Corpus and ruled the murder charges against David Middleton would not be dismissed. He also rejected the defense motion to have both murders tried separately, so the cases would stay joindered for purposes of prosecution. Middleton's trial date remained February 12, 1996.

The ruling was a major victory for the prosecution, and Viloria met with Jenkins and Douglas later that evening for a celebration dinner of burgers and beers at a local pub. While they were waiting for their dinners, Jenkins asked, "What do you think their next move will be?"

Viloria replied, "Whatever it is, I'm sure it won't happen till the Supreme Court gets off their asses and rules on Frutiger. We're not out of the woods yet, but I'll be ready for them when we get to trial."

Douglas said, "Since it looks like we're gonna have some downtime in the case, I say we go out and arrest the devil's disciple. We may never tie her to the murders, but we've got her solid on the Good Guys case."

"I agree," said Jenkins. "But I'm not sure whether she's the devil's disciple or an unwitting angel of mercy. After going through everything we've got on her involvement with Middleton, I think she might have actually chased away a couple of his potential victims with her jealousy."

"I almost forgot about Suzy the bartender," Douglas said. "I wonder how many other girls out there are alive today because Middleton's girlfriend is a raving bitch."

Viloria finished his beer and said, "I'm betting on the devil's disciple angle. Anyway, there's no reason to leave Haley running free anymore. She's not gonna do us any good testifying against Middleton and the statute of limitations is ticking on her involvement at Good Guys. Bring me the case when you get it wrapped up and I'll get you an arrest warrant."

Douglas said, "If nobody ends up killing anybody tonight we'll be able to jump on this first thing in the morning. The sad part about this is we have a stronger case against Haley than we do against Middleton. It's gonna be a bitch if she ends up doing time and he walks on a technicality."

Jenkins slowly rapped his knuckles three times on the wooden tabletop and then threw some grains of salt that had spilled on the table over his right shoulder. He said, "It's a good thing I'm not a superstitious man or else I might think my partner just jinxed us. Is anyone up for another beer?"

Chapter 49

FOR WHOM THE BELL TOLLS

Three uniformed Washoe County Sheriff's deputies accompanied Jenkins and Douglas when they went to Evonne Haley's trailer at 10:00 in the morning on Friday, October 27, 1995. She initially would not open her door for them, but she acquiesced after Jenkins used his cell phone to call inside and calmly explained they had a warrant for her arrest and weren't leaving without her.

The arrest warrant signed an hour earlier by Judge Salcido charged Evonne Haley with one count each of burglary, fraudulent use of a credit card and possession of stolen property—all related to her involvement in the Good Guys' case. To say Haley was a bit upset when she learned she was being arrested would be like saying the sinking of the Titanic was a minor boating accident.

Haley appeared extremely disheveled in the booking photo that was printed on the front page of the *Reno Gazette Journal* the next morning, but much to her credit she learned a valuable lesson during her arrest. She now knew that punching a uniformed deputy in the mouth would earn her a quick trip to the carpet, a patch of rug burn on her face and an added charge of obstructing an officer.

Haley's arrest warrant carried a one hundred thousand dollar cash only bail since she was considered a flight risk with no roots in the community. She could not come up with this amount, so she remained in custody until her arraignment on Wednesday, November 1, 1995. Standing in front of Judge Salcido, Haley said she understood the charges against her and entered a plea of not guilty. Haley's court appointed public defender requested a bail reduction since she had a teenage daughter at home and was a responsible member of the community.

Prosecutor Tom Viloria pointed out to the court that Haley's daughter was now in the care and custody of relatives in Colorado which is most likely where Haley herself would head if she were to be let out on bail. After hearing both arguments, Judge Salcido denied the bail reduction and set a trial date for Evonne Haley of May 30, 1996 in the District Courtroom of the Honorable Judge Deborah Agosti.

With both Middleton and Haley now in custody, there was not much more work for the detectives assigned to the case to do. They had exhausted every investigative tool they could think of attempting to tie Haley to the two Reno murders. There was no doubt in anyone's mind that Haley at least had knowledge of the murders even if she wasn't an active participant in them, but proving it was another matter. Chasing a weak case could ruin the strong one they already had against her, so they decided to cut their losses and take what they could get.

The task force was disbanded and the detectives moved on to other cases. On Friday, November 3, 1995 the investigation into the murders of Kathy Powell and Thelma Davilla were officially listed as closed by arrest and pending prosecution. The detectives who worked the two cases had expended a tremendous amount of effort and displayed extroadonary investigative talents in order to solve the murders. They were proud of their accomplishments, but each of them knew a piece of the investigation would remain with them forever. They say when you look into the eyes of the devil, part of the devil will stare into your soul forever. None of them would ever forget the face of David Middleton.

Tom Viloria busied himself preparing for the upcoming trials of Middleton and Haley. Prosecuting Haley would be a fairly easy process since there was so much physical evidence against her. The evidence against Middleton was mainly circumstantial, but Viloria remained confident he could win a conviction against him. His flair for courtroom dramatics would allow him to present what evidence they did have in front of the jury in a way that would maximize its impact.

During his case preparation Viloria was contacted several times by the prosecutor's office from Montrose, Colorado. They were following the progress of the case with great interest and Viloria hoped they would eventually decide to prosecute Middleton for the murder of Buffy Rice-Donohue. At one point, Viloria told the Montrose District Attorney he was convinced Middleton had murdered Buffy and would assist in any way possible with prosecution in Colorado after the Reno case was finished. The District Attorney told Viloria that no decision had been made yet on whether they would be seeking an arrest warrant for Middleton in the Buffy Rice-Donohue case, and that was where the discussion ended.

On November 30, 1995 the prosecution was dealt their first major blow in the David Middleton case. The Nevada Supreme Court issued a decision to reverse the murder conviction of Clinton Frutiger. They agreed with the Public Defender's office that probable cause the involvement of criminal agency was involved in the death of Peggy Poulter had not been established at the grand jury phase, so the case never should have gone to trial. Clinton Frutiger was now a free man, and the popular opinion was that David Middleton would not be far behind.

Tom Viloria took the Supreme Court decision in stride. He expected it, so he was prepared. Viloria went into action before Mike Speccio could file another writ based on the Frutiger decision. On Friday, December 1, 1995 Viloria filed a motion with Judge Breen requesting the Public Defender's office be removed from Middleton's defense based on a conflict of interest. Evonne Haley was also being represented by that office and she and Middleton were being tried on a case where they were co-conspirators. Viloria requested that an attorney not associated with the Public Defender's office be appointed by the court to represent Middleton.

Speccio argued that his office had more time invested in Middleton's defense than Haley's, so they should remain on the Middleton case and appoint another attorney for Haley. Since Viloria's ex-parte motion was already filed, Judge Breen could not take Speccio's arguments under consideration. He would have to rule on the prosecution's motion as it stood, and the defense would not be able to take any further action until he did so.

Viloria beat Speccio to the punch, but he knew his preemptive strike was nothing more than a delay tactic. It would buy him time, and time was the one thing he needed most in order to prepare for the inevitable appeal that would be filed on Middleton's behalf based on the Frutiger decision. Rocky won round one, but the fight wasn't over until the final bell rang.

Chapter 50
OUTSIDE THE BOX

The day after Viloria filed his motion he went to work with a vengeance trying to find evidence that would strengthen his criminal agency argument in the murders of Kathy Powell and Thelma Davilla. Jenkins and Douglas were unofficially put back on the case with instructions to help Viloria in any way possible.

In a murder trial the defense has the leeway of bringing in as much expert testimony as the defendant can afford in order to prove his innocence. Nowhere was this better illustrated than in the acquittal of O.J. Simpson two months earlier. The prosecution in that case had more than enough evidence to convict Simpson of a double homicide, but his money bought him his freedom. David Middleton didn't have O.J.'s money, but the notoriety his attorneys would gain by getting him acquitted would be an investment in their future.

Viloria was well aware of the tactics utilized by Simpson's "Dream Team" defense and the furor still raging over the racial overtones resonating from that case. It was big news and he was certain Middleton's defense team would try to capitalize on the tidal wave of press the case generated. He needed to line up expert witnesses to bolster his own case, but he didn't have the assets available to the defense.

The main problem for the prosecution in the Middleton case would be proving criminal agency was involved in the deaths of Powell and Davilla. The first step in doing this would be dealing with the coroner's ruling of undetermined cause of death. Reasonable doubt that Kathy Powell could have died of natural causes would blow both cases out of the water. Viloria needed to convince a jury that Kathy Powell had been murdered in order to make criminal agency believable in the Davilla case. Without Powell, he would lose Davilla, so that was where he started with his preparations.

After lengthy research Viloria located someone who might be able to help him. Dr. Vincent Di Maio was the Chief Medical Examiner in San Antonio, Texas and was a certified expert witness in deaths by suffocation. Dr. Di Maio was fascinated by the Middleton case after Viloria called and asked him for help. He agreed to review the coroner's autopsy report pro bono and testify in any subsequent court proceedings if needed.

Viloria faxed all the documentation he had to Dr. Di Maio and heard back from him two days later. Dr. Di Maio first addressed the coroner's concerns about Kathy Powell possibly dying from a heart attack because she had been taking lithium. It was his expert opinion that even though Kathy Powell had some mild perivascular fibrosis in her heart, lithium use would not have caused heart failure. He said studies done in the 1990's showed long-term users of lithium did not die from heart disease at a rate greater than the general public.

Dr. Di Maio next addressed the bruises found on Kathy Powell's elbows and knees. He said these were the result of a struggle to free herself from a confined space—which in this case would have been the refrigerator. He said petechiae was only found in thirteen percent of the deaths caused by asphyxiation he had investigated, so the absence of it in Powell's case did not preclude this as cause of death. Dr. Di Maio said he would gladly testify under oath that it was his opinion the circumstances of Powell's disappearance and the condition of her body when found indicate that her death was a homicide. He also said the circumstances surrounding Thelma Davilla's disappearance and the discovery of her skeletal remains indicated her death was also a homicide.

The report by Dr. Di Maio was good news, but Viloria knew the defense could easily find an expert witness of their own to contradict that opinion. Such was the nature of expert testimony, so he needed more. It was only a matter of time before Judge Breen ruled on the motion to remove the Public Defender from Middleton's defense. Whoever ended up with the case would file a motion to drop the charges based on the Frutiger decision, so time was running out.

The National Homicide Investigators' conference takes place the first week of December every year. 1995 was Reno's turn to host the conference and the Middleton case was a hot topic with the detectives in attendance. As with most police conferences, most of the meaningful discussions take place at bars after the classes. True to form, Jenkins and Douglas were sitting at a bar in the El Dorado Casino with a group of detectives from different agencies filling them in on the Middleton case on Tuesday evening, December 5, 1995.

Jenkins explained the problem they were having proving criminal agency and asked if anyone had any suggestions. A redheaded Irish N.Y.P.D. detective with a ruddy complexion and too much Bushmills in him said, "You should check with the Canuks. I hear they are doing some weird shit with knot investigations up there."

The N.Y.P.D. detective's partner was slightly more sober. He said, "What Timmy meant to say is you might want to give the Royal Canadian Mounted Police a call. They have a guy in Vancouver who is a knot expert and he might be able to take a look at your case."

The next morning Jenkins called the North Vancouver office of the Royal Canadian Mounted Police and was put in touch with an investigator named John "J.J." Van Tassel. He was not only a knot expert, he was currently the *only* knot expert in modern law enforcement who had offered testimony in a court of law on the subject. He took an interest in the Middleton case and agreed to fly to Reno the next day to examine the ropes and knots that were used to bind the victims.

After thorough examination of all the knots used in both cases, Van Tassel submitted a report that would greatly aid the prosecution. He could not say all of the knots were tied by the same person, but he could accurately say all of the knots were the same type. He said he could testify that in his experience a killer in a frenzied state will use the same knot on every occasion as part of the modus operandi of his crime because his subconscious mind reverts back to the state of euphoria he experiences during his criminal acts.

More importantly, Van Tassel said the knots on both Powell and Davilla had tightened after they had been tied. He determined this after comparing the knots used to bind the bodies to the knots used on the ropes tied around the exterior of the sleeping bag Kathy Powell's body was secreted in. Even though these ropes were used as handles to lift the dead weight of her body, the knots did not tighten as much as those that were in the ropes used to bind her. That showed she must have struggled against the ropes for a prolonged period of time prior to her death. The knots found on the skeletal remains of Davilla were in the same strained condition.

They now had expert witnesses who could challenge the coroner's ruling and also say that Powell and Davilla were both alive when they were tied up. They still needed more, and another innocuous conversation was about to give it to them.

To show Van Tassel their appreciation Jenkins and Douglas took him out to dinner before his flight left for Vancouver. While discussing the case Jenkins said, "I still have the feeling we're missing something with the cause of death, but I think we have to get outside of the box to find it."

Eddie Dixon had accompanied the detectives to dinner. He said, "I don't know much about thinking outside the box, but I do know I can't stop thinking about what was going through that poor lady's head while she was dying *inside* of that box. That shit is gonna creep me out forever!"

Jenkins smiled and said, "Once again Eddie, you have proven you are a genius of your own sorts. We'll never know what Kathy Powell's thoughts were while trapped inside of that refrigerator, but we certainly owe her an effort to find out how long she was thinking them."

Chapter 51

THE GEEK SQUAD

An idea popped into Jenkins' head after Eddie Dixon made his innocent statement about Kathy Powell's thoughts while she was being held inside of the refrigerator. They had proof she was alive at some point while being held inside of the refrigerator, but if they could prove exactly how long she could remain alive they might be able to establish her cause of death in spite of the coroner's ruling.

There had to be a way to calculate how much oxygen a person Kathy Powell's size needed to sustain life, and just how much oxygen was available to her inside of the refrigerator. They already had expert witnesses and physical evidence to show she was held captive inside of the refrigerator with the door closed, so naturally the air supply would be limited to what was flowing through the two small holes drilled into the sides of the refrigerator.

The detectives working the Middleton case were knowledgeable enough to solve almost any criminal or legal problem thrown at them, but they all agreed this one was out of their realm of expertise. Since it was Eddie Dixon who sparked the idea in the first place, he went to the crime lab with Jenkins the next morning to see if they could get an answer to their question.

The forensic investigators listened intently while Jenkins explained the information he was looking for. The refrigerator was wheeled out of the evidence room and into the crime lab, and they spent the next hour taking measurements and doing calculations. After several exhaustive attempts the technicians relented that this type of problem was over their heads too.

One of the crime scene investigators who had come into the room to see what was going on said she had taken some night courses at the University of Nevada Reno's Engineering School. She told the detectives what they were looking for seemed more of an engineering problem than a forensic one, so maybe they should check there for help. It was a long shot, but it was better than none at all.

Jenkins called the University and was put in touch with Dr. Tariq Ahmed, the assistant professor in charge of the Civil Engineering program. Dr. Ahmed agreed to see them, and an hour later the two detectives were standing in his office waiting for him to return from instructing a morning class.

Dixon studied the framed certificates covering the office walls and remarked, "This guy has more degrees than a thermometer and enough letters behind his name to start his own alphabet. I always though of engineers as geeks, but if he can help us put Middleton away, I'll trade in my holster for a pocket protector in a heartbeat."

Dr. Ahmed walked into the office and introduced himself to the detectives. He was tall and lean with a dark Middle Eastern complexion, curly black hair, and wore black horn-rimmed glasses on his youthful looking face. He looked more like a student than a professor, but Jenkins and Dixon both smiled when they spotted the telltale pocket protector holding three pens in it in the pocket of his white button-down shirt.

When Jenkins finished explaining what they needed he expected to be told there was nothing the professor could do to help them. Instead, Dr. Ahmed calmly said, "This will be a very simple problem to solve. I will need to take a few measurements of my own of course, but then all I will have to do is prepare an oxygen flow in a confined space for human respiration calculation. If you need this quickly I can calculate the survivability time to fifteen minutes either way, but I can narrow that down to a more accurate time through further calculations."

Jenkins assured Dr. Ahmed that a fifteen-minute window of survivability would be more than adequate for what they needed. Dr. Ahmed opened his desk drawer and took out a common tape measure and a large calculator. He put them both into his briefcase and told the detectives he would be more than happy to accompany them right then to take the measurements. If the request surprised the doctor he certainly did not show it. His demeanor was so calm that one would have thought the detectives had asked him to solve a simple multiplication problem instead of calculate how long it took a murder victim to breath her last breaths.

The next day Dr. Ahmed presented a twelve-page report containing his calculations to the detectives. After reading through it they realized the only numbers they could understand in the report were the page numbers, but Dr. Ahmed agreed to explain his calculations in court if needed. The information the detectives needed the most was written in layman's terms on the cover page of the report. It read:

Subject: Oxygen Flow Calculation In A Confined Space For
          Human Respiration

Dear Ed,

With reference to our discussion, I am writing this letter to inform you of the results of my analysis regarding the subject mentioned above.

As shown in step 9 of my calculation, the oxygen utilization rate for human respiration is about 13.8 L/hr, (liters per hour), which is about 180 times greater than the conservative estimate of oxygen flow through the two holes in the refrigerator, (0.076 L/hr). Therefore, we can neglect this flow.

So my conclusion is that a person the size of your victim would die within about 5.5 hours. However, if oxygen partial pressure for human survivability is made available to me, I can calculate a more accurate time if you need it.

Sincerely,

Tariq Ahmed, Ph.D, P.E.

The detectives were elated by the report. They now had an expert witness who would testify that the maximum amount of time Kathy Powell could have survived inside of that refrigerator was 5.5. hours. Jenkins pulled out the first murder book they'd prepared and flipped it open to the section detailing the times Middleton visited his storage shed after Kathy Powell first disappeared.

His first visit to the storage shed was at 5:47 A.M. on Saturday, February 4, 1995. This was when they theorized he brought Kathy Powell to the shed and locked her in the refrigerator. Throughout that day he made periodic visits to the storage unit, but there was only an hour or two between visits. They would never know what he did to Kathy Powell during those visits, but they were certain she was alive and held captive inside of the refrigerator.

The timeline showed a gap of over twelve hours between Middleton's visit to the storage shed at 5:38 P.M. on Saturday, February 4th and his next visit at 6:19 A.M. on Sunday, February 5th. All the evidence they had gathered thus far led them to believe Kathy Powell had been held captive inside of the refrigerator whenever she was left alone in the storage shed. Based on the report from Dr. Ahmed, they could now say there was no way she could have survived inside of the refrigerator during that twelve hour time span between visits.

Even if Middleton hadn't planned to kill Kathy Powell, they could now prove she died at his hands during the commission of a felony. This was enough to prove criminal agency under the felony murder rule, and that was all they needed to get past any appeals based on the Frutiger decision. The only downside to the engineering report prepared by Dr. Ahmed was that word traveled fast in police circles, and the Major Crimes Unit quickly became known as *The Geek Squad.*

Chapter 52

JUSTICE

On Friday, January 5, 1996 Judge Breen issued his ruling on the removal of the Public Defender's office from Middleton's defense. He agreed with Viloria's motion and removed Mike Speccio and his staff from Middleton's defense.

A private attorney named Fred Pinkerton from Reno was appointed by the court to defend Middleton. Pinkerton was a skilled trial lawyer and would be a worthy adversary for the prosecution. His first act as Middleton's attorney was about as predictable as the January snow in the Sierra Nevada Mountains surrounding Reno.

On Wednesday, January 17, 1996 Pinkerton re-submitted Speccio's original Writ of Habeas Corpus to Judge Breen and asked him to take another look at in light of the Frutiger decision. The gauntlet was thrown down and the fight was now in Judge Breen's court.

The resubmission of the writ started a new media frenzy. The newspapers speculated that the murder charges against Middleton would be reversed just as they were in the Frutiger case. Interviews were done with the relatives of Kathy Powell and Thelma Davilla, and they all expressed their displeasure with the fact the court was even considering a reversal of the murder charges.

Kathy Powell's brother was quoted as saying, "I am very upset that there is even a remote possibility the court would reverse the murder charges against Middleton. If that decision is made, I think the people of Nevada have reason to be seriously concerned about their safety."

The television media also jumped on the case. The Maury Povich show televised taped interviews of the Rice family in Colorado and Middleton's Florida victim Alyssa Cervantes from her home in Miami. The interviews portrayed Middleton as a murdering predator who had been slipping through the cracks in the justice system his entire life, and it now appeared another chasm had just opened for him in Reno.

Tom Viloria seemed unfazed by the publicity or the possibility the murder charges might be reversed. Middleton's trial had once again been postponed until June 6, 1996, and Viloria had other matters to keep him occupied while he awaited Judge Breen's decision. Evonne Haley was set to go to trial soon and Viloria wouldn't allow anything to distract him from vigorously prosecuting her case.

Haley went to trial in Washoe County District Court on Monday, April 29, 1996. Her attorney filed a pre-trial motion that precluded the prosecution from mentioning anything about the Powell-Davilla murder investigations other than to say Haley was accused of using the credit card of a deceased person. Due to the publicity surrounding the case it was ludicrous to think anyone on Haley's jury panel did not know about the murder investigation, but the fact Viloria could not mention it made his job more difficult.

Viloria presented the two Good Guys employees, Detective Dave Wood and Detective Dave Jenkins as prosecution witnesses. He was allowed to introduce some photos of Middleton's storage unit into evidence, but only those that showed the location of evidence pertinent to the crimes Haley was charged with. The ominous refrigerator could be seen in the background of the photos, but no mention of it was made in court.

The stereo equipment, the red hand truck, the yellow messenger service windbreaker and the handwritten phone order receipt from Good Guys were also introduced into evidence. The last piece of evidence introduced were photos of Middleton's distinctive looking International Harvester truck that started the initial chain of events in the case rolling.

The defense only called one witness to the stand. Haley's nineteen-year-old son had flown in from Colorado to testify in his mother's defense. He had no knowledge of the crime, but testified to the fact his mother was an honest person who would never knowingly commit a crime. He said Haley had been manipulated by Middleton since she met him and he believed his mother honestly thought she was picking up legitimately purchased items at the Good Guys store.

Viloria did not cross examine the witness because the teenager appeared to be the only person in the courtroom to actually believe his mother was an honest person. Proving him wrong would do nothing to help his case, but keeping him on the stand might provoke sympathy for Haley from the jury.

Haley did not take the witness stand in her own defense, and never so much as looked at the jury throughout the two-day trial. She appeared nervous and jittery, and spent her entire time in the courtroom staring down at the table in front of her. Closing arguments in the case concluded at 2:00 in the afternoon on Tuesday, April 30, 1996. At 2:30 the jury informed Judge Agosti they had reached a verdict. Evonne Haley was found guilty on all counts and sentencing was set for May 31, 1996.

The pre-sentencing report prepared by the Nevada Department of Parole and Probation on Evonne Haley was favorable. They could not consider any other allegations of Haley's involvement in the Middleton case for their report since she wasn't charged in the murders. This was her first felony conviction, so they recommended she be given probation for the Good Guys case. Probation is the standard sentence in Nevada for a first time offender in a property crime.

Fortunately Judge Agosti was not bound by the report and she knew Evonne Haley was very much involved in other aspects of the Kathy Powell murder case. Judge Agosti sentenced Evonne Haley to seven years in the Nevada State Prison based on her conviction in the Good Guys case. She also sentenced her to another three years in prison for her initial charge of being under the influence of methamphetamine when Jenkins arrested her at the beginning of the investigation. Even though the sentences would run concurrently, Evonne Haley would not be eligible for parole for at least three and a half years.

Viloria closed the book on the devil's disciple and hoped to never again set eyes on her. He was pleased with the sentence, but not as much as the husband and wife from Colorado sitting in the spectators' section behind the prosecution table were. They still wore the buttons bearing their daughter's photo pinned to their shirts, and they prayed Buffy was smiling down from heaven as she watched a hysterical Evonne Haley being led from the courtroom in handcuffs.

Chapter 53

I'M READY FOR 'EM

On Monday, June 3, 1996 Judge Breen contacted all involved parties and advised them he had made a decision on the Writ of Habeas Corpus filed on Middleton's behalf. He scheduled a hearing in his courtroom at 9:00 A.M. on Thursday, June 6, 1996 to discuss his findings. The early rumors circulating from the courthouse were the news would not be good for the prosecution.

By 8:00 A.M. on the morning of the hearing, the white marble steps leading to the front entrance of the courthouse were crowded with spectators and news crews waiting to get inside. News trucks sporting satellite antennas were parked on side streets, and reporters were going over last minute instructions with their camera crews. All the local networks as well as FOX and CNN were represented. The press smelled a story, and they were on it like sharks on chum.

Tom Viloria sat calmly in the District Attorney's office discussing the prosecution's options with Dick Gammick and Chief Deputy District Attorney David Stanton. The unofficial word had already filtered down that Judge Breen would be reversing the murder charges against Middleton, but even without the murder charges he would not walk away a free man like Clinton Frutiger had.

The prosecution still had two strong kidnap cases and the credit card crimes to charge Middleton with. It was the District Attorney's opinion that they should move forward with prosecution on these charges and cut their losses on the murder charges. He was certain they could win a conviction resulting in life in prison for Middleton if they prosecuted him on these charges alone, but they might lose everything if they tried to fight the decision to drop the murder charges.

Viloria pointed out that a life sentence wouldn't really mean life, because Middleton would have the possibility of parole. A more realistic timeframe for his prison sentence if he *was* convicted of these crimes would be twenty years. That would put him at fifty-five-years-old when he became eligible for parole, and that was definitely still young enough to kill again. Not fighting the ruling would also set a precedent for some very poor case law, and that was something Viloria wanted no part of.

The only way to possibly fight Judge Breen's inevitable ruling on the murder charges was to get the Nevada Supreme Court to reverse their own ruling in the Frutiger case. Court decisions often get reversed due to the interpretations of different judges looking into new and changing laws. But as District Attorney Gammick pointed out to his young prosecutor, *no one* had ever gone in front of a group of Supreme Court judges and asked them to reverse a decision they themselves had made less than six months prior.

Viloria shrugged his shoulders and simply said, "I'm ready for 'em."

Gammick gave Viloria the go ahead to file an appeal as soon as Judge Breen announced his decision, but made it perfectly clear that other employment options might be on the horizon for him if his plan backfired. Viloria already had most of the appellate paperwork prepared in anticipation of the decision and he would spearhead the fight while Gammick and his chief assistant handled the press.

Viloria was seated at the prosecution table when Middleton was led into the courtroom at 8:45 A.M. Middleton was once again dressed in a blue jail jumpsuit with his hands cuffed to a belly chain. But this time he was smiling like a kid at Christmas as he took a seat next to his attorney Fred Pinkerton at the defense table.

The second row of spectator seats behind the prosecution table had once again been reserved for the families of the victims. Bonnie and Walt Rice were in attendance and had been accepted into this group of survivors. They still wore their pins with Buffy's photo on them, but there was a new twist at this proceeding. The members of Powell's and Davilla's families had followed suit and made pins with photos of their own loved ones on them. They wore them on their shirts in plain view so there was no doubt which side of the conflict that particular row of spectators were routing for.

None of the task force detectives were in attendance. There would be no testimony offered in this proceeding, and they already were reasonably certain what Judge Breen's decision would be. They wanted to avoid the media circus that would certainly follow the proceeding and trusted Viloria to speak for them in the case.

At precisely 9:00 Judge Breen entered the courtroom through the door leading to his chambers behind the judge's dais. After everyone was seated, he addressed his audience. He said, "I have reached a decision in this matter, but I would first like to explain what the State law has given me to work with while reaching my conclusion.

Based on the recent Frutiger decision I have had to divide the evidence in this case into two categories. The first is that the two victims were murdered, and the second is that it was the defendant who murdered them."

The courtroom was eerily quiet as Judge Breen continued. "Now the prosecution has assured this court they have plenty of evidence to prove the second category, but in light of the Frutiger decision I am not allowed to consider any of that. The only thing I can focus on is the corpus delicti, which in the case of murder is the body. I can only ask myself one question, and that is 'what does the body tell us?'

Viewed alone, the body of Ms. Davilla tells us nothing, and the body of Ms. Powell tells us very little. Based on the recent Supreme Court decision this is the only evidence I can consider, so I must rule in favor of the defense on their Writ of Habeas Corpus. Based on the new standards of evidence set forth by the State Supreme Court, I find the prosecution has not adequately shown criminal agency was involved in either of these deaths. The two counts of murder Mr. Middleton has been charged with will be dropped, but the other charges will remain."

There was an uproar in the courtroom and Judge Breen banged his gavel to bring the crowd to order. Middleton smiled broadly and shook hands with his attorney. Pinkerton then stood up and asked Judge Breen to set bail in the amount of ten thousand dollars for his client since this was now not a murder case.

Viloria stood and objected to bail in any amount. He reminded Judge Breen that Middleton was still being charged with two kidnaps, one of which involved torture. He also informed the judge he would be filing an appeal to the State Supreme Court on his decision before the end of the work day.

Judge Breen sided with the prosecution and ruled Middleton would be held in custody without bail until trial. The date of that trial would be set after the State Supreme Court ruled on the prosecution's appeal. The judge then adjourned the proceeding and the reporters rushed outside to begin their interviews with people as they left.

Viloria left the courthouse undetected through a side door, but Gammick met with the press on the front steps of the courthouse to give a statement. He said, "The dismissal of Middleton's murder charges shows me the justice system is broken and it is up to us to fix it."

Chief Deputy District Attorney Dave Stanton added, "There are some very savvy criminals out there, and I think this gives them a recipe for how to commit murder and not be held responsible."

A reporter shouted out a question asking Gammick what he thought of Judge Breen and the Frutiger decision in general. Gammick answered, "I hate to seem like I'm ducking and dodging you, but we're just not ready to comment on anything in that area. All I can tell you is we're going to put this right back on the Supreme Court. They can let Middleton go on these murders if they want, but I'm sure as hell not gonna."

The attorneys for the defense had a different view of Judge Breen's decision when they were interviewed. Fred Pinkerton said, "Frankly, I'm proud. It's good to see that the system is working and we're dealing with the law instead of popular opinion."

Attorney John Petty who wrote the original writ said, "We don't want judges who make decisions based on what's politically popular, we want them to make decisions on the law. That is what Judge Breen did here today."

The reporters then moved on to interview some of the victim's family members. Kathy Powell's brother Jeff said, "Naturally I'm very upset with the decision. I was kind of expecting it, but now the reality is sinking in. I think Middleton's background as a police officer gives him knowledge a lot of people wouldn't have and helps him to manipulate the system. I just hope we can turn this around."

Walt Rice said, "It really sinks hard in my heart that this can happen. I have a lot of faith in the District Attorney's office in

Reno, so I don't think this is the end of the line for Middleton. But still, I'd like to see Montrose file murder charges against him in case he gets away with it here."

Dave Jenkins had a different opinion than those being interviewed, perhaps because he was looking at a bigger picture. Privately he said, "Judge Breen made the only decision he could based on what he had to work with. He dropped the charges against Middleton so we could go after the Supreme Court on Frutiger. If he would have let the murder charges stand at the District Court level, Middleton would have beat his conviction on appeal. Then we'd never get him because of double jeopardy. Judge Breen is a stud."

Chapter 54

ROCK AND ROLL TIME

It is said that the wheels of justice turn slowly, but this was not the case in the Nevada State Supreme Court ruling on the appeal of Judge Breen's decision to dismiss the murder charges against David Middleton. With speed that even surprised the District Attorney's office, the court ruled in favor of the prosecution and reinstated the murder charges against Middleton on July 25, 1996.

Some attribute the speedy decision to Viloria's gathering of expert witnesses and his excellent documentation of facts related to the involvement of criminal agency in the deaths. Others say the court anticipated the appeal and they were waiting to overturn what they knew to be a bad decision in the first place. Whatever the reason, Middleton was once again facing murder charges.

The State Supreme Court stopped short of reversing their entire decision on the Frutiger appeal, but they did say every case needed to be looked at on its own merit and corpus delicti should be based on any relevant evidence available. In the Frutiger case the Court said evidence used by the prosecution linked the suspect to the victim, but not to his involvement in her death. They specifically cited that even though he was driving Peggy Poulter's car and using her credit cards, it did nothing to establish criminal agency being involved in her death.

The Court also cited the medical evidence presented by the defense in the Frutiger case. Peggy Poulter did have identifiable medical problems that could have caused death by natural causes. This was not the case with either Kathy Powel or Thelma Davilla because both women were reasonably healthy.

The State Supreme Court decision also clarified Judge Breen's opinion that he could not look at any evidence not offered by the bodies themselves in determining criminal agency. The Supreme Court decision read in part:

> This conclusion is not mandated by our decision in Frutiger. The court must consider and weigh all evidence offered which bears on the question of death by criminal agency. In this case, the circumstances of the disappearance of the women, the discoveries of their bodies in remote locations, tied with ropes, wrapped in garbage bags, bitten severely, clearly creates a reasonable inference of criminal agency. Furthermore, unlike in Frutiger where the weight of medical evidence indicated a likelihood of death by natural causes, in this case there is no evidence to rebut the inference of death by criminal agency. The District Court erred in not considering at least the circumstances of the disappearances of the women and the discoveries of their bodies. There is ample evidence by those

circumstances alone tending to prove that Powell and Davilla died by criminal agency.

With respect to the question of the felony murder charges, we conclude that at the preliminary hearing the State met its burden of proving corpus delicti for the two felony counts of kidnapping and murder during the commission of a felony.

We reverse the District Court's order granting respondent's pretrial petition for a Writ of Habeas Corpus and we remand this matter to the District Court for further proceedings. It will be up to the trial jury to weigh all relevant evidence presented and then conclude if corpus delicti has been met beyond a reasonable doubt.

Nev. 1996
Sheriff, Washoe County v. Middleton
112 Nev. 956, 921 P.2d 282

With that decision the State Supreme Court was able to save face by not admitting they had erred in the Frutiger case, while at the same time clarify the facts of their ruling so they did not hinder future murder prosecutions. Also important was the State Supreme Court did not refer to any of the expert witness documentation Viloria had gathered for his appellate motion. They simply ruled that only probable cause of criminal agency and not proof beyond a reasonable doubt was needed at the preliminary hearing, and the State had met this burden of proof.

Since the expert witness evidence wasn't referenced in the decision, it was not yet divulged to the defense. Viloria could now keep that information to himself and bring it out only when needed. This was a major victory for the prosecution in general, but especially for Tom Viloria. Not only did he go into the ring the underdog, he beat the odds and came out on top.

It was a very happy Dick Gammick who called a press conference that afternoon to announce murder charges against David Middleton were being reinstated. He said, "We're back in business, and it's rock and roll time!"

Fred Pinkerton was much more subdued during his interview regarding the State Supreme Court decision. He said, "I try not to act emotionally in these things. My own reaction is the Supreme Court's decision is its decision, so now it's time to go to work." Pinkerton acknowledged his client might now face the death penalty, but said he probably wouldn't go to trial for at least a year and a lot could happen in that time.

Kathy Powell's brother Jeff acted as spokesperson to the press for his family and the family of Thelma Davilla. He said the families were elated the murder charges had been reinstated and they were happy with the State Supreme Court ruling.

Bonnie and Walt Rice also expressed similar sentiments during a telephone interview. Bonnie added the only downside to the decision was now that Middleton was back on trial for murder in Reno, she feared the Montrose District Attorney would not file charges on him for murdering their daughter in Colorado. The authorities in Montrose were still taking a wait and see approach on the Buffy Rice-Donohue case.

The most moving interview came when a reporter from the *Reno Gazette Journal* called Florida victim Alyssa Cervantes and asked her what she thought of the latest development. She said, "I feel a little bit more at ease. I was a little bit edgy when I found out they could drop the charges and he could just walk away from everything. He ruined my life and he practically walked away from what he did to me. It's really scary if you think about it. I thank God every day for the detectives in Reno who took that monster off the street, and I also pray to Him to give attorney Tom Viloria the strength and courage to make sure Middleton never goes free again."

The detectives and the prosecutor felt a bit guilty when they read that quote in the paper the next day. While Alyssa Cervantes was thanking God and praying for them, they were in various states of inebriation sitting at a bar celebrating while they discussed how nice it would be if the court ruled Middleton could get death by suffocating inside of a refrigerator instead of by lethal injection. Then they thought about it and stopped feeling guilty at all. Like Douglas said, "Even the Big Man would understand that one."

Chapter 55

INVISIBLE VICTIMS

At a hearing on Friday, August 30, 1996 Dick Gammick advised Judge Breen that the District Attorney's office would be seeking the death penalty for David Middleton. He based this decision on the aggravating circumstances of torture and depravity of mind.

Judge Breen set a trial date of May 5, 1997, but everyone knew this was not a realistic timeframe for the defense case preparation. They were now facing a capital murder case and nine months would not be enough time to mount a defense in a case such as this. The police murder book alone totaled in excess of 2,500 pages, and that did not include evidentiary reports or expert witness testimony.

The prosecution's case was built mainly on circumstantial evidence, so the job of the defense would be to prevent as much of that as they could from being introduced in court. The way to do that was through pre-trial motions, and those took time. It was said from the start that this case would be won or lost long before the jury heard the first witness, so the pre-trial motions were the most important job of the defense and the prosecution.

Fred Pinkerton was one of Reno's top defense attorneys and no stranger to murder trials built on circumstantial evidence. In 1985 he represented former world-class skier Craig Holliday in a

Reno case where he was accused of murdering his mother for her estate. The Holliday case was based largely on circumstantial evidence, and Pinkerton gained an acquittal for his client.

Pinkerton told a reporter, "I'm a trial lawyer, and a circumstantial case is a trial lawyer's dream. After you go through a couple of them you learn a lot about presentation and analysis of evidence."

Pinkerton went back to the beginning of the case and started taking apart the prosecution's arguments one piece at a time. This meant Viloria would also have to go back to the beginning to defend the State's case. It was a time consuming process, but one that needed to be done in order to get a conviction.

The first motion Pinkerton submitted to the court was to sever the Davilla case from the Powell one and try them separately. He argued the joinder of the cases could prejudice his client, because the jury might cumulate the various crimes charged and find guilt when they might not do so if the crimes were tried separately. There was also a possibility the jury might develop feelings of hostility toward Middleton since they were hearing testimony about several crimes he was being charged with instead of one crime.

Even though this argument had been made at the Justice Court level, Judge Breen had to rule on it again for the trial court. After reading Viloria's briefs and hearing lengthy discussion from both sides, he ruled the joinder of the two cases was proper. The cases would be tried together and any further discussion on the matter could be taken up in appeals court should the case get to that level.

The next defense motion requested a change of venue for the trial based on pre-trial publicity. Pinkerton cited interviews done with the victim's families as well as the Maury Povich interviews done with the Rice's and Alyssa Cervantes. Viloria pointed out that Middleton himself had done a television interview with *Inside Addition* proclaiming his innocence, and a large part of the pre-trial publicity had come from his former defense attorney Mike Speccio. The case already had achieved national news coverage, so moving it out of Reno would have no effect on the outcome whatsoever.

Judge Breen denied the change of venue request citing the fact modern electronic media would expose potential jurors to pre-trial publicity no matter where they moved the case. They would have to rely on their voir dire of the jurors and jury instruction to keep the publicity from having an effect on the trial.

The process dragged on at a snail's pace until the defense and prosecution found themselves still doing battle outside of the courtroom as the court date approached. On April 9, 1997 Pinkerton went to Judge Breen and asked for an extension on the trial date. There had been so many pre-trial motions that he and his staff were not prepared to go to trial in April. He blamed this partially on the fact that the District Attorney's office had just turned over an abundance of documentation that they allegedly *forgot* to give the defense during the initial discovery phase of the proceedings.

Judge Breen was not happy about the request, but he set a new trial date for August 11, 1997. He cautioned both the defense and the prosecution that this would be the last extension he would give, and trial would start on that date regardless of whether or not they were ready.

The new court date was more than two years after the initial discovery of Kathy Powell's body. Witness testimony could be unreliable even if the events were fresh in their minds, but time caused people to forget certain things. A good defense attorney could make a witness who was completely credible right after an incident look like he was a liar in front of a jury if he became confused. Any contradiction in witness testimony, no matter how slight, could cause a reasonable doubt in the mind of a juror and end up with an acquittal or hung jury. Viloria was ready to go to trial, and he was even less happy with the postponement than the judge was.

He also wasn't happy with some of Judge Breen's rulings on the defense pre-trial motions. The court ruled the prosecution could not introduce any of Middleton's prior acts from his conviction in Florida or any of his allegations of police on-duty misconduct during the case-in-chief. This included the Santeria priest testimony and ritualistic rape of the civilian police employee. The prior acts might be brought in during the penalty phase, but Judge Breen ruled Santeria was a religion protected under the First

Amendment so Middleton's involvement in it could not be used against him.

Viloria moved to introduce the animal head voodoo dagger since it had been found in Middleton's storage shed and was possibly used in the commission of the crimes he was being charged in. Pinkerton objected, saying this was a tool used in the Santeria religion so it was also protected by the First Amendment. After more lengthy debate Judge Breen ruled a photo of the dagger could be introduced into evidence, but the long horn at the end of the animal skull handle would have to be cut from the photo.

Viloria relented to the judge's decision, but the horn was what he wanted to get in front of the jury since this is what Middleton allegedly used to anally rape his victim in Florida. He was confident he would have been able to steer the testimony about the dagger to that crime if he could get in front of the jury, but he now lost that option.

Judge Breen also ruled that no testimony or evidence related to the Buffy Rice-Donohue murder could be introduced during trial. Since Middleton had been neither charged nor convicted in that crime, anything related to it could not be used against him. If the Montrose Police had at least charged him with the murder, Viloria might have been able to introduce evidence showing prior bad acts. Middleton was not even listed as a suspect in that case, so he had the right to claim innocence until proven guilty.

The one major battle Viloria won was Pinkerton's motion to deny Bonnie and Walt Rice access to the court proceedings. They still wore the buttons with Buffy's photo on them every time they showed up in court, and Pinkerton said this would prejudice the jury since Middleton had not been charged in that crime. Judge Breen had already denied a defense motion to keep the press out of the courtroom since this was an open proceeding. He cited the same precedent and denied the request to keep the Rice's out of the courtroom. As long as they did not disrupt the proceedings, they had the right to be there.

Viloria wasn't concerned with the presence of Bonnie and Walt Rice influencing the jury, because he knew it wouldn't. He knew he was going to get a guilty verdict no matter who was sitting in the courtroom. He wanted Bonnie and Walt Rice in that courtroom because in their eyes David Middleton was being tried for three murders—not two. The third victim David Middleton was on trial for murdering would be invisible to the jurors, but she would be seen clearly in the eyes of her family, her killer *and* the man who was prosecuting him.

Chapter 56

SQUEAK

Jury selection began at precisely 9:00 A.M. on the morning of Monday, August 11, 1997. During the trial phase a defendant is allowed to dress in a manner that does not make him look guilty in the eyes of the jury, so Middleton's attorney supplied him with an appropriate outfit. He wore a dark blue suit, white shirt and blue and red striped tie. His curly hair was pulled into a ponytail and he wore gold wire-rimmed glasses. He looked more like an attorney than a murderer as he sat at the defense table—except very few attorneys wore a belly chain and handcuffs under their suit coats.

Webster defined the word *peer* as a person of equal standing, so to say Middleton would be tried by a jury of his peers would be a euphemism. In order to make the statement correct the jury would have to be made up of twelve sociopath serial killers who just happened to be pathological liars in addition to their other attributes.

Nevertheless, by the end of the day a jury agreed upon by both the defense and the prosecution had been selected to hear the case. The panel consisted of six males and six females. Two of the women were African American and one of the males was Hispanic. An African American male and an Oriental female were also selected as alternates. This diverse group proportionately reflected the demographics of the area.

Before jury selection began Judge Breen cautioned the prospective jurors that the case would probably last at least two weeks, and much of the testimony and evidence offered during the trial would be graphic. He also informed them the District Attorney's office had filed intent to seek the death penalty if Middleton was convicted, so the jurors would be ruling on that issue too. The fourteen people ultimately selected as jurors agreed to stay in for the long run.

The trial began at 9:00 the next morning when Viloria presented his opening arguments to the jury. Dressed in an impeccably pressed grey pinstriped suit and crisp white shirt, Viloria stood in front of the jury box and outlined the prosecution's case for the twelve people who would ultimately decide David Middleton's fate.

He told the jurors the defense would be trying to convince them Kathy Powell and Thelma Davilla both died of natural causes that had nothing to do with David Middleton. He then assured them that by the time the prosecution completed its case, there would be no doubt in any of their minds that both women would be alive and well had Middleton never crossed their paths.

Viloria admitted the prosecution's case was made up of mainly circumstantial and forensic evidence. He said the reason for this was the only other type of evidence available was eyewitness testimony, and Middleton had made sure none of that existed. There were only three people who knew exactly what happened to Kathy Powell and Thelma Davilla. Two of them were dead, and the other wasn't talking. Viloria assured the jurors that by the time he finished laying out all of the State's evidence, there would be no doubt in their minds David Middleton caused the deaths of Kathy Powell and Thelma Davilla.

When it was Pinkerton's turn to address the jury he told them the State built their case on nothing but pure conjecture in an attempt to pin two unsolved deaths on Middleton. He said they would hear testimony backed up by expert witnesses that Kathy Powell's death wasn't a homicide. And no one had *any* idea how Thelma Davilla died, because her body yielded no evidence.

Pinkerton said the defense did not condone the actions Middleton took after discovering Kathy Powell had died and they would stipulate to the fact he made a mistake by disposing of her body in the manner he did. But that mistake did not constitute the crime of murder, or any other crime currently written into statute. He then alleged the charges related to Davilla's death were nothing more than a matter of the police finding a scapegoat already in custody to close the case with.

As to the charges relating to the Good Guys case, Pinkerton told the jurors the police already had a suspect in custody for that. He said the defense would show Middleton was guilty of nothing more than using poor judgment and putting trust in the woman he loved. Pinkerton's last statement caused Bonnie Rice to grimace as if a foul odor just entered the room.

At 10:00 A.M. Viloria called Officer Pat Dreelan as the first witness for the prosecution. Dreelan described in great detail

every aspect of his dumpster-diving adventure the night Kathy
Powell's body was discovered. Viloria asked his witness how he
could so vividly remember the incident in such great detail more
than two years after the fact. Officer Dreelan stated under oath that
he still had nightmares about finding Kathy Powell, so
remembering that night was all too easy for him. The defense
declined to cross examine.

Detective Dave Jenkins was the next witness to take the
stand. The jury did not get to hear testimony regarding the original
incriminating statement Middleton made to Jenkins during his first
interview. The defense had won a motion to keep the spontaneous
statement Middleton made about possibly having knowledge of
Kathy Powell's death out of court, since it was their opinion
Miranda Rights should have been given to him before he was
physically taken to the Police Records section that day.

But Jenkins *was* allowed to testify to everything else he did
during the investigation, and his testimony alone seemed like it
would be enough to convict Middleton. Several jurors shook their
heads in disgust when Jenkins told of Middleton's statement that
he found Kathy Powell bound and dead when he returned to her
apartment after going to the store to buy liquor. Middleton didn't
seem to notice the jurors' looks of disbelief because he never made
eye contact with them throughout the proceedings.

Viloria led Jenkins' testimony to the discovery of the
storage shed just before court was about to recess for the day. The
timing of the testimony relating to the discovery of the torture

chamber and the refrigerator was carefully planned by the prosecutor so the imagery would remain with the jurors throughout the night and become ingrained in their subconscious. What happened next was *not* planned, but since Viloria was known to have a flare for dramatics at trial, everyone who knew him swore it was.

The Judge ruled that the prosecution could have the refrigerator brought into the courtroom so Viloria could show it to the jury. The photos introduced at the preliminary hearing of the demonstration using the forensic investigator inside of the refrigerator to reenact Kathy Powell's body position were already on display in the courtroom along with the other crime scene photos. But the refrigerator itself would be the most compelling piece of evidence introduced by the prosecution.

An evidence technician was standing by in a storage room down the hall from the courtroom with the refrigerator loaded onto a wooden dolly. The dolly was the type used by furniture movers and was nothing more than a carpeted wooden rectangle with a plastic coaster-type wheel mounted on each corner. The bailiff phoned the evidence technician to tell him they were ready for the refrigerator, and the courtroom was deathly quiet as everyone waited for its arrival.

An eerie sound could be heard in the distance as everyone in the courtroom turned their attention to the doors leading to the hallway. The sound was faint at first, but grew steadily louder by the second. It was a rhythmic staccato sound of *eak, eak, eak.*

Ordinarily the sound probably wouldn't have attracted much attention, but in a silent courtroom filled with murder photos and stories of death, the noise was almost as frightening as the man seated at the defense table himself.

The noise seemed almost deafening by the time the evidence technician wheeled the refrigerator into the courtroom, and it was then the origin of the sound was discovered. One of the wheels on the dolly was badly in need of lubrication, and the steady squeaking noise drew even more attention to the refrigerator of death as it was brought to the front of the courtroom.

One of the jurors later said the most memorable part of the trial for him was that steady *eak, eak, eak* as the refrigerator was wheeled into the courtroom. He said it was almost as if Kathy Powell was calling to them from her place in the afterlife.

The squeaky wheel was probably nothing more than coincidence, but unfortunately cops don't believe in coincidences. Tom Viloria became a legend in police folklore that day, because by the time the story made its way to the cop watering holes that night there was no coincidence about it. The story of a young prosecutor sitting in a darkened aisle of a Home Depot the night before trial searching through racks of wooden dollies until he found one with just the right *squeak* would live forever. Viloria never admitted having anything to do with the squeaky wheel—but he never denied it either.

Chapter 57

DON'T CHEAT THE HANGMAN

The prosecution finished direct examination of Dave Jenkins at 10:00 A.M. on Thursday, August 14, 1997. After hearing two full days of testimony from Jenkins, the jury had a good understanding of why the deaths of Kathy Powell and Thelma Davilla were investigated as homicides, how they were linked together and attributed to one suspect, and how that suspect came to be identified as David Middleton.

During cross examination the defense hammered Jenkins on the marathon interview and made allegations that the only reason Middleton talked to the police at all is that he was promised he would not be charged with murder. Jenkins remained poised and confident during this cross examination. He assured the court the interview was purely voluntary, no promises were made and it was ended as soon as Middleton said he didn't want to talk to them anymore. He then added that Middleton really didn't tell them anything helpful to the investigation during the interview anyway.

The defense then changed course and asked Jenkins if the police had ever explored the possibility that a third person was involved in the murder of Kathy Powell. The inference was that Middleton was telling the truth about returning to Powell's apartment and finding her dead, but the police were so focused on him that they did not investigate the involvement of another person in the murder.

Jenkins simply stated that once they identified Middleton as a suspect, the evidence they gathered was so overwhelming that it would have been a waste of resources to look anywhere else. There were no further questions, and Jenkins was excused from the witness stand.

Viloria spent the next day and a half bringing detectives, crime scene technicians and forensic investigators to the stand to testify about their involvement in the investigation. By the time court recessed for the weekend at 4:30 P.M. on Friday, August 15, 1997, all of the forensic evidence linking Middleton to the two murders had been introduced.

The jury was not sequestered, but Judge Breen instructed them not to talk about the case or pay attention to any publicity generated by it. Given the amount of news coverage the trial was getting, that was akin to telling a child not to look under the tree on Christmas morning.

The court reconvened at 9:00 in the morning on Monday, August 18, 1997. The jury first heard testimony from the two Good Guys employees who completed the transaction where Kathy Powell's credit card was used. The fact that Evonne Haley had already been found guilty of using Middleton's truck to pick up the stereo equipment was allowed into testimony since her case was already adjudicated. Pinkerton also did not fall prey to the trap his predecessor landed in by questioning whether a salesperson who talks to hundreds of people a day on the phone could tell whether the caller was a man or a woman, so neither witness was cross examined.

Viloria then began calling his expert witnesses to the stand. The first to testify was John "J.J." Van Tassel of the Royal Canadian Mounted Police. None of the jurors had ever seen a Mounty in person, and they seemed a bit disappointed when Van Tassel walked into court wearing a dark blue business suit instead of a red serge uniform and black riding boots. Their disappointment ended after Van Tassel took the stand and recited his resume to the court.

In addition to offering testimony on knots in several Canadian cases, Van Tassel had just returned from Boulder, Colorado where he assisted investigators by examining knots in the John Bennett Ramsey murder case. That case was on the forefront of every American newspaper, so the fact Van Tassel had been called in to help on it lent more credence to his testimony in the Middleton trial.

Viloria used a PowerPoint projector to display photos of the knots tied in the ropes used to bind Kathy Powell and the ropes found on the remains of Thelma Davilla. Van Tassel patiently explained the similarities in all of the knots and how he could tell the victims had been struggling against the ropes. The jury seemed mesmerized by the testimony as Van Tassel's explanation made the knots almost seem to come alive before them. The effective display of knot imagery was more Viloria theatrics—and it worked.

Pinkerton only asked Van Tassel two questions during cross examination. Could Van Tassel tell if all the knots he examined where tied by the same person, and could he tell if any of the knots were tied by David Middleton? Van Tassel answered no to both questions and Pinkerton said he had nothing further for the witness.

Since Viloria had anticipated this line of questioning, he asked Van Tassel on re-direct just what he could tell about the person who tied the knots. It was then that Van Tassel introduced his testimony about a person's frenzied state of mind reverting to the knot he was most familiar with and the feelings of euphoria a killer might get each time he tied that knot. These statements coming from the world's foremost and possibly *only* knot expert were damaging to Middleton, and the look on Pinkerton's face said he knew he'd made a mistake by opening the line of questioning.

The next witness called to the stand by the prosecution was Dr. Vincent Di Maio. After being sworn in Dr. Di Maio told the jury that in addition to being the Chief Medical Examiner in San Antonio, Texas, he was also a consultant in forensic pathology. Dr. Di Maio said he had personally performed roughly two thousand autopsies and had been offering expert testimony in cause of death cases for five years.

Viloria then asked Dr. Di Maio what his opinion was on the cause and manner of the deaths of Kathy Powell and Thelma

Davilla. Dr. Di Maio said, "Based on all the evidence I have examined in these two cases, if the deaths would have occurred in my jurisdiction the causes of death would have been listed as undetermined, and the manner of death would be homicide. I feel the method of death for Ms. Powell was asphyxia most probably due to suffocation."

When asked about the method of death for Thelma Davilla, Dr. Di Maio said, "In view of the circumstance surrounding her death and the fashion in which her body was found, it is my opinion this death was also a homicide. Due to the condition of the body I could not go any further with the manner of death. Knowing what happened to Ms. Powell suggests that Ms. Davilla was also asphyxiated, but I would not be able to rule out shooting or stabbing either."

Dr. Di Maio's last statement weighed heavily with the jurors. They had already been shown photos of two guns and the voodoo machete—minus the menacing horn of course—that were taken from Middleton's storage shed. Viloria didn't have to convince the jurors *how* Middleton killed his victims, only that he *did* kill them. The fact he had now shown the jurors three possible scenarios involving the manner of Thelma Davilla's death greatly strengthened his case.

The defense elected not to cross examine Dr. Di Maio since they would be calling expert witnesses of their own to refute his testimony. Judge Breen then recessed the court for lunch, but before trial resumed in the afternoon the bailiff brought him a note from the jury foreman. The note said the jurors were somewhat confused by the description of the area where Thelma Davilla's remains were found, and they requested a site visit before they heard any further testimony.

The judge granted the request, but since Middleton and his attorneys had the right to be present during the site survey it would take time to put the trip together. Court was adjourned for the day and all parties were told to meet at the courthouse at 9:00 the next morning for the trip to the site. Due to safety concerns he advised the attorneys of this in his chambers so the press and public would not know about it. He also placed a gag order on this particular part of the proceedings until the trip was completed.

At 9:00 A.M. on Tuesday, August 19, 1997 the twelve jurors and two alternates were loaded onto a chartered bus for their twenty-five mile ride to the gravesite. Armed deputies were placed in the seats directly in front of and behind the jurors for security. Judge Breen along with the defense and prosecution attorneys rode in the front of the bus. Two marked sheriff's cars each carrying four heavily armed S.W.A.T. officers were used as escorts in front of and behind the bus.

A sheriff's van with blacked out windows and a heavy mesh screen separating the driver and passenger compartments trailed the motorcade. The van was driven by another S.W.A.T. officer and his partner sat in the passenger seat with a twelve-gauge shotgun cradled in his lap. Middleton rode in the back seat of the van with Dave Jenkins and John Douglas sitting on either side of him. Sitting in the seat directly behind Middleton was Eddie Dixon, dressed in black Reno P.D. S.W.A.T. fatigues with a C.A.R.-15 assault rifle hanging from his neck in a tactical sling.

Detective Larry Canfield was waiting for the jurors when the bus and escort vehicles pulled up Dog Valley Road and stopped at the location where Thelma Davilla was found. It was a bright sunny morning and the temperature was already hovering around ninety degrees. The Sheriff's S.W.A.T. team ringed the perimeter of the area for security as Detective Canfield led the judge and jurors on a tour of the site.

Middleton stood in the shade underneath a group of trees with Jenkins, Douglas and Dixon watching the jurors examine the area. Middleton was allowed to dress in a suit for the trip since he would be visible to the jurors. His hands were cuffed to the belly chain under his jacket, but the judge agreed with the defense team that for appearance reasons the police could not use ankle cuffs on him.

At one point Middleton looked over his left shoulder away from the activity and toward the glistening Truckee River running through the valley below them. Eddie Dixon patted his C.A.R.-15 and said, "Please don't think about running, Mr. Middleton. I'm too old and out of shape to chase you and I'd hate to cheat the hangman."

Middleton turned and smiled his evil grin at Dixon, but the smile quickly faded when he saw Evidence Eddie had a look in his eyes that scared even the devil himself. There was no doubt in his mind a morning run would not be in his plans for the day.

Chapter 58

REST

The field trip to the Verdi dump site set the trial back one full day. When court reconvened at 9:00 A.M. on Wednesday, August 20, 1997 Viloria told Judge Breen the prosecution had only four witnesses left to testify. He then called Dr. Louis Patetta as his first witness of the day.

Dr. Patetta was the orthodontist who took the dental impression of Middleton. He testified that he took the mold after Detectives Jenkins and Douglas brought Middleton to his Reno office with a seizure order. He said he personally took the impression and subsequently turned it over to Forensic Dentist Raymond Rawson.

The only questions the defense had for Dr. Patetta were regarding chain of custody for the dental impression. Once that was established the witness was excused.

The next prosecution witness was Dr. Rawson, who testified that he examined the bite marks found on Kathy Powell's torso and later matched them to the dental impression taken from David Middleton. Viloria used his PowerPoint projector to display a large color photo of the bite mark to Kathy Powell's left breast on the screen in front of the courtroom. Blood and bruising could be clearly seen in and around the teeth marks in the photo.

Because of the bleeding Dr. Rawson said he could tell the victim was still alive when she was bitten. He then told the jury that the depth of the teeth marks and the bruising meant the victim would have been in a great deal of pain when she was bitten.

Viloria asked Dr. Rawson if in his opinion a bite such as that would have caused a person to scream in pain. The defense objection to the question was overruled, and Dr. Rawson said a person would definitely scream in pain if they were bitten with the force used to cause the bite mark in question.

Viloria then asked Dr. Rawson if in his opinion a scream such as that would be stifled if the victim had been gagged with a rubber ball in her mouth. This time Judge Breen sustained the defense objection to the question being speculative. Viloria withdrew the question, but it still hung in the air as plain as the blue rubber ball gag displayed on the evidence table.

Dr. Rawson next testified that when he examined the bite he could tell it was caused by a person with a distinctive under bite. He was provided with a dental X-ray from Middleton and noted he did in fact have a distinctive under bite. When he was subsequently provided Middleton's dental impression he matched it to the bite and concluded it was caused by David Middleton. He said his observations were further confirmed through the DNA match to Middleton based on the saliva found around the bite mark.

What the prosecutor did next was the epitome of Tom Viloria theatrical productions. With the push of a button on the

PowerPoint remote, a set of winged teeth came flying slowly into the photo displayed on the screen. The teeth made chomping motions as the red wings mounted on them quickly fluttered and carried them toward their final destination. The last chomp was when the teeth bit down firmly on Kathy Powell's left breast and came to rest perfectly matching the bite mark. Viloria simply said, "I have no further questions for this witness."

An act like that would be impossible to follow, so the defense declined to cross examine Dr. Rawson, and he was excused. The next witness called by the prosecution was Professor Tariq Ahmed from the U.N.R. Engineering School. Professor Ahmed cut an impressive figure as he strode through the crowded courtroom toward the witness stand. He was dressed in a grey pinstriped suit, and his curly hair was trimmed short and impeccably groomed.

After Professor Ahmed was sworn in he walked the jurors through his calculations on oxygen flow and human respiration. Viloria displayed PowerPoint photos of the calculations as the witness spoke, and Dr. Ahmed was able to break everything down into layman's terms for them. He finalized the report with the most important calculation of all—Kathy Powell would suffocate if held in that refrigerator for more than five and one half hours.

On cross examination Pinkerton asked the professor how accurate his estimation of five and one half hours was. Professor Ahmed's answer was honest and genuine. He said he was one hundred percent certain this estimate was correct because he believed the victim would have actually died within three and one half hours since the holes drilled in the refrigerator were so small. He said he calculated the equations based on the best case scenario in order to give Mr. Middleton the benefit of doubt, but since Ms. Powell was obviously struggling to get out of the refrigerator her oxygen use would have been greatly increased.

Middleton had just been shot down by a round fired from an engineer's calculator—not from a cop's gun. Every juror now had the picture of Kathy Powell desperately trying to scratch and kick her way out of the refrigerator while gulping down the last precious breaths of fetid air available to her inside of the coffin Middleton placed her in. It was a gruesome image, but exactly the one Viloria wanted them to take into deliberations with them.

Professor Ahmed was excused and Viloria called his last witness to the stand. Detective John Douglas testified to the dates and times Middleton visited his storage shed after Kathy Powell disappeared. Using the timeline retrieved from the storage facility security system, they determined there was a twelve-hour gap between Middleton's visits to the shed from Saturday, February 4, 1995 to Sunday February 5, 1995. It had been proven that Kathy Powell was alive inside the refrigerator at some point, so based on Dr. Ahmed's calculations there was no way she could have survived that twelve-hour time span.

Having Douglas testify to this instead of one of the other detectives was another calculated decision by Viloria. Not only was Douglas a believable and likeable witness, he was also an

African American. Since the summation witness for the prosecution was the same race as the defendant, the defense would look foolish if they tried to insinuate racial issues were involved in the case.

The defense asked Douglas some perfunctory questions about the accuracy of the security clock, but since the self-calibrating system proved to be functioning properly, this was a moot issue. After Douglas was excused Viloria told Judge Breen the prosecution was resting their case. But the case was the only thing that rested that night, because the trial was far from over.

Chapter 59

HOUSE OF CARDS

The prosecution had done a good job laying a nasty trail of evidence leading toward Middleton's involvement in the deaths of Kathy Powell and Thelma Davilla. Pinkerton had only one option available to him when it came time to present his case. He had to attack the manner of death because if he could raise a doubt about criminal agency all the evidence the prosecution had presented would be meaningless.

Court was back in session at 9:00 A.M. on Thursday, August 21, 1997. Middleton himself was not on the defense witness list as testifying on his own behalf. Before the jury was brought into the courtroom, Judge Breen asked him if he wished to testify.

Middleton replied, "I really do want to testify, but just on the Davilla case part of it. But I guess I can't because the cases are joined. I can't testify to one without looking bad on the other, so I guess I just can't testify at all."

With Middleton's response read into the record, Judge Breen had the jury come in and asked the defense to call their first witness. Pinkerton called Dr. Robert Bucklin to the stand. Dr. Bucklin was a deputy medical examiner for Clark County, Nevada and an expert in forensic pathology. He testified that after examining Powell's autopsy results he found she suffered from heart disease and this could have contributed to her death. He said he did not think she died of asphyxiation.

On cross examination Viloria asked Dr. Bucklin if he was one hundred percent certain Kathy Powell did not die from asphyxiation. He answered no, but it was his opinion the chances were extremely remote. Viloria next asked if struggling to get free from a confined space while gasping for air in an environment with limited oxygen could exacerbate a person's heart condition. The witness answered in that scenario a heart condition could definitely be worsened, but he could not say if that was actually what happened.

The next witness called by the defense was a psychiatrist named Dr. Jerry Howle. He testified that since lithium was found in Kathy Powell's system during autopsy it could have been a contributing factor in her death. He said lithium could cause cardiac arrhythmia and carried some risk of sudden death.

When it was Viloria's turn to question the witness he asked Dr. Howle if he was familiar with a 1991 study by the American Heart Association that found long-term users of lithium did not die from heart disease at a greater rate than the general public. Dr. Howle said he was familiar with that study, but it was his experience a person should get an E.K.G. test done before they started taking lithium. Since Kathy Powell did not do this there was still a possibility that taking lithium contributed to her death.

After Dr. Howle was finished testifying the defense rested their case. Judge Breen recessed the court for lunch and told the attorneys to be ready to present their closing arguments to the jury at 2:00 that afternoon.

Viloria thought it was a good move on Pinkerton's part to keep his defense simple. Manner of death had been the week point of the case from its inception, so attacking that was a sound course of action. All the defense needed to do was raise doubt about the manner of Kathy Powell's death to have them find Middleton not guilty on the murder charge.

Viloria knew all along if he lost Powell the rest of the case would come tumbling down like a house made of playing cards. He rolled the dice when he decided to fight the manner of death issue, and now he stood a good chance of losing everything. He always had the Good Guys case to fall back on so Middleton wouldn't walk away totally free, but the most he'd get for that crime was five years in prison.

There was no time to think about that because in two hours he would have to present a summation of the most important case he had ever been involved in to the twelve people who would decide Middleton's fate. As he read through his notes one last time, the photo of Buffy Rice-Donohue propped up on his cluttered desk reminded him there were more people depending on him than just those in the courtroom. It was time to head back into the ring for the final round.

Chapter 60
STRINGING PEARLS

Prosecuting a case built almost entirely on circumstantial evidence is akin to a jeweler crafting a fine necklace out of individual pearls. Each piece of evidence laid out in front of the jury is like a pearl gently placed on the black felt covering the jeweler's work table. The closing argument is the braided gold strand that runs through the pearls and pulls them all together to form the finished product.

When Viloria finished his closing arguments at 4:00 that afternoon everyone in the courtroom could see that he was the equivalent of a master jeweler. He took each piece of evidence in chronological order and pulled them together in a way that convinced his listeners there was no way the deaths of Kathy Powell and Thelma Davilla were anything *but* brutally sadistic murders.

Viloria's last statement to the jurors was the gold clasp that would hold his necklace in place, and hopefully win a guilty verdict for Middleton. He said, "Kathy Powell did not tie herself up and place herself in that refrigerator, just like Thelma Davilla did not bind and bury herself in that field you walked through. The manner in which these women died would suggest involvement of criminal agency to any reasonable person, and I see twelve reasonable persons seated before me.

Your job is to decide proof beyond a reasonable doubt of criminal agency—not what the exact means of that criminal agency was. Kathy Powell and Thelma Davilla call to you from their graves with that proof, and with the proof of who that criminal agent was. Thank you."

After Viloria took his seat at the prosecution table, his most memorable event of the trial occurred. Middleton turned and looked at Viloria from his seat at the defense table and gave him the thumbs up sign. He then mouthed the words, "You got me."

There was not enough time left in the day for the defense to present their closing arguments, so Judge Breen recessed the court for the day. At 9:00 A.M. on Friday, August 22, 1997 Fred Pinkerton took his turn summing up the defense case for the jury. It was his job to pull apart the necklace Viloria built the day before and send the pearls scattering in different directions before the jury left for deliberations. It was a job he had done many times before, and one he did very well.

Pinkerton started out with the Thelma Davilla case. He said the prosecution did not present one single witness at trial who could positively establish a link between David Middleton and Thelma Davilla. He reminded the jurors they heard testimony from two witnesses who said they had seen Davilla with a woman who resembled Middleton's girlfriend, and there was possibly an African American man with her on one of these occasions. But at no time did anyone ever point a finger at Middleton and say "I saw *that* man with *that* woman."

As to the cause and manner of death for Thelma Davilla, Pinkerton emphasized there was none—because there was no way to determine it. There were several explanations on how Thelma Davilla could have died and came to be buried in that field, but the police did not explore any of them. Likewise, the police did not explore any of the myriad of possibilities about how evidence from Thelma Davilla ended up in Middleton's storage shed.

The reason for this was the police had already focused on Middleton because of his involvement with Kathy Powell. They became oblivious to the fact they were dealing with two separate cases and made the mistake of investigating them as one case with two victims. Because of this, they possibly missed important clues and evidence that would have led them to the real story behind Thelma Davilla's death.

Pinkerton then moved onto Kathy Powell. He said there was a very simple solution for how Kathy Powell ended up inside of that dumpster on the night of February 11, 1995. He said the reason it was simple was that Middleton himself already told it to the police.

Pinkerton said, "Mr. Middleton admitted to having kinky sex with Kathy Powell, but the sex was consensual. We've already heard testimony that Ms. Powell was not a well woman, and we know that sometime while she was with Mr. Middleton she expired.

"The defense does not condone the fact that Mr. Middleton admittedly panicked and hid Kathy Powell's body. We certainly do not agree with his decision to eventually dispose of her body in a dumpster either. But you are here to decide whether Mr. Middleton is guilty of *murder*, not to judge the sexual acts of two consenting adults, or the poor decision Mr. Middleton made after Kathy Powell expired."

In his summation Pinkerton told the jurors that without the Kathy Powell case being classified as a murder, the Thelma Davilla case would have been listed as nothing more than a suspicious death. He said the prosecution did not establish proof beyond a reasonable doubt that Kathy Powell's death was a murder, and their entire theory in the Davilla case was built around the fact that it was. Lastly, he reminded the jurors it wasn't the defense's job to prove a murder didn't occur—it was the prosecution's job to prove one *did* occur. Pinkerton then thanked the jury and took his seat next to Middleton.

After a fifteen minute recess Judge Breen began his jury instructions. He told the jury it was now time for them to review all of the supporting evidence presented in this case and make their determination whether guilt beyond a reasonable doubt had been proven by the prosecution. Since there were multiple charges stemming from two different cases, it was their responsibility to address them separately and determine guilt or innocence for each crime charged.

The judge also reminded the jurors they had heard much conflicting testimony during the trial and gave them instructions on how to deal with this. Citing a Nevada Supreme Court ruling titled

Bolden v. State, he told the jurors it is up to them to determine the credibility of the evidence and what weight to give it when deciding on guilt or innocence. When Judge Breen was through with his instructions, he excused the jury to begin their deliberations and adjourned the court for the day.

Viloria stopped to talk to Bonnie and Walt Rice before leaving the courtroom. They told him he was doing a great job and they were confident the jury would rule in favor of the prosecution. They said they were remaining in Reno until the verdict was reached and asked Viloria if he would call them if he heard anything.

Walt Rice then told him a prosecutor from Montrose had sat through his closing arguments, but they didn't want to distract him by telling him sooner. There was still no word about whether Middleton would be charged in Colorado for Buffy's murder, but they weren't holding much hope the authorities in Montrose would change their minds.

As Viloria walked to his office he wished he was as confident as the Rice's that the jury would find Middleton guilty. Pinkerton had fought a clean fight while defending Middleton, but he also put up some good arguments that might interject reasonable doubt into the jury's thought process. It only took one juror to wreak havoc during deliberations, and a hung jury was just as good as a not guilty verdict for the defense.

Prosecuting the case for a second time due to a hung jury would be far too costly, so the charges would have to be amended to exclude murder if that were to happen. Viloria would consider anything less than a guilty verdict a loss, and he'd already decided to walk away from the case if that were to happen.

Although the jury was not sequestered during the trial, they would be during the deliberation phase. Deliberations would go through the weekend, if needed, but Viloria and everyone else following the case hoped it wouldn't go that long. The common rule of thumb was the longer the jury deliberated, the better the charge of acquittal. As Viloria locked up his office for the day he had the feeling it was going to be a long weekend.

Chapter 61

THE KNOCKOUT PUNCH

Deliberations went on through the weekend as the jurors quietly discussed the case inside a locked conference room on the second floor of the Washoe County Courthouse. On four different occasions during their first day of deliberations they sent the bailiff to retrieve articles of evidence and evidentiary photos related to the case so they could review them.

On the second day they sent word to Judge Breen asking him to clarify a point of law dealing with the two-pronged test for criminal agency. When Viloria heard that, he became even more nervous than he had been at the beginning of deliberations. The fact the jury needed clarification on *any* point of law was never a good sign for the prosecution.

Each day lunch and dinner were brought to the jurors in the conference room, and they deliberated straight through until 8:00 P.M. At that time they were escorted to their rooms at a local hotel, and then returned to the jury room at 9:00 the following morning.

By Sunday night Viloria heard unofficially that the jurors were close to a decision. They had nearly deadlocked at one point, but had now apparently worked through their problems and supposedly would have a decision sometime the next morning. Viloria shared the news with the task force detectives and they all spent their third long sleepless night since the trial had ended.

On Monday, August 26, 1997 at 9:00 A.M. Jenkins and Douglas joined Viloria in his office and anxiously awaited news of the jury's verdict. They all cleared their calendars for the day so they would be free to go to the courtroom when the jury announced they were ready. On the outside, the three men appeared calm and collected as they waited for the news, but every time Viloria's phone rang they all practically jumped out of their chairs with anticipation.

At 11:00 the call came through that the jury had reached a decision. Judge Breen would convene court at 2:00 in the afternoon so the jury could announce their verdict. Calls were made to the other task force members as well as the victim's families to tell them the verdict had been reached. They did not have to call the Rice's because they were patiently waiting in the courtroom cafeteria for word about the jury deliberations.

The courtroom was packed with spectators and reporters by 2:00, and everyone rose to their feet when Judge Breen entered the room. After he took his seat at the bench and everyone else was seated, the jury was led into the courtroom. The calmest person in the room appeared to be David Middleton as he smiled and nodded at the jurors. He looked more like a man greeting people at a social function than someone who was waiting to hear his fate.

Judge Breen looked at the jurors and asked, "Mr. Foreman, has the jury reached a verdict?"

The jury foreman was a forty-six-year-old postal worker who looked much more pale and tired that he did when he was last in court the previous Friday. He stood and answered, "Yes, Your Honor, we have."

The foreman gave a sealed envelope to the bailiff, who then walked to the bench and handed it to Judge Breen. The courtroom was silent as the judge tore open the envelope and quietly read the paper inside of it. After a moment, he looked at Middleton and said, "Will the defendant please rise?"

Middleton and Pinkerton slowly stood up and faced the judge's bench. It was so quiet Viloria swore he could hear his heart pounding as he waited for the judge to announce the verdict. Finally, Judge Breen said, "In regard to count number one, this jury has found the defendant, David Stephen Middleton, *guilty* of the first degree murder of Katherine Powell."

A loud chorus of cheers erupted from the courtroom and Judge Breen waited until the crowd quieted before continuing. Viloria's head was spinning and he almost didn't hear the judge say, "Regarding count number two, this jury also finds the defendant *guilty* of the first degree murder of Thelma Davilla."

And that was the last thing Viloria heard. Judge Breen had to quiet the crowd by threatening to clear the courtroom, but even after the noise settled Viloria could only hear two things in his head. *The jury finds the Defendant guilty of the first degree murder of Katherine Powell, and guilty of the first degree murder of Thelma Davilla.*

When all was said and done the jury had found Middleton guilty of every crime he was charged with. He now faced sentencing on two counts of first degree murder, two counts of first degree kidnapping, one count of grand larceny and one count of fraudulent use of a credit card. Viloria had won the fight with a knockout.

Middleton remained standing and showed no emotion as the judge polled the jurors to make sure the verdicts he read were correct. After the polling was complete, he dismissed the jury and told them to return at 9:00 the next morning for the penalty phase. He thanked them for what was certainly a difficult job and told them he would not keep them sequestered during the penalty phase.

Judge Breen then dismissed the court, and the escort deputies flanked Middleton as he stood motionless with his head held low at the defense table. He was then led out of the courtroom looking more like a beaten dog than the devil's incarnate.

The families of Kathy Powell, Thelma Davilla and Buffy Rice-Donohue stood silently with their heads bowed while they thanked whatever God they prayed to that Middleton had been found guilty. Viloria was swarmed by the task force detectives who congratulated him while escorting him through the group of reporters waiting for interviews. He wasn't in this for the glory, so the interviews would be left up to the district attorney.

When Douglas suggested a celebration was in order, Viloria replied, "Maybe just a small one. The hard part starts tomorrow, and I've still got work to do."

Chapter 62

THE OLD RAG

During the penalty phase the prosecution would be able to introduce some of Middleton's prior criminal acts and put family members on the stand to testify to victim impact. Viloria planned to put relatives of both Kathy Powell and Thelma Davilla on the stand. He also made arrangements for Alyssa Cervantes to fly to Reno from Florida to testify about the crimes Middleton committed against her when she was sixteen.

Viloria also petitioned the court to allow him to introduce evidence from the Colorado investigation of Middleton's involvement in the Buffy Rice-Donohue case and his alleged rape of the civilian employee when he was a Miami cop. The witness lists for the prosecution and the defense as well as any motions before the court would have to be discussed outside the presence of the jury. Even though the jurors reported at 9:00 A.M. on Tuesday, August 27, 1997, it was highly doubtful they would hear a word of testimony until later that afternoon.

Since this was a death penalty hearing Pinkerton relinquished the lead of Middleton's defense to another attorney from his office who had more experience in this area. Attorney Patrick Flannigan took over the case and immediately began making motions to the court against Viloria's planned strategy for the penalty hearing.

Outside the presence of the jury, Flannigan moved to preclude evidence that Middleton had been charged with sexual assault and kidnapping in Florida in 1990. The Florida case resulted in the conviction of one count of aggravated battery and one count of false imprisonment, so it was Flannigan's opinion that any mention of sexual assault would violate Middleton's constitutional rights. He also argued there was no reason for the victim in that crime to testify since only the fact Middleton had been convicted was relevant to the penalty hearing.

Viloria objected to this, but Judge Breen sided with the defense. He said, "I'm not going to allow testimony concerning sexual assault in the State's case. However, I warn defense counsel that any explanation of this conviction is going to open up the door to Mr. Viloria's ability to explain what he perceives as the facts of this case."

The defense then motioned that no mention of the Buffy Rice-Donohue case or the alleged rape in Florida could be made during the penalty hearing. Middleton was not charged in the Colorado case and the victim could not be called as a witness to testify to Middleton's criminal behavior. Even though the alleged victim in the Florida case could testify about what Middleton did to her, she believed it was a Santeria religious ritual, so testimony was precluded by the First Amendment.

Viloria argued that the defense was hiding behind the Constitution, but Judge Breen again sided with the defense. No mention of either incident could be made in front of the jury, and

Viloria's strategy to argue for the death penalty was slowly being chipped away.

The next defense motion concerned testimony by the victim's families. Flannigan voiced concern that members of Powell's family might get on the stand and ask for the death penalty, which in turn might influence the jury's decision.

Viloria said he would instruct the family members not to specifically ask for the death sentence, but argued that they could ask for the maximum sentence. He then argued that if defense witnesses asked for a penalty less than death he could recall the family members to ask for the death sentence.

Judge Breen asked Viloria if it was his interpretation of the Constitution that he could do that. Viloria had heard enough about the protection the Constitution was giving Middleton and flew into a lengthy tirade about it. He said, "The rights of the defendant have wallowed the Constitution, making it meaningless. I would submit that it is just that, an old rag that needs to be modified. It has no meaning."

Judge Breen ruled for the defense, and the reporters listening to the arguments had a field day with Viloria's comment about the Constitution. He meant it in the context that the Constitution was now being used to protect the criminal and not the victim, but that was not how it read in the morning papers.

Even if Reno wasn't a fairly conservative town, the headline "PROSECUTOR CALLS CONSITTUTION AN OLD RAG" was never a good thing to read. It was the first bad press

Viloria had during the case, but it was bad press that would stay with him for a long time.

Chapter 63

GOING HOME

The Jury was led into the courtroom at 1:00 in the afternoon and the proceedings began. Since this was the same jury that had already heard the case at trial, Viloria dispensed with a lengthy opening statement. He told the jury that in considering the death sentence for the two murders, there were four aggravating circumstances in the Davilla case and five in the Powell case.

In Davilla they could consider that Middleton had two prior felony convictions—one in Florida and his weapons conviction in Reno. One of those convictions involved the use of threat of violence. The murder was also committed in the commission of or the attempt to commit first degree kidnap, and Middleton was convicted of more than one murder during the proceeding.

In the Powell case the same four aggravating circumstances were present, but there was also a fifth they could consider. Powell's murder involved torture and depravity of mind. Viloria was reasonably confident that he could win a death sentence based just on these aggravators, but he wished the judge would have ruled in his favor on introducing Middleton's past criminal history.

When it was Flannigan's turn to address the jury he reminded them that even though the death penalty was an option, they were under no obligation to use it when sentencing Middleton for the crimes he had been convicted of. He said he would be calling a character witness in support of Middleton and offering testimony from the Board of Pardons.

Viloria kept his case simple since he had to alter his original strategy. The first witness he called to the stand was Kathy Powell's brother Jeff. He testified to the fact his sister was a good and caring person, and the lives of her family members had been devastated by her murder.

Viloria was not allowed to ask Mr. Powell what his opinion was of the proper sentence for Middleton. He did ask the witness, "How do you think a person who took someone like your sister from the world should be treated?"

Powell said, "I can't see giving that person any more respect, dignity, or mercy than he showed Kathy."

The defense objected, but Judge Breen overruled and allowed the statement to remain on record. Flannigan did not cross examine.

The second and last witness Viloria called was Thelma Davilla's sister, Dora Valverde. Ms. Valverde broke down in tears on the witness stand. She said all her sister ever wanted was to live free in this great country, but now she would never live anywhere again because of David Middleton. Once again, the defense did not cross examine.

When it was Flannigan's turn he called only one character witness to the stand for Middleton. His step-mother Margaret* had married Middleton's natural father, and had known Middleton since he was ten years old. She testified that Middleton was always a good and caring person and that something must have gone terribly wrong in his life for him to have become involved in crimes such as these. She said she believed Middleton could become a functioning member of society again if he were allowed to do so.

Flannigan then asked, "And did you know he got in trouble in Miami?"

The woman answered, "Oh yes, but that was a long time ago."

Viloria saw this as his opening. On cross examination he asked, "So you are aware then, ma'am, that your stepson took a sixteen-year-old girl to a remote area, kept her in his car and engaged in sexual activity with her?"

Flannigan sprang to his feet and immediately objected to Viloria's question. He was red- faced with anger and moved for a mistrial. The aggravation showed on Judge Breen's face as he ordered the bailiff to remove the jury from the courtroom.

When the jury was gone, Judge Breen asked, "Why now Mr. Viloria? Why now without my advanced permission?"

Viloria argued that the defense opened the door for the question by asking an explosive question about Middleton getting in trouble in Florida. Judge Breen didn't buy his explanation. He said, "I'm questioning your motives here. You are precluded from asking any questions, any further questions of this witness or you'll pack this to the ninth circuit on your back."

When the jurors returned to the courtroom Judge Breen admonished them that Middleton's prior conviction did not relate to sexual activity and asked if anyone would have trouble disregarding Viloria's question. None of them indicated they would.

Viloria's tactics earned him a complaint to the State Bar's ethics review board, but it was worth it. Were it not for a 1990 plea bargain resulting from a sloppy investigation in Florida, the jury would have gotten to hear from the victim herself. At least he got the gist of the case out in front of them. The jurors could say they'd have no trouble disregarding the question—but there was no doubt they'd heard it.

Flannigan then called Susan McCurdy, Executive Secretary of the Parole and Pardons Board to the stand. He asked Ms. McCurdy, "If Middleton were sentenced to life imprisonment without the possibility of parole, could that sentence ever be commuted to parole?"

"No it could not," she replied.

On cross examination, Viloria asked, "Ma'am, that assumes that the legislature doesn't change the law during the next session, or the next session after that, or the next session after that, doesn't it?"

"That is correct," she answered.

Viloria asked, "They are always free to change the law as they do every year, right?"

"That is also correct," she said.

"So there is no guarantee that life without won't be subjected to change and no longer be life without. Is that also correct, Ms. McCurdy?"

"Yes," she replied, "that is also correct."

"No further questions," Viloria said.

The defense made no objections and both sides rested their cases. Judge Breen adjourned the court for the day and said they would reconvene at 9:00 A.M. the next morning for jury instructions.

At precisely 9:00 A.M. on Thursday, August 28, 1997 the jury was led into the courtroom to hear their sentencing instructions from Judge Breen. Guilt or innocence was no longer an issue. The only thing the jurors were to discuss was what sentence David Middleton would get for each of the crimes he was convicted of. Judge Breen told the jurors the latitude of sentencing and the guidelines for issuing those sentences, and then excused them for deliberations.

This time there was no need to sequester the jury. At 10:30 A.M. the jury foreman advised the bailiff they had reached their decision and all parties were ordered back into the courtroom.

Judge Breen took the sealed envelope containing the sentences from the bailiff. He opened the envelope, read the sentences to himself and then had the defendant stand to hear them.

Judge Breen said, "Mr. Middleton, for both murders the jury found no mitigating circumstances sufficient to outweigh the aggravators. You are hereby sentenced to death for the murders of Kathy Powell and Thelma Davilla.

"For the two counts of first degree kidnapping, one count of grand larceny and one count of fraudulent use of a credit card, you are sentenced to the following prison terms: life without the possibility of parole, life without the possibility of parole, ten years and ten years. May God have mercy on your soul Mr. Middleton. This court is dismissed."

A Nevada State Appellate Court was asked to review the death penalty ruling based on prosecutorial misconduct on the part of Tom Viloria. On November 28, 1997 the Appellate Court issued its ruling. The conclusion of the appellate decision reads, *"We find Middleton's claims to lack merit. We therefore affirm his judgment of conviction and sentence of death."*

It was time for the devil to return to hell…maybe.

Chapter 64

JABBA

It takes approximately fifteen years to kill a person in the state of Nevada once they've been given the death sentence, and David Middleton is no exception. As of the writing of this book, David Middleton is still very much alive and heavily involved in scripting the continuing appeals of both his conviction and death sentence.

After Middleton's conviction, Judge Breen ruled there was no longer a conflict of interest and moved the responsibilities for the appeal process back to the Public Defender's Office. Middleton's string of appeals has addressed issues such as ineffective counsel, prosecutorial misconduct, Miranda rights, improper evidence handling, search and seizure, and the wrongful joinder of the cases. He's gone through several attorneys on his quest to beat his charges and the death sentence, but so far all of his appeals have been denied.

As soon as Middleton lost his last appeal in August of 2007, his newest and most current appeal was filed. This will be his last appeal at the State level, but then the arduous process of Federal Court appeals begins. The one avenue of appeal that worries everyone associated with the case is the same one that worried Dave Jenkins the first time he heard it—*undetermined cause and manner of death.*

Case law changes often, and all it will take is one ruling like the Frutiger decision to cast a shadow of doubt over Middleton's murder conviction. There will be no guarantees that Middleton won't win an appeal until the day an executioner injects him with a lethal cocktail. And for some of the people whose lives Middleton has destroyed—that day can't come soon enough.

Until then, Middleton has found a new home on Death Row in the Ely Nevada State Prison. He has become what is described as a model prisoner with charismatic charm that has made more than one prison guard wonder if maybe he really *didn't* kill those two women in Reno. One female prison guard said she was actually relieved when she was moved off of her assignment on Death Row because she felt herself getting a little *too* close to David Middleton. After all, as Middleton often reminded the guards, he used to be *one of them.*

During Middleton's last appearance at the Washoe County Courthouse in August of 2007, one of the jail deputies working the transport van was also working in the courthouse during the trial in 1997. He said he almost didn't recognize Middleton, who now went by the moniker of "Big Dave."

The deputy said, "He was so fat we had to give him his own row of seats on the bus. If it wasn't for Middleton's name on the paperwork I wouldn't have even known it was him. Big Dave my ass. He looked more like Jabba the Hut!"

Chapter 65

THE MATRON

Evonne Haley also appealed her conviction on the charges from the Good Guys case. The Nevada State Supreme Court affirmed her conviction in a proceeding titled Haley v. State on July 28, 1998. She was then returned to the Southern Nevada Women's Correctional Institute in Las Vegas to serve the remainder of her seven year sentence.

On July 23, 1999 Haley received news that she was going to be released from prison early. Before she could celebrate the good news, she was told the reason she was being released from her sentence early was that she was being extradited to Colorado on charges related to her part in the murder of Buffy Rice-Donohue.

The Rice's at first were ecstatic when they found out Haley was being returned for prosecution. But then they learned through their attorney Keith Killian that Montrose District Attorney Wyatt Angelo had cut a deal with Haley. If she took the stand and told the truth about what happened to Buffy, Angelo would only charge her with four felony counts of being an accessory to murder after the fact. She would be sentenced to eleven years in prison, but the District Attorney would stipulate she would be released no later than November 15, 2003.

A tearful Haley took the stand in Montrose, Colorado on September 10, 1999. Prison had not been good to Evonne Haley. The words pretty or even good looking had probably never been used to describe her, but a reporter for the *Denver Post* described her as looking "frumpish and matronly" at her trial.

Haley described herself as being like an older sister to Buffy. She said she did pick Buffy up the last day she was seen alive and drove her to the apartment she shared with Middleton because Buffy wanted to buy cocaine.

Haley said Buffy left the apartment alone with Middleton and she stayed behind. She said two hours later, a distraught Middleton returned to the apartment and said he had accidentally killed Buffy during an argument in a wooded area near Colona, approximately twenty miles from the apartment.

Haley said Middleton begged her to keep quiet about the murder, because as a black man in a white town he would never get a fair trial. Haley said she believed Buffy's death was an accident and helped Middleton dispose of the body because she feared she would lose her daughter if anyone found out about the killing.

District Attorney Angelo never addressed the facts that Buffy had been sexually assaulted, her body was bound with rope or that the duct tape gag over her mouth when she was found had teeth marks in it to show she was alive when she had been gagged.

And then there was the matter of the witness who saw Middleton carrying what looked like Buffy's body out of his apartment—not out of a wooded area twenty miles away. Angelo accepted Haley's story as the truth and told the judge the State was willing to abide by the plea bargain.

Bonnie Rice was incensed. She stepped in front of the defense table, pointed a finger at Evonne Haley and shouted, "That is an outright lie! I condemn you for the murder of my daughter!"

Bonnie Rice was forcibly removed form the courtroom by two deputies. Evonne Haley walked out of the courtroom on her own to begin serving her token sentence for what she said was her part in the death of Buffy Rice-Donohue.

Attorney Keith Killian was quoted in the *Denver Post* as saying it was routine to have a forty-five day span between a trial and the acceptance of a plea bargain in order to examine a pre-sentencing report and to consult with the victim's family regarding the sentence. In this case, Evonne Haley was sentenced on the same day she testified. No one ever asked the Rice's or Mason Donohue how they felt about the plea bargain.

The Rice's had requested through an appellate court that a special prosecutor try Haley in this case. The court was supposed to rule on their request the following Monday, but Angelo took Haley to court on a Wednesday.

Killian told the *Denver Post* he couldn't help wonder if Angelo purposely hustled the case through court before the appellate court could rule on the Rice's request. He said by entering into a plea agreement that resulted in a conviction, Angelo took the pressure off the Montrose Police Department for doing an inept investigation of Buffy's death in the first place.

Whatever the reason for offering Haley the plea bargain, Angelo now had co-conspirator testimony that Middleton killed Buffy Rice-Donohue. This testimony could be used against Middleton because it could be corroborated by a veritable mountain of independent evidence.

And yet, Angelo refused to file charges on Middleton. He said, "You can't kill a man twice, so why waste good money prosecuting someone who is already on Death Row in Nevada?"

I will not insult the intelligence of my readers by answering that question for them. I will say that perhaps the biggest travesty of justice and the saddest part of this story is the fact that the Buffy Rice-Donohue murder file still says—*open and unsolved*...

CONCLUSION
JULY 21, 2008

No one will ever know what caused David Middleton to change from being a respected member of the law enforcement community to a convicted serial killer. The reason for this is the killer himself is not talking. To this day David Middleton proclaims his innocence to anyone who will listen. Well, not just anyone. He declined to be interviewed for this book, so maybe he only proclaims his innocence to those who might actually believe him—or those he can intimidate.

There a lot of questions surrounding the murders committed by David Middleton that will forever go unanswered. One of those questions is just how many people he has killed over the years. Law enforcement knows of three, but they speculate there are more. There is one fact the law enforcement officers close to this investigation are certain of: Big Dave wore a badge at one time, but he was never *one of us.*

Middleton still has not been charged with the murder of Buffy Rice-Donohue, and according to the Montrose District Attorney's Office he probably never will. But as the saying goes, never say never. Perhaps the Colorado authorities might change their mind about prosecuting Middleton if someday enough people voice their opinion about this injustice.

Evonne Haley was released from prison in November of 2003. She is now a free woman and lives with relatives in Grand

Junction, Colorado. A reporter from the *Denver Post* recently went to Haley's house to try to interview her. Haley's aunt answered the door and said, "Oh, that thing. That happened so long ago that we try not to talk about it."

She then closed the door and the reporter never got her interview. It seems Evonne Haley didn't have as much trouble forgetting about the Buffy Rice-Donohue case as everyone else did.

Many people's lives have been dramatically changed because David Middleton's path crossed theirs. His victim's lives ended, but their loved ones continued with theirs and had to adjust to the horrific tradgeties he inflicted on them.

Mason Donohue spent many years alone and lonely after Buffy's murder. She was his first and only love, and he has never truly moved on after losing her. Eventually he earned his Masters Degree in education, and in 2005 he married and moved to a small town in Wyoming to start a family. They say there is a difference between moving away and moving on though.

Bonnie and Walt Rice spent everything they had trying to get the Montrose authorities to investigate the murder of their daughter and prosecute her killer. They sued the Montrose Police Department and District Attorney Wyatt Angelo. Even though the court found evidence of malfeasance in some of their claims, they were forced to issue summary judgment due to statute of limitations and issues of clemency.

Walt now works as a long haul truck driver and Bonnie stays busy babysitting her grandchildren. Losing a child is every parent's worst nightmare, but the living hell the Rice's went through is unfathomable. But true to the words carved on Buffy's gravestone—they will never stop fighting for her.

Bonnie Rice was instrumental in starting the First Victim Advocate Group in Montrose. She said she never wanted to think of another victim's family being treated the way they were, and wanted to see at least one good thing come from Buffy's death. Bonnie recently sat down and had coffee with Lieutenant Tom Chinn from the Montrose Police Department. She said she would never forget, but she was not above forgiving.

Tom Viloria continued on with a successful career in the Washoe County District Attorneys office before moving on to an even more successful private practice. His law offices in downtown Reno are the most prestigious in the city. But of all the cases he's been involved in, it is the Buffy Rice-Donohue case that still haunts him.

After Middleton was sentenced in the Powell and Davilla cases, Viloria felt so strongly about his guilt in the Buffy Rice-Donohue case that he called the Montrose District Attorney and offered to prosecute Middleton *pro bono.* He said the entire Middleton prosecution in Reno only cost $400,000, so if Colorado swore him in as a special prosecutor and he gave his services for free, prosecution would be more than affordable.

Sheriff Bill Masters from San Miguel County, Colorado heard about Viloria's offer and donated $50,000 to the Montrose D.A.'s office to help with costs of prosecuting Middleton. The money was spent elsewhere, and Viloria's offer was declined. Viloria said he never could figure that out and it will always bother him.

John Douglas left the Reno Police Department shortly after the Middleton case was adjudicated. He took a job with the Nevada Division of Parole and Probation, and quickly worked his way into an upper management position. He retired from law enforcement in May of 2008. His hair was grayer than the day he booked David Middleton for the murders of Kathy Powell and Thelma Davilla, but Eddie Murphy still would have envied his smile when he announced his retirement.

All of the other detectives who worked the Middleton case have also since retired—except one. Dave Jenkins recently hung up his trademark suit and tie and donned his dress blue uniform to attend his daughter Ali's graduation from the Reno Police Department Academy. Jenkins' daughter was twelve-years-old the night he became a dumpster diver, but pinning her shiny new badge on her uniform shirt at her graduation was by far the high point of his career. Secretly, he hoped she'd never become a *corpse cop*.

After thirty-one years with the department, Detective Dave Jenkins is still slaying monsters. Right now he is engulfed in the investigation of another possible serial killer dubbed the "Co-Ed Stalker," but that is a story for another time…